American Language Hub

LEVEL 5
Student's Book

JEREMY DAY
GRAHAM SKERRITT
KIERAN DONAGHY

macmillan education

Contents

Welcome

GRAMMAR

Verb tenses and structures

A Choose the correct option to complete the conversation.

A: Hello. Could you tell me [1]*where is the conversation class* / *where the conversation class is*?

B: Yes, just follow me! [2]*I'm going* / *I'll go* there now. I actually study here myself.

A: Cool. [3]*Did you* / *Have you* been studying English for long?

B: Let me think. Actually [4]*I'll have been* / *I'll be* at this school for two years at the end of this month. Don't worry. You [5]*don't have to* / *must not* bring anything. Just yourself. And there is only one rule: you [6]*don't need to* / *must not* speak in your own language in class.

A: Great, that's really important. In my last school we [7]*used to* / *get used to* do a lot of grammar. But I wasn't [8]*taught* / *didn't teach* any speaking or pronunciation. So I really need to [9]*used to* / *get used to* speaking more.

B: Yes, me too. I [10]*was learning* / *am learning* on my own for a little while, but stopped because I didn't feel like I'd made much progress.

Articles, determiners and quantifiers

B Find and correct the mistakes in the sentences.

1. It's ~~the~~ good to watch videos in English to practice your listening.
2. A lot problems when learning a language come from lack of confidence not lack of ability.
3. It's best to get personal recommendations when finding the English courses.
4. When you first learn a language you should spend a great deal time on grammar.
5. A childhood is a good time to start learning a language.
6. There's never time enough when you're working and learning at the same time.
7. Most the people feel demotivated at some point when learning a new language.
8. Every languages has it own unique pronunciation and grammar and you can't easily compare them.
9. Languages are neither fixed and completely stable but are constantly changing.

C SPEAK Work in pairs and discuss the questions.

1. Do you agree with the speakers in Exercise A? Why/Why not?
2. Do you agree with the statements in Exercise B? Why/Why not?

VOCABULARY

Collocations

A Choose the correct words to complete the collocations.

1. It's *highly* / *deeply* / *absolutely* likely that even jobs in education will be automated in the future.
2. Concerning future problems, I'm *bitterly* / *deeply* / *ridiculously* concerned about extreme weather conditions.
3. There is the possibility *for* / *of* / *about* colonizing another planet to relieve human overpopulation.
4. Young people should have *knowledge* / *ideas* / *opinions* of news sources and searching online to deal with the problem of fake news.
5. Understanding your *focus* / *target* / *regular* audience is important for being an entrepreneur.
6. Not all regeneration projects get a *positive* / *high* / *key* reaction from local communities.

Compound adjectives and nouns

B Complete the sentences with the compound adjectives and nouns in the box.

community spirit	last-minute	old-fashioned
six-bedroom	street parties	up-to-date

1. Visit our website for the most ________ travel times and ________ deals.
2. Mark and Susan have just bought a huge ________ house in the country. It's a little ________, but they're planning on renovating it.
3. There is great ________ in my town. The local council usually organize ________ for national holidays.

C SPEAK Work in pairs. Do you agree with the statements in Exercise A?

PRONUNCIATION

0.1 **A** Circle the arrows to predict which intonation will be used. Then listen and check.

1. Is this meeting finishing soon? [↗] / [↘]
2. How often do you come to these classes? [↗] / [↘]
3. Unless there is a good reason [↗] / [↘], you shouldn't work late. [↗] / [↘]
4. Take some chocolate bars [↗] / [↘], in case you need a quick snack. [↗] / [↘]

0.2 **B** Listen to the sentences. Draw (‿) between any words that link together.

1. He's improved a lot despite having a few problems.
2. We went out at night a lot to see the city.
3. Plenty of people find it difficult at first.
4. Hundreds of people came out to see her talk.

C Practice saying the sentences in Exercise B.

1 TRENDS

The majority have no other reason for their opinions than that they are the fashion.

Samuel Johnson

A flamingo among geese, egrets, swans and herons.

OBJECTIVES

- talk about style and fashion
- give fashion advice
- compare different trends
- make a podcast or vlog
- pitch your own business idea
- write a blog post

Work with a partner. Discuss the questions.

1 Look at the picture. How does it relate to trends?

2 Read the quote. What do you think it means? Do you agree?

3 How important are trends in the following areas to you?

- fashion
- music
- design
- lifestyle

1.1 Dress for success

- Talk about style and fashion
- Give fashion advice

V– clothes and fashion; metaphors   G– nominal clauses   P– linking /r/   S– listening for recommendations

VOCABULARY
Clothes and fashion

A Work in pairs. Take the quiz.

B Go to the **Vocabulary Hub** on **page 142**.

1 Do you carefully plan your **outfits** or just wear the first thing on hand?
2 Have you ever had to attend an event with **a dress code**?
3 If you had to go to a **costume** party, what costume would you wear?
4 Are people more productive when they wear a **uniform** or **casual** clothing?
5 Would you describe yourself as a **trendsetter** or a **trend follower**?
6 Is it better to **fit in with** or **stand out** from **the crowd**?
7 Do you ever wear **baggy** or **scruffy** clothes to relax at home?

READING

A PREDICT Work in pairs. Read the title of the article. Look at pictures 1–3. How might what the people are wearing affect their behavior?

B SCAN Read *Style speaks* and check your predictions from Exercise A.

STYLE *speaks*

We've all heard the old adages ... *Dress for the job you want, not the job you have. Look good, feel good.* These clichés are somewhat worn out. How can the way we dress affect our lives? But it seems there may be some truth in them after all. People do form first impressions based on what we're wearing. Not only that but maybe even part of our own self-worth is tied up in the clothing choices we make.

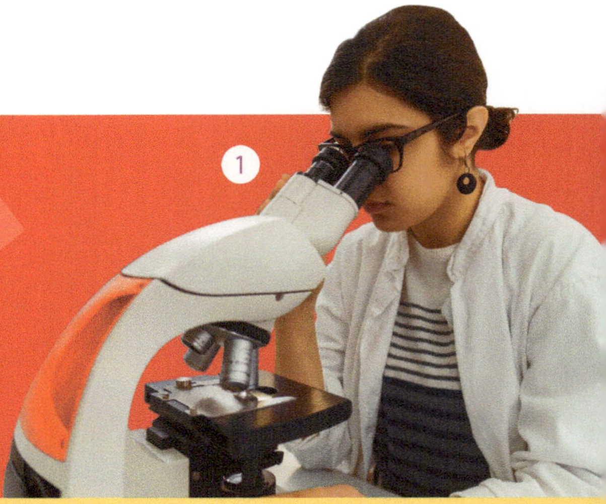
1

Power dressing

Not convinced? Imagine turning up for an interview at a big city firm, or company in the jeans you've been wearing for the past three days and an old baggy T-shirt. Would you be successful in getting the job? Unlikely. Would you feel self-conscious about what you're wearing? Very likely. It seems that wearing dress clothes, such as a well-made suit, could help you feel more confident. And when we're feeling confident we negotiate better, we respond better to questions and we put other people at ease.

2

Breaking free

On the flip side, wearing fitted or tailored clothing is not what most of us would choose to wear when we are trying to be creative. Can you imagine writing the next great novel, or coming up with a great innovation while sitting and typing away in a $2,000 designer suit? This is why many leading tech companies have an ultra-relaxed dress code and encourage casual clothing. Mark Zuckerberg isn't topping any best-dressed lists but his billions of dollars make up for it. Furthermore, many workplaces have 'Casual Fridays' to encourage employees to let their hair down a little and get creativity flowing.

Uniform thinking

Wearing a uniform can make us feel part of something – provide us with a sense of belonging, but also one of duty. Many people argue that wearing school uniforms encourages us to work harder. While this is not necessarily true, there is no doubt that when, for example, a firefighter puts on a helmet or a doctor puts on a white coat, it comes with a responsibility. So fundamentally, to dress the role is to start to live it.

Glossary

adage (n) a well-known phrase that says something about life and human experience
clique (n) a small group of people who seem unfriendly to other people
unconsciously (adv) without realizing or being aware of one's actions

C READ FOR DETAIL Read the article again. Complete each statement with one to three words from the article.

1 People should wear ______________ when they're feeling down.
2 ______________ could help people come up with new ideas.
3 People sometimes wear ______________ clothing to fit in.
4 ______________ may encourage people to make healthier choices.
5 People should wear ______________ to feel more persuasive.
6 ______________ may make people more careful at work.

D SPEAK Discuss in small groups.

1 What surprised you most about the blog post?
2 Do you think your own choice of clothes affects how you think and behave?

Gym ready

It's not just work that clothing affects, but lifestyle as well. Professional and semi-professional athletes tend to stick rigidly to an 'athleisure' style. Their reasoning? They don't enjoy wearing formal clothes. And they want to be able to work out whenever they feel like it. And for many, having the clothes on reminds them to make healthier choices … to choose the fruit salad over the fruit pie.

Pack mentality

Have we really evolved that much away from our primal, tribal instincts? Visit any city center at lunchtime on a Saturday and your answer will be probably not. The packs of roving teenagers are dressed in a pseudo uniform of name-brand clothing, like Ray-Bans and Hollister T-shirts. We unconsciously imitate the clothing of people we look up to. A shared sense of style builds rapport and helps you to instantly feel part of a clique. Maybe it's self-preservation, or maybe it's a hope that you will be infused with the qualities you admire.

Lift your mood

That our mood impacts what we choose to wear will not come as a surprise. How many of us think about it the other way around? What we wear could affect how we are feeling for the better or worse. One of the best cures for when you're feeling down is to wear that cozy, bright yellow sweater. More people than you might think are great believers in wearing bright colors to boost positivity. It seems simple, but why not give it a shot next time you're having a bad day?

3

GRAMMAR

Nominal clauses

A Read the sentences. Is the underlined part of each sentence the subject or the object?

1 They don't enjoy wearing formal clothes.
2 Wearing a uniform can make us feel part of something.

B Work in pairs. Underline the nominal clauses in sentences from the article. Use the information in the box to help you. The first two have been done for you.

Nominal clauses

Nominal clauses are clauses that work like nouns. They are very common as objects, but they are also possible as the subject, after a preposition or the verb *be*, and in the following ways.

a nominal *-ing* clause ___
b nominal *that* clause ___
c nominal question-clause ___
d nominal infinitive ___
e We frequently use a phrase like *the fact/idea that* or *the experience/problem of* to introduce a nominal clause and make it easier to understand. ___
f *That* clauses and infinitive can sound unnatural as the subject. We can use *it* as an empty subject instead. ___

1 Luke is upset that he didn't pass.
2 Lisa doesn't enjoy watching horror movies.
3 It wasn't surprising that Tara came in first place.
4 The fact that the team won the tournament shows how good the manager is.
5 Where you go to college is your choice.
6 To tell a lie about something so important was wrong.

C WORK IT OUT Match sentences 1–6 in Exercise B with the rules (a–f) in the box.

D Go to the **Grammar Hub** on **page 122**.

E Complete the sentences so they are true for you. Then discuss in pairs.

1 What I like doing most of all in the evenings …
2 How a person is dressed …
3 Spending a lot of money on …

SPEAKING

DISCUSS Work in groups. To what extent do you agree with the following statements? Give reasons for your answers.

- Wearing a uniform affects what grades you get in school.
- Buying expensive clothes is the best way to succeed in life.
- Spending a lot of money on luxury goods makes people more generous.

LISTENING

A SPEAK Work in pairs. Look at the infographic from a fashion magazine. What do you think the results would be in your country?

1.1 **B LISTEN FOR RECOMMENDATIONS** Listen to a conversation between two friends. What nine tips does Carly give Dan? Use the information in the box to help you.

> **Listening for recommendations**
>
> When listening for recommendations, pay attention to phrases like *it's a good idea to*, *it's always worth*, or *don't forget to*.
>
> Also listen for phrases that signal a shift from main points to examples (e.g. *for instance*, *let's say*) and those that move from examples to new main points (e.g. *more generally*, *that's an example of*).

1.1 **C LISTEN FOR DETAIL** Listen again. Choose the correct answers (a, b or c).

1. Why is Dan worried?
   - a He doesn't know what to wear for his new job.
   - b He thinks people won't respect him.
   - c He won't earn enough to buy nice clothes.
2. What's good about the suit Dan wants to buy?
   - a the price
   - b the fit
   - c the quality
3. Why did Dan wear baggy sweatpants for his job interview?
   - a He knew the interviewers couldn't see them.
   - b He wanted to create a good impression.
   - c He didn't have any other pants.
4. What should Dan do with his suit pants?
   - a mend them
   - b sell them
   - c put them in the trash
5. According to Carly, what's good about ugly sales pages?
   - a You can charge more money.
   - b You appear inexperienced.
   - c You can buy things cheaply.
6. Where does Carly say you can find good second-hand bargains?
   - a expensive parts of town
   - b trendy neighborhoods
   - c areas near colleges

D SPEAK Work in small groups.

1. Which of Carly's tips do you already follow?
2. Would you try any of them in the future? Why/Why not?

FASHION TRENDS
in the US according to our readers

75% of you only buy **NAME-BRAND** sportswear

45% believe **QUALITY** is more important than **VALUE** for money

IMAGE is the first thing that **85%** of you notice about someone the first time you meet them

65% **THROW** ripped clothing away rather than **MENDING** it

40% of our readers think **FASHION** is more important than **COMFORT**

VOCABULARY
Metaphors

A SPEAK Work in pairs. Look at the sentences. What do the underlined words and phrases mean?

1. a I'd love to come out tonight, but I'm on a tight budget. ___
   b They had some nice suits, but they were all too tight. ___
2. a The dress was so finely stitched that it looked seamless. ___
   b It needs to be a seamless process for your customers. ___
3. a Instead of buying a cheap off-the-rack suit, save up for a tailor-made suit. ___, ___
   b Don't use an off-the-shelf template for your company's website. We can design a tailor-made site to help you stand out from the competition. ___, ___

B Work in pairs. Decide whether the underlined words in Exercise A are literal (l) or metaphorical (m). Use the information in the box to help you.

Metaphors

A metaphor is a word or phrase that's used in a different context from its literal meaning. It's easier to understand a metaphor when you know the literal meaning. For example:

Literal: *There is a **breeze** outside. (= a light wind)*

Metaphorical: *It was a **breeze**! I got the job. (= easy and pleasant)*

C Complete the sentences with the correct form of the words in the box.

catch drain peanut run snap wind

1. I'm getting very ________ up about it.
2. You're throwing money down the ________.
3. It's much better in the long ________.
4. Then you'll have two suits in your closet for ________.
5. Choose a template that ________ your eye.
6. All the best stuff will be ________ up immediately.

D Work in pairs. What is the metaphorical meaning of each sentence in Exercise C?

E Complete the questions with the correct form of a word from Exercises A or C.

1. When one person leaves a job and another person takes over, how can they make the transition as ________ as possible?
2. Are you the kind of person who plans for the long ________? Or do you tend to make snap decisions?
3. Have you ever bought anything that was ________ especially for you? Or do you always buy ________ products?
4. Which current trends really ________ you up?

F SPEAK Work in pairs. Discuss the questions in Exercise E.

PRONUNCIATION
Linking /r/

A Work in pairs. Read the sentences below aloud. Draw a (‿) between any words that you think are connected by a /r/ sound.

1. I saw a nice suit yesterday for 40% off.
2. You're only saving money if you buy something you need.
3. I just wore a jacket from an old suit.
4. They had no idea I was wearing sweatpants.
5. Are auction sites the best place to pick up cheap clothes?
6. Avoid stores in a trendy area or one with a lot of students.
7. Many sales clerks are authorized to offer discounts.

1.2 **B** Listen to check. Then practice saying the sentences.

SPEAKING HUB

A PREPARE Choose one of the following roles. Spend a few minutes thinking about your character (e.g. your age, background, ambitions, the problems you face, etc).

- **Role 1: The fashion victim.** You always want the latest designer fashions, but you're worried you would spend far too much.
- **Role 2: The reluctant shopper.** You hate shopping and don't care what you wear, but all your clothes are old and scruffy.
- **Role 3: The trendsetter.** You like to take risks and experiment with your clothes. Just one problem: you've run out of ideas!

B DISCUSS Work in groups of two or three. Role-play a conversation between your characters. Ask your partners for more information about their situation. Offer each other (good or bad) fashion advice.

I know it feels good to snap up a bargain, but in the long run, it's just money down the drain, don't you think?

C REFLECT Report back to the class on the best and worst advice for each character.

Talk about style and fashion

Give fashion advice

1.2 Trendsetting

- Compare different trends
- Make a podcast or vlog

G – comparatives and superlatives
P – emphatic stress
V – experimenting with prefixes and suffixes
S – using contrasts to work out meaning

READING

A SPEAK Work in pairs. Think of as many trends from the past five years as you can in one minute. Use the topics below to help you.

- technology
- music
- fashion
- culture

B READ FOR MAIN IDEA Read *The life cycle of a trend* quickly. Match the paragraphs (1–7) with the topics (a–d). Some paragraphs cover more than one topic.

a musical styles ___
b music formats ___, ___, ___
c games ___
d human needs ___, ___, ___

THE LIFE CYCLE OF A TREND

1 Technology trends are very simple at first sight: older technologies become <u>outdated</u> and <u>anachronistic</u>, to be replaced by **newer**, **<u>funkier</u>** technologies, until they are rendered <u>obsolete</u> with the next cycle. In this way, the vinyl records of the 1970s gave way to cassettes in the 1980s. By the 1990s, cassettes were <u>old hat</u> and CDs were <u>state-of-the-art</u>. By the 2000s, we all loved <u>novel</u> gadgets like MP3 players. But by the 2010s, we had cloud-based music streaming services like Spotify. Why limit yourself to the music you own, when you can stream every song ever recorded?

2 But in 2016, the unexpected happened: sales of vinyl records in the UK outstripped digital music sales for the first time. The renewed interest in vinyl is a powerful reminder that trends don't always flow in a straight line from <u>fringe</u> products to mass-market <u>blockbusters</u>. It also reminds us to pay attention to the durability of trends over decades, not just the short-term ups and downs of **the latest** fads.

3 These trends are **clearest** in the world of popular music, which seems to be on a 20-year cycle. In the 1980s, music from the 50s and 60s was cool, while 70s music was <u>tacky</u>. By the 1990s, 70s music was enjoying a revival, but 80s music had become the height of uncool. After 2000, it was OK to like 80s music again but now 90s music was for losers. The 20-year cycle makes **somewhat more sense** when you remember that the average trendsetter is about 22 years old. They <u>feel sheepish about</u> the music they enjoyed when they were 12, but they can look back **a great deal more fondly** at the music from their early childhood.

4 There's a key difference between a trend, a flash-in-the-pan and a fad. A flash-in-the-pan pops up suddenly, grabs everyone's attention, and then disappears again **almost as suddenly**. A few years ago, the whole world went crazy for a new smartphone app called 'Pokémon Go'. At one point, people were playing it everywhere you looked. But within a few months, almost everybody had abandoned it, leaving only a handful of <u>die-hard fans</u> to persevere with it.

Vinyl LP Sales and Market Share

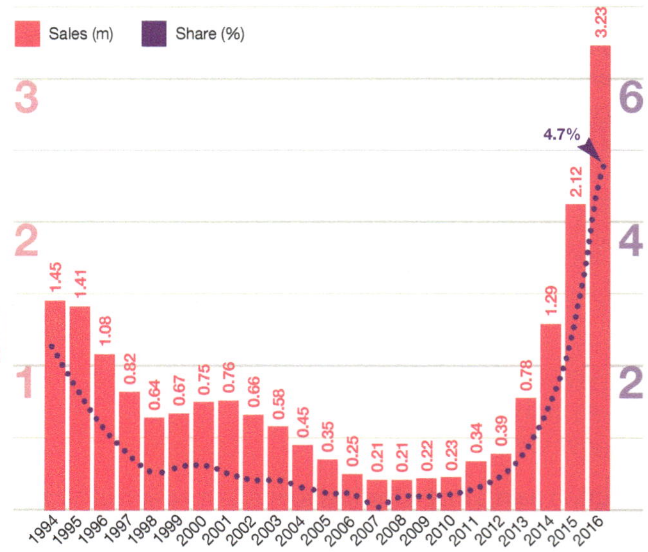

Source: British Phonographic Industry

5 A fad, on the other hand, may be **a little more <u>enduring</u>**, but it too is doomed to disappear sooner or later because it serves no useful purpose. It may be <u>quirky</u> or amusing, but unless it fulfills a basic human need, like 'convenience', 'social status', 'self-expression' or 'security', it will never be **more than a <u>gimmick</u>**.

6 In contrast, an <u>authentic</u> trend always fulfills one of **our very deepest** needs – something that's shared by every human that's ever lived. Of course, nobody really needs **a slightly thinner than usual phone** or every song ever recorded, but we do need things like relaxation, creative stimulation, self-confidence and a sense of belonging to a social group, which those products and services satisfy.

7 This idea of basic human needs also goes some way toward explaining **by far the most curious** feature of the vinyl revival: almost half of buyers of vinyl records never actually listen to them according to a poll by ICM Unlimited! As long as we see vinyl as 'a music format' to fulfill our need for 'relaxation' and 'creative stimulation', this makes no sense. But don't forget, we also have a need to own beautiful physical objects to express our personality, and this is **every bit as important as** those other needs. And of course, the large-sleeved LPs **more than meet** that particular need, to **a much greater extent than** either <u>diminutive</u> CDs or <u>intangible</u> digital downloads.

Glossary

doom (v) to make someone or something certain to fail, be destroyed, be extremely unhappy, etc
durability (n) the ability to continue to exist or work for a long time.
outstrip (v) to become larger than something else
revival (n) the process of becoming active, successful, or popular again

C WORK OUT MEANING Read the article carefully and answer the questions. Use the information in the box to help you.

Using contrasts to work out meaning

It's usually possible to work out the meaning of new words and phrases by looking for contrasts with known words and phrases. Look out for linking words (e.g. *while, but*) that signal a contrast.

1 Which underlined adjectives in paragraph 1 mean *old-fashioned*? Which mean *new*?

2 What do the two underlined words in paragraph 2 contrast?

3 What do the underlined words and phrases mean in paragraph 3?

4 What does the underlined phrase in paragraph 4 mean? What is it being contrasted with in the same sentence?

5 Which two verbs are being contrasted in the last sentence in paragraph 4?

6 Which of the underlined words in paragraphs 5 and 6 have a positive meaning? Which have a negative meaning?

7 What do the underlined adjectives in paragraph 7 mean? Which words in the same paragraph have the opposite meanings?

D Work in pairs. Compare your answers to Exercise C.

E SPEAK Work in pairs. Discuss the questions.

1 Do you agree that all successful trends are popular because they fulfill a basic human need?

2 Can you think of any examples or counterexamples to support your opinion?

GRAMMAR

Comparatives and superlatives

A Are these statements true (T) or false (F)?

1 After a comparative adjective (e.g. *bigger*), we always need *than*. T / F

2 We form the comparative and superlative of *-ly* adverbs (e.g. *quickly*) by changing *-y* to *-ier*/*-iest*. T / F

3 We always need *the* before a superlative (e.g. *fastest*). T / F

B Work in pairs. Justify your choices in Exercise A with examples in bold from the *The life cycle of a trend*.

1 ____________________

2 ____________________

3 ____________________

C WORK IT OUT Complete the rules with an example in bold from the article.

Advanced comparatives and superlatives

1 Some modifiers start with *a/an* (e.g. *a little*). When we use these together with *a/an* + noun, the second *a/an* goes after the comparative: ____________________

2 Only a few words (*anticipated / expected / hoped for / necessary / usual*) can come between *than* and a noun:
____

3 We can use the structure *more than* with a small number of verbs (*double, make up for, meet*):
____

D Go to the Grammar Hub on page 122.

E SPEAK Tell your partner about one of the following. Use comparative and superlative structures.

- a movie that you enjoyed more than you thought you would
- a concert that you went to or an album you really love
- the most enjoyable vacation you've ever had

SPEAKING

DISCUSS Work in pairs. Compare the following things. Use structures from this lesson.

1 fashion from 1 / 5 / 10 / 20 / 50 years ago

2 popular music from 5 / 10 / 20 / 30 years ago

3 technology now / 10 / 20 / 50 years ago

4 society now / 10 / 20 / 100 years ago

LISTENING

A SPEAK Work in pairs. Discuss the questions.

1 What's the difference between the types of people in the box? Do you know any of these types of people?

blogger influencer podcaster trendsetter vlogger

2 Do you listen to any podcasts or watch any vlogs? If so, which ones?

B LISTEN FOR GIST 1.3 Listen to a podcast about trendsetting. Which topics do the speakers give advice about?

- ☐ 1 making money
- ☐ 2 choosing a focus
- ☐ 3 using social media to build a community
- ☐ 4 the problem with perfection
- ☐ 5 designing your own website
- ☐ 6 learning from statistics
- ☐ 7 long-term planning
- ☐ 8 learning from mistakes

C LISTEN FOR DETAIL 1.3 Listen again. Are the statements true (T) or false (F)? Correct the false statements.

1 Dora and Adam are in the same room. T / F

2 Dora regrets that she made so many mistakes. T / F

3 Hardly anyone watched Dora's videos at first. T / F

4 Dora releases a video at the same time every week. T / F

5 Dora replies to every comment on her videos. T / F

6 Dora sees herself as an overnight success. T / F

7 Adam is unsure about filming himself. T / F

D SPEAK Discuss in pairs.

1 Do you think the idea of an 'overnight success' is a myth?

2 Have you ever had a blog or vlog? If not, would you ever consider starting one? Why/Why not?

VOCABULARY

Experimenting with prefixes and suffixes

A Complete Dora's advice using the words in the box.

amateurish disaster-prone hyper-influential largish re-editing super-lucky tech-savvy unmute user-friendly

VLOG AWAY!

A lot of the vlogs on the web are very [1] ______________. Stand out by editing and [2] ______________ until your vlog is as slick and professional as possible.

If you're not particularly [3] ______________, do some research into [4] ______________ software – one with clear instructions.

Look at some of the videos made by the most [5] ______________ vloggers and some with a [6] ______________ number of subscribers. Success isn't down to being [7] ______________, it's about hard work and perfecting the craft.

You don't have to be a [8] ______________ person to sometimes forget to [9] ______________ the mic. Remember not to be too hard on yourself. We all make mistakes, the important thing is to learn from them. You'll get more confident with experience.

B Complete the information in the box with examples from Exercise A. Use the information in the box to help you.

Experimenting with prefixes and suffixes

1. Some prefixes (e.g. *un-*, *re-*) allow you to invent completely new verbs: ________, ________
2. *Super-*, *hyper-* and *ultra-* all mean 'much more than usual': ________, ________
3. You can add *-y* or *-ish* to nouns to invent new informal adjectives: *trashy*, *babyish*, ________
4. You can add *-ish* to an adjective or number to mean 'more or less': *twentyish*, *smallish*, ________
5. *Friendly*, *prone*, *proof*, *resistant* and *savvy* can be used as suffixes to make adjectives: *environmentally friendly*, *waterproof*, *heat-resistant*, ________, ________, ________

.4 **C** Replace the underlined phrases in these extracts with a word with a prefix or suffix. You may need to change the word order in some sentences. Then listen to check.

1. You actually need to forget all you learned about all those rules about perfection!
2. Whenever I have a fairly good idea for a podcast, then I try to make it within a few days.
3. You also need to be far more aware of how to use social media.
4. Well, there are plenty of people who post offensive comments that are like spam.
5. Your content would work much better as videos that work well on smartphones.
6. I really think you should think again and become a vlogger instead.
7. I feel incredibly exhausted just thinking about it.

D Go to the **Vocabulary Hub** on **page 142**.

E **SPEAK** Work in pairs. Think of examples of the following.

- websites that aren't very user-friendly / smartphone-friendly
- a person who's tech-savvy / fashion-savvy
- any objects you own that are waterproof or water-resistant
- any objects you own that are damage-prone

PRONUNCIATION
Emphatic stress

1.5 **A** Listen to the extracts from the recording. Underline the words that are stressed.

1. One of the most common mistakes that new vloggers and podcasters make is to expect everything to be perfect.
2. But after a while, it got a lot easier!
3. … if nobody cared after a year, I'd give up. And it did take a while to get noticed.
4. … you've found your niche and you've created some excellent content.
5. Every Wednesday at ten o'clock, there will be a new video on my channel.
6. I suppose in many people's eyes, I am an overnight success.
7. I felt awkward at first, too, but you do get used to it.
8. Dora Cho, thanks so much for joining me today.

B Work in pairs. Why did the speaker use emphatic stress in the extracts in Exercise A? Practice saying the sentences.

1.6 **C** Decide where to add emphatic stress in these sentences. Then listen to check.

1. That's one of the most popular vlogs on the web.
2. When you reach one million subscribers, it will be worth it!
3. Is it possible to be a trendsetter and an influencer?

SPEAKING HUB

A **PLAN** Work in small groups. You are going to make a podcast or vlog episode about trends. Discuss the following questions.

- What will it be about?
- Why will anyone want to listen/watch?
- What topics could you cover?
- How will you add your own personalities?

B **DISCUSS** Share your initial ideas with the class. Ask your 'audience' what the next episodes should focus on. Try to engage with them to generate enthusiasm.

C **PREPARE** Plan an episode of your podcast/vlog. Don't simply write a script – you'll need to stay spontaneous.

D **PRESENT** Make your podcast/vlog. If you have recording equipment, e.g. a phone, you can use that. Otherwise, present your episode to the class.

- Compare different trends
- Make a podcast or vlog

Café Hub

1.3 Diet and lifestyle

A – *give it a go* **S** – using circumlocution

Veganuary

A Work in pairs. You are going to watch a video titled *Veganuary*. What do you think *Veganuary* means?

B ▶ Watch the video and check your answers to Exercise A.

C ▶ Watch the video again. Complete the sentences with one word or a number.

1. There are now more choices for vegans when they eat out and at ______________.
2. The food which Tabitha says she misses most is ______________.
3. Tabitha initially became a vegan because of ______________ reasons.
4. Many cafés sell a wider selection of products to appeal to ______________.
5. Some people limit eating meat to one or two times a ______________.
6. In the UK ______________ people attempted *Veganuary*.

Glossary

boom (v) to experience an increase in activity, interest or growth

ethics (n) a set of principles that people use to decide what is right and what is wrong

mainstream (adj) considered ordinary or normal and accepted or used by most people

niche (n) a specialized segment of the market for a particular kind of product or service

AUTHENTIC ENGLISH

A Read the sentence from the video. What do you think the phrase in bold means?

Health, ethics, there are just so many reasons, I think, to ***give it a go****.*

B Read the information in the box to check your answer to Exercise A.

give it a go

We use *give it a go* to express it's a good idea to attempt something you haven't done before. We also use *give it a try*, *give it a shot* and *take a stab at it* to express the same idea.

C Work in pairs. Respond to the sentences using *give it a go* or one of the other expressions from the box in Exercise B.

1. We're not sure whether to try skiing when we're in Switzerland.
   Why not give it a shot and see if you like it?
2. Sam would like to study French but he's always found languages difficult.
3. I've never traveled to another country alone before.
4. Nina's always been too shy to introduce herself to complete strangers.

D **SPEAK** Discuss three things you would like to start doing that you have never tried before.

The big pitch

SAM MALCOLM AMANDA HARRY EMILY

A Watch the video. Work in pairs. Discuss the questions.

1 Who is Sam and how does he spend his day?
2 What do the following people do?

Emily Malcolm Amanda Harry

B Watch the video again. Complete the sentences with the best option.

1 Emily feels *confident about / unprepared for* her pitch.
2 Emily would like to *grow her current business / start a new sustainable business*.
3 Emily's yoga experience package will include *two / three* meals a day.
4 Emily's business will focus on *yoga and food / outdoor yoga*.
5 Emily thinks *she will make profits evenly every year / her profits will equal her costs in the first year*.

SPEAKING SKILL

A Work in pairs. Look at the example from the video. Why has Emily used this phrase?

Emily: ... Well, it's kind of like my yoga classes that I teach, but with the idea that you would be getting more than just exercise.

B Look at the information in the box. Then underline examples of circumlocution in the sentences from the video.

Using circumlocution

We frequently use circumlocution, the use of many words where fewer would do, in a deliberate attempt to be vague or evasive, when we are nervous or can't think of the exact word, or even to make an idea sound more impressive. Look at these other sentences from the video and underline examples of circumlocution.

1 I mean what I really want to do is to expand my business into something more sustainable, you know, a yoga retreat where people can stay for a few days.
2 Full body cleansing, you know the physiological withdrawal of toxins from the body.

C Why do you think Amanda uses circumlocution in the sentences from Exercise B?

D Work in pairs. Ask each other about the following things. When you answer try to be evasive or vague. Use the expressions from Exercise B to help you.

- your favorite café
- your diet
- your job or studies

SPEAKING HUB

A PLAN You are going to make a short pitch for a business you would like to set up. Think of a business idea.

B PREPARE Write notes on what you are going to say. Consider the following points.

- product/service
- USP (Unique Selling Point)
- market
- profitability

C PRESENT Work in groups. Pitch your business idea.

Well, I'd like to give running my own exercise boot camp a try.

D REACT Once everyone in the group has pitched their idea, decide which is the best. Give reasons.

Pitch your own business idea

Turn to page 156 to learn how to write a blog post about a trend.

Unit 1 Review

GRAMMAR

A **Put the words into the correct order to make nominal clauses.**

A: Why are you getting rid of those pants? There's nothing wrong with them!

B: Well, the fact [1]**aren't / in the knees / holes / that / there** doesn't mean I can wear them forever. These pants are so last year!

A: Come on! [2] **your clothes / people / think about / what** isn't important! What counts is [3]**on / what's / inside / the**!

B: Exactly! But you know what they say: [4]**on / good / to look / outside / the** is to feel good on the inside. And anyway, [5]**fashion / gives / following** me a lot of pleasure.

A: Yeah, apart from the fact [6]**you can afford / that you spend / more than**.

B: [7]**much / I spend / How** is up to me!

B **Choose the correct options (a, b, c or d) to complete each sentence.**

1 This is the ___ worst movie I've ever seen.
 - a just
 - b marginally
 - c somewhat
 - d absolute

2 There was a slightly larger than ___ crowd at the game.
 - a anticipated
 - b believed
 - c hope for
 - d previous

3 Some online stores are ___ as cheap as high-end stores.
 - a by far
 - b double
 - c far and away
 - d twice

4 My achievements are ___ as impressive as yours.
 - a considerably
 - b every bit
 - c rather
 - d significantly

5 The hotel offers ___ best views across the bay.
 - a at least
 - b fractionally
 - c the very
 - d dramatically

VOCABULARY

A **Match numbers (1–6) to letters (a–f) to form full sentences.**

1 If Jon decides to come to the wedding,
2 If you get a new job in an office,
3 If celebrities dress in a stylish way,
4 If you wear creative and original clothes,
5 If you want to stay cool in the summer,
6 If you're going away for the weekend,

a wear light, baggy clothes.
b you'll fit in well here – everyone has a very unique style.
c pack at least four outfits.
d make sure he doesn't wear his usual scruffy clothes.
e check the company's dress code before you start.
f they usually set a trend.

B **Complete the words in the sentences. Some of the letters have been given to help you.**

1 I can't afford to eat out again this week – I'm on a very ___ ___ g ___ ___ budget.
2 We offer a range of ___ ___ ___-the-___ ___ ___ ___ and ___ a ___ ___ ___ ___-m ___ ___ ___ suits for our customers.
3 I got really ___ ___ u ___ ___ up this morning when I couldn't find a parking space.
4 I know it seems expensive now, but it's worth it in the long ___ ___ ___.
5 If we are late getting to the store, all the bargains will have been ___ ___ ___ p ___ ___ ___ up!
6 If you have the time to look, you can buy great clothes for p ___ ___ n ___ ___ ___ in thrift stores.
7 The exam was an absolute ___ ___ ___ ___ z ___ – I'm sure I got a great grade!

C **Complete the ad using a prefix or suffix from the box with the words in parentheses. Each prefix or suffix may be used more than once. Other changes may be necessary.**

-ish ultra- -savvy -prone -y -friendly -proof

TRENDY KID

Are you looking for an [1]_______________ (*cool*) fashion gadget for an [2]_______________ (*accident*) child?
Our new unbreakable 'Trendy Kid' smartwatch is completely [3]_______________ (*child*).

No need to be [4]_______________ (*tech*)!
This watch uses the latest skeuomorphic design principles to make it as [5]_______________ (*user*) as possible.

Available in [6]_______________ (*flower*) pink or [7]_______________ (*mud*) brown.

Do you love the design but worry that you'll look too [8]_______________ (*child*) wearing a 'Trendy Kid' watch? Head over to our store for a huge range of on-trend adult smartwatches!

2 CREATIVITY

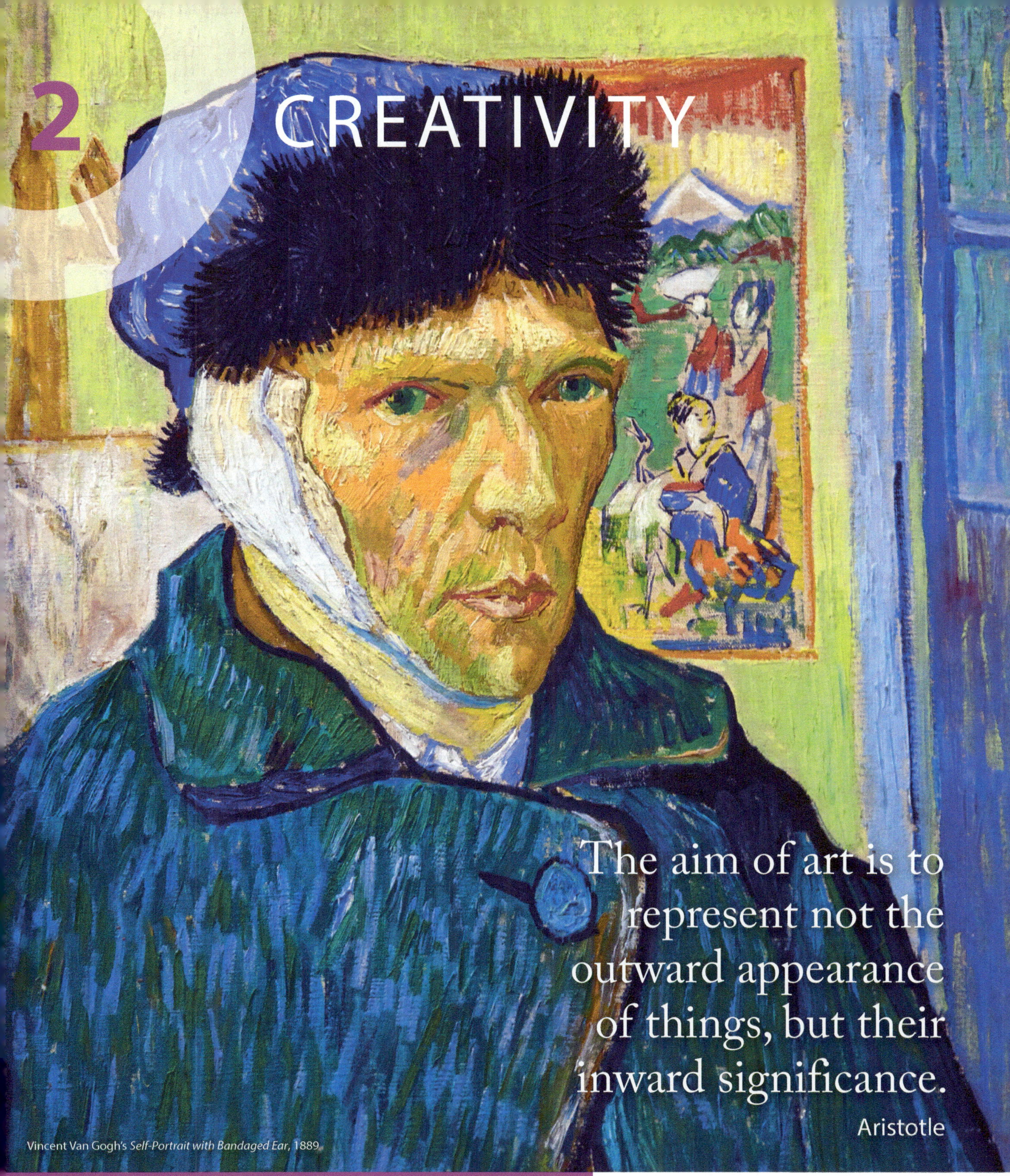

> The aim of art is to represent not the outward appearance of things, but their inward significance.
>
> Aristotle

Vincent Van Gogh's *Self-Portrait with Bandaged Ear*, 1889

OBJECTIVES

- give a presentation about art
- talk about creative projects
- talk about finding inspiration
- describe a life-changing moment
- discuss a work of art
- write a review

Work with a partner. Discuss the questions.

1 Look at the picture. What is your opinion of works of art like this?

2 What does Aristotle mean in the quote? Do you agree with him?

3 Is the main aim, or goal of art:

- to tell a story
- to express emotion
- to persuade
- to celebrate an event
- to create beauty
- to entertain?

2.1 The story behind it

- Give a presentation about art
- Talk about creative projects

V – describing art **P** – contrastive stress **G** – narrative tenses **S** – anticipating content before listening

VOCABULARY
Describing art

A SPEAK Work in pairs. Look at the pictures (a–e) and discuss the questions.

1 Do you know any of these works of art?
2 Which do you prefer? Why?

B Choose the correct adjectives to complete the comments (1–5).

C Go to the Vocabulary Hub on page 142.

D What art forms are being described in Exercise B?

1 ______ 2 ______ 3 ______ 4 ______ 5 ______

E SPEAK Think of an example of an art form from Exercise D. Describe it to your partner.

I find this installation groundbreaking. It makes you think about space in a different way.
It's actually fairly … It's not that … It's somewhat …

1 I think some famous works of art are ***overrated / repetitive***. But that isn't the case here. The artist's use of light and shade in this composition was different from anything that had come before – it was truly ***pretentious / groundbreaking***.

2 It was ***hilarious / tedious***! I couldn't stop laughing. OK, the same jokes again and again become a little ***underrated / repetitive***, but the comic performances were ***awesome / appalling***.

3 It's a very ***unconventional / repetitive*** piece. I can see why some people wouldn't want something so big and strange put up in a public space. They probably think it's a little ***acclaimed / pretentious***, as if the artist is trying too hard to be different.

4 Most people recognize this image. It's so ***iconic / hilarious***, capturing the mood of the time it was taken. It's ***thought-provoking / unconventional***, too – it really makes you consider the human story behind this historical event.

5 The risk with performances like this is if the songs are ***appalling / iconic*** then it's really not enjoyable. It just makes them really ***tedious / awesome*** – so long and slow. Fortunately the music, lighting and costumes in this show were really special. It was a truly ***sensational / iconic*** experience. I can see why it's been ***overrated / acclaimed*** by critics and audiences.

a

b

LISTENING

A Work in pairs. Read a review of the radio show *More than meets the eye*. Are there similar radio shows in your country?

> ### *More than meets the eye*
> ★★★★★ ★★★★★
>
> gives an analysis of one different piece of groundbreaking fine art each week. The guest speakers make these discussions unique and sometimes fairly unconventional. They don't just have specialist knowledge of the artist, but also some personal connection to the pieces.

B **ANTICIPATE CONTENT** You're going to listen to an episode of *More than meets the eye* about picture b. Work in pairs and answer the questions below. Use the information in the box to help you.

> **Anticipating content before listening**
>
> You can use different types of information to predict what you will hear.
> - Read notes, reviews, handouts, etc.
> - Look at titles or images for clues about what the speaker will cover.
> - Use your own knowledge to predict topics or themes.
> - Use information to think of questions you expect to be answered.

1 What topics will be discussed in the show?

____

2 What questions will be answered?

____

C **LISTEN FOR GIST** Listen to the show and check your predictions in Exercise B.

D **LISTEN FOR DETAIL** Listen and write down the different ideas about who the main subject of the painting is.

1 ________________

2 ________________

3 ________________

E **SPEAK** Work in pairs and discuss the questions.

1 Who do you think the subject of the painting is?

2 Why do you think the artist chose this composition?

PRONUNCIATION

Contrastive stress

2.3 **A** Listen to these extracts from the radio show. Draw arrows to show whether the intonation rises (↗) or falls (↘).

1 Yes, we can see her entourage on the right (__), but to the left (__), we can see the artist himself, standing next to a gigantic canvas.

2 So, it's a portrait of the King and Queen (__), not the Infanta (__).

2.4 **B** Underline the words you think will be stressed and draw arrows to show where you think the intonation will rise (↗) or fall (↘). Then listen to check.

1 Actually, Mondrian wasn't American, he was Dutch.

2 Although I like his landscapes, his portraits are much better.

3 Why don't we watch a movie instead of going to the gallery?

4 I don't think it's tedious. I just think it's overrated.

5 It was painted in 1656 – you said 1666.

6 **A:** You study art history, don't you?
B: No, I study fine art, not art history.

C **SPEAK** Guess whether your partner likes these things or not. Respond to your partner's guesses. Use contrastive stress when appropriate.

> classical music · comic books · crime novels · heavy metal · Hollywood movies · modern art · musicals · science fiction movies · soap operas

A: You like Spider-Man comicbooks.
B: No, I like Batman not Spider-Man.

SPEAKING

A Choose a work of art that you really like. It could be a painting, a sculpture, a photograph, a movie, a book, a play, a poem or a song.

B **PLAN** Write notes so that you can talk about:

- information about the artist / writer / singer
- a description of the work of art
- your interpretation of the work of art
- the reasons why you like this work of art.

C **PRESENT** Give a short presentation to your partner about the work of art you have chosen.

D **DISCUSS** Ask your partner about the work of art he or she chose.

c

d

e

READING

A PREDICT Look at the pictures in the article. What kind of place is this? Do you know anything about it?

B SKIM Read the box below about the Eden Project. Check your answers to Exercise A.

C READ FOR DETAIL Read *How we made the Eden Project*. Put the events (a–h) in the correct order. Two events are not needed.

___ **a** They hired a lot of people to work on the project.
___ **b** They did a lot of tests to make sure the building would be safe.
___ **c** They tried out some innovative techniques.
___ **d** They had to stop working until they found more money.
___ **e** They started working on designs without a specific location in mind.
___ **f** Tim Smit had the inspiration for the project.
___ **g** They found the ideal location.
___ **h** They conducted a feasibility study.

The Eden Project is a spectacular tropical garden housed inside huge plastic bubbles within a crater the size of thirty soccer fields.

How we made the Eden Project

Tim Smit, *founder*

We started the construction with just $3000 in the bank. To persuade government officials to part with public funds, you have to do a feasibility study and that's expensive. So we simply progressed on faith, and hope, promising ourselves that we'd never use the word *if* only *when*.

The idea for a huge horticultural expo had come to me as I worked on the Lost Gardens of Heligan. [1]I'd always loved the thought of a lost civilization in a volcanic crater, and when I saw the lunar landscape of the old Cornish clay pits, [2]I realized they'd be the perfect site.

A friend put me in touch with an architecture firm. I hadn't received a penny in funding at that point, or even a site, just a belief that the idea of a lost world in a crater would appeal to anyone who's ever been 12. They thought the idea was crazy, but it struck them as an adventure and they agreed to start work for nothing. Meanwhile, a construction firm put some money into the project in return for a share of the profits. Everyone was now suddenly highly motivated.

Our two horticultural directors recruited anyone they'd ever worked with and debated what to put in the buildings. I'd envisaged rainforest and Mediterranean areas, eager for it to be the greatest ever collection of plants useful to humans. But it was also a question of finding a balance between the wow factor and more meditative moments. So we have a giant waterfall along with a prairie that, in the winter, is about the most boring thing you can see – then, for six weeks a year, it bursts into spectacular life.

Glossary

arch (n) a structure with a curved top and straight sides that you can walk through
camaraderie (n) friendship and trust between people in a group
crater (n) a large round hole in the ground
pioneer (n) one of the first people to do something important
pit (n) a very large hole dug in the ground in order to obtain a particular substance or type of stone
quarry (n) a place where stone is dug out of the ground.

D SCAN Read the article again. What were the obstacles they had to overcome to build the Eden Project?

E SPEAK Work in pairs. Discuss the questions.

1. Why do you think people agreed to work on the project while funding was uncertain?
2. Why do you think this project succeeded?
3. Would you like to have worked on this project?
4. What other kinds of projects would you like to work on?

Jolyon Brewis, *architect of Grimshaw Architects*

Most architects dream of creating a new world on a scale that eclipses all that's gone before. So, in the early days, when there was always the threat of construction being stopped because of lack of money, all the companies involved carried on regardless: we were so enthralled by the vision.

Our first designs were for different locations, including a tent-like structure for a hillside, then Smit discovered the china clay quarry at Bodelva. It had a romantic, lost world feel since it would be hidden from view until you were almost upon it. For a long while it all seemed like a terrific gamble. Usually, the one thing an architect can rely on is solid ground, but since it was still a working quarry there was a lot of movement. What's more, to figure out costs, we had to design our buildings right down to the last detail, even though no one knew if there'd even be enough money to buy the site.

[3]<u>We'd been working</u> on a series of snaking arches linked with glass, but while one of our design teams [4]<u>were cleaning up</u>, they realized that bubbles would have far more stability on the shifting soil. Building on such a huge scale involved untried technology: this was a leap into the unknown. Glass would have been too heavy so we pioneered 11-meter hexagonal pillows of inflated plastic. It had never been used so big before and we had no idea how it would behave. So we had to work through various disaster scenarios, such as what would happen if one deflated, then filled up with water and brought down the entire structure.

The worst moments were at the beginning when we [5]<u>hadn't been given</u> the funding yet and some of the foundations [6]<u>got washed away</u> during one of the wettest winters in memory. But there was a great feeling of camaraderie. We felt there was nothing we couldn't cope with.

GRAMMAR

Narrative tenses

A Match the underlined words (1–6) in the article with the tenses.

simple past	___	past perfect progressive	___
past progressive	___	simple past passive voice	___
past perfect	___	past perfect passive voice	___

B WORK IT OUT Complete the rules with the tenses in Exercise A.

Narrative tenses

1. When we tell a story, we use the ______________ and ______________ to explain the main events.
2. We use the ______________ and ______________ to give background information for actions that were completed before the main events of the story.
3. We use the ______________ and ______________ to give background information for actions that were in progress before the main events of the story.

C Go to the **Grammar Hub** on **page 124**.

D Choose a sentence and continue the story. (It doesn't have to be a true story!)

1. I had been working for several hours when …
2. I had been planning to go to … for months, but …
3. I had just gone to bed when …
4. It had been raining all day, so …
5. I had been feeling sick all day because …
6. I had already eaten a big breakfast, but …

SPEAKING HUB

A PREPARE Think of an anecdote about an interesting project you worked on or a piece of work you have done. Use the ideas below to help you prepare what you are going to say.

- what was the project or piece of work
- what went well
- what went badly
- what would you do differently if you could do it again

B PRESENT Work in groups. Tell your anecdote about the project or piece of work.

C DISCUSS Listen to your classmates' anecdotes, react to what they say and ask questions.

D REFLECT Choose the best anecdotes.

Give a presentation about art
Talk about creative projects

2.2 Creative people

- Talk about finding inspiration
- Describe a life-changing moment

V – ideas and inspiration; compound adjectives
G – future in the past
P – questions for comment or criticism
S – inferring meaning

VOCABULARY
Ideas and inspiration

A Read the blog post *Sparking ideas*. Choose the correct definition (a or b) for the underlined phrases (1–10).

1 a find the right location
  b find the right mood
2 a abandon an idea
  b develop an idea
3 a working from nothing
  b working with no equipment
4 a steal someone's ideas
  b discuss something with someone
5 a get ideas from
  b paint a picture of
6 a escape a problem
  b help you to think of some ideas
7 a become very involved with something
  b are about to finish
8 a feel more energetic about
  b get a different view of
9 a find a good idea
  b am unable to progress
10 a think carefully
  b rely on your feelings

SPARKING IDEAS

Jasmine, artist

'Some people are very practical about finding ideas. But not me. I need to [1]get into the right state of mind, whatever it takes. It means traveling miles to get away from everyone, working through the night or going for a walk – until I find inspiration or it finds me. Then I just [2]run with an idea and see where it takes me.'

Leo, dancer and choreographer

'[5]I draw inspiration from other art – movies, paintings, even books are great ways [6]to jump start your creativity. They're not just sources of inspiration for my dance. When [7]you immerse yourself in other art forms, you get the distance you need from your own work. You [8]get a fresh perspective on it.'

Michelle, director

'[3]Working from a blank canvas, with no idea where you are going to start, can be really scary. So, … I call my mom! It's great [4]to bounce ideas off someone. Even if you disagree, it can help you move forward.'

Sam, playwright

'Although writing is my job, when [9]I hit a wall and just can't find the ideas, I start doodling cartoons, shapes. It really helps me to think. Then when the ideas start to come, [10]you trust your instincts. You just know which ideas to use, which to combine and which to just forget.'

B Choose the correct phrases to complete the sentences.

1 I've just ***gotten into the right state of mind / hit a wall*** with this project. I have no inspiration and can't get any further with it.

2 With art projects, you can't always know for certain you have the best idea. Sometimes you just have to ***trust your instincts / work from a blank canvas***.

3 When you're feeling uninspired, talk to other people. ***Bouncing ideas off someone / Running with an idea*** can only help.

4 When there are no distractions and you are completely focused, you can truly ***get a fresh perspective on / immerse yourself in*** something.

5 We had no idea where we could begin with the design. We were ***jump starting our creativity / working from a blank canvas***.

C SPEAK Work in pairs. Do you ever have to be creative in your daily life? How do you come up with ideas?

LISTENING

A LISTEN FOR MAIN IDEA Listen to Mark and Lauren discussing an article about inspiration. What seven tips for getting inspiration do they discuss?

SEVEN TIPS FOR GETTING INSPIRATION

1 ____________________

2 ____________________

3 ____________________

4 ____________________

5 ____________________

6 ____________________

7 ____________________

B LISTEN FOR DETAIL Listen again. Which of the tips does Mark like?

C SPEAK Work in pairs. Have you ever tried any of the ideas mentioned in Exercise A? Why/Why not?

PRONUNCIATION

Questions for comment or criticism

A Listen to the questions from the discussion. Draw arrows in the parentheses to show whether the intonation rises (↗) or falls (↘) at the end of each sentence.

1 Isn't that somewhat pretentious? ( )

2 Is he crazy? ( )

3 Why does she keep writing if it's terrible? ( )

4 Don't you think? ( )

5 Is she serious? ( )

6 How can you make something when you don't know what you're doing? ( )

2.7 **B** Choose the correct intonation for the questions. Then listen to check your answers.

1 **A:** Do you think it's sensible to schedule time for creativity?

B: What's the point of that? (*rise / fall*) You can't be creative if you're not in the right state of mind.

2 **A:** Do you ever have creative ideas while you're dreaming?

B: Yes, but I can never remember them. Isn't that frustrating? (*rise / fall*)

3 **A:** Do you find it easier to be creative when you're listening to music?

B: Are you serious? (*rise / fall*) I can't think properly unless it's quiet.

4 **A:** Do you feel more creative early in the morning or late at night?

B: Late at night. Definitely. Who feels creative first thing in the morning? (*rise / fall*)

C SPEAK Ask your partner the questions in Exercise B. Try to use a question for comment or criticism in your answer.

SPEAKING

A Look at the infographic. Think of an advantage and disadvantage for each suggestion.

B Work in pairs. Compare your ideas with your partner.

C Now decide which is the best suggestion for finding ideas. Talk for about one minute.

D DISCUSS Work in pairs and discuss the questions.

1 Are you a creative person?

2 How important is the ability to be creative?

3 Do you think everyone should try to do something creative from time to time?

VOCABULARY
Compound adjectives

A Complete the fame quiz.

ARE YOU CUT OUT FOR FAME?

RATE YOURSELF ON A SCALE OF 1 to 5.
1 = Strongly agree 5 = Strongly disagree

1. You would trade having privacy for being world famous. 1 2 3 4 5
2. You are very focused on one kind of career. You are not open-minded to other career choices. 1 2 3 4 5
3. You would describe yourself as a highly-motivated person. 1 2 3 4 5
4. You are thick skinned. You don't mind being criticized. 1 2 3 4 5
5. You would rather be self-employed than do part-time work for someone else for the same money. 1 2 3 4 5
6. You'd prefer to be paid less in a fun creative job than well paid and bored at work. 1 2 3 4 5
7. You can handle working long days and doing late-night shifts. 1 2 3 4 5

B Work in pairs. Turn to page 149 of the Communication Hub to see what your answers say about you.

C Find eight compound adjectives in the quiz. Use the information in the box to help you.

Compound adjectives

Compound adjectives can be formed in several ways, including:

- adjective + noun: *last-minute*
- adjective + participle: *left-handed*
- adverb + participle: *never-ending*
- noun + adjective: *sun-dried*
- noun + participle: *career-ending*

We always hyphenate compound adjectives before a noun, but not after a noun. However, some compound adjectives are written as one word (e.g. *heartwarming*) or always hyphenated (e.g. *self-important*).

D Go to the Vocabulary Hub on page 142.

E **SPEAK** Work in pairs and discuss the questions. Use some of the adjectives in Exercise C.

1. Would you like to be famous?
2. What do you think are the good and bad points of being famous?

CHANGE OF PLANS

Some people choose a career at a young age and stick with it. However, here are four famous people who ended up with very different careers from what they expected.

CHARLIZE THERON

Charlize Theron, originally from South Africa, was to have been a ballerina. However, she suffered a career-ending injury to her knee that meant she had to abandon her childhood dream. Instead, she decided she would turn to acting. After finding it difficult to land speaking roles, she watched hours of television to try to pick up an American accent. But, the roles still didn't come and although she was getting modeling work, money was tight. One day she was trying to cash a check at the bank but the teller said he was not going to accept it. Theron started to argue with the teller, making a scene in the bank as she tried to explain that she was about to be thrown out of her apartment if she couldn't cash the check. Eventually a man in the line behind her came over to help resolve the situation and, after she had her money, he gave her his business card – he was an agent. A couple of months later, Theron had landed her first movie role.

ANDREA BOCELLI

World-famous opera singer Andrea Bocelli was supposed to have a very different career. Although he displayed a clear talent for music from an early age, his parents encouraged him to study law so that he would always have a steady income. Following his parents' advice, he attended law school and became a lawyer. However, he also continued with his music – playing in piano bars in the evenings to earn money for singing lessons. It was at one of these bars where he got the lucky break that was to launch his career. Zucchero, a famous Italian singer, heard him sing, and thought that he would be perfect for a demo he wanted to make. As a result of that meeting, Bocelli ending up going on tour with Zucchero. Bocelli even sang at Zucchero's birthday party – and was immediately signed up by an agent at the party. The agent knew he was going to be a big star – and she was right.

Glossary

renovate (v) to make something old look new again by repairing and improving it, especially a building

embroidery (n) the activity of decorating cloth with colored stitches

READING

A SPEAK Look at the pictures of the people in the article *Change of plans*. What do you know about them?

B READ FOR DETAIL Read *Change of plans*. What do the four people's stories have in common?

C INFER MEANING Read the article again and answer the questions. Use the information in the box to help you.

Inferring meaning

Writers do not always explain everything in detail. They sometimes provide readers with the facts and allow them to infer the meaning by drawing a conclusion from the available information.

1 Why was Charlize Theron unable to get speaking roles?

2 Does Andrea Bocelli still work as a lawyer?

3 What do we know about Harrison Ford's personality when he was younger?

4 How did Grandma Moses learn to paint?

D SPEAK Work in pairs and discuss the questions

1 Which was the most interesting story? Why?
2 Which person do you think was the luckiest?

HARRISON FORD

Harrison Ford first became interested in acting at the age of 18 because he thought it would be an easy way to get a good grade on his English course. He dropped out of college and moved to Hollywood in his early 20s. He managed to get some small acting jobs, but after a few years he became frustrated with the kind of roles he was being offered. While renovating his house, he decided to use the tools he had bought and the skills he had learned to become a self-employed carpenter. One day, movie director George Lucas hired Ford to make some cabinets for his home and after meeting him, decided to cast him in a movie he was making called *American Graffiti*. When Lucas was auditioning actors for his next movie, he was one actor short so he asked Ford to help out. In the end, he cast Ford and the movie, *Star Wars*, would go on to become a huge hit and make Ford a star.

GRANDMA MOSES

Grandma Moses (Anna Mary Robertson Moses) became a famous painter at the age of 80 – despite not having had any formal training. She was born in 1860 and raised on her parents' farm. She didn't attend school regularly, because she knew she would be leaving home to start working on another farm when she was 12. She married at 17, was widowed at 47, and retired at 76. In fact, she didn't start painting until she took it up as a hobby at the age of 78. She only started because she was giving up embroidery due to pain from arthritis. She painted rural scenes from her childhood, which she gave away or sold cheaply. However, one day an art collector saw her paintings in a local store. He drove straight to her farm and asked to buy all the paintings she had, and, later that year, he exhibited some of her paintings at a show for new painters. This led to solo exhibitions, and soon her shows would break attendance records around the world. She died in 1961.

GRAMMAR

Future in the past

A WORK IT OUT Look at the underlined phrases in the article. Then choose the correct words to complete the rules.

Future in the past

1 When we talk about plans, intentions and predictions that we had in the past, we use ***past / present*** forms of the verbs we usually use to talk about the future.

2 We use *be* + *to* + base form for events that ***came true / didn't come true*** and *be* + *to* + *have* + past participle (or *be* + *supposed to* + verb) for events that ***came true / didn't come true***.

B Go to the **Grammar Hub** on **page 124**.

C Write sentences using the future in the past to explain the situations (1–5). Then share your ideas with a partner.

1 You didn't get up early today.
2 You missed your train or bus this morning.
3 You didn't eat lunch yesterday.
4 You got lost in the city.
5 You went to see a movie with a friend.

I was going to get up early, but I forgot to set my alarm clock.

SPEAKING HUB

A PLAN Think of a time when a change of plans had a big effect on your life. Choose one of these situations or think of your own idea.

- You changed your mind about something.
- You suddenly had an unexpected opportunity.
- Something did not go as you had planned.
- Something good came out of a bad situation.

B PREPARE Write notes to prepare to talk about this event.

C PRESENT Tell your partner about what happened.

D DISCUSS Listen and ask your partner questions.

– Talk about finding inspiration
– Describe a life-changing moment

2.3 Art and design

A– *nowhere* phrases S– managing a discussion

City design festival

a

b

A Work in pairs. Look at the pictures (a and b) and discuss the questions.

1 Where are they?

2 What do you think they are?

B Watch the video and check your answers to Exercise A.

Glossary

accessible (adj) art, music, literature, etc, which is easy to understand and enjoy
ceramic (adj) made from clay baked at a high temperature so that it has become hard
eccentricity (n) the state of behaving in a strange and unusual way, sometimes in a humorous way
installation (n) a piece of art that consists of several objects or pictures arranged to produce a particular effect

C Watch the video again. Check (✓) the things you see.

1 People walking inside an installation. ☐
2 A designer creating an installation. ☐
3 An indoor design exhibition. ☐
4 A man sitting at a table with a cup of coffee. ☐
5 Children playing on the installation. ☐
6 A person taking a photo of an installation. ☐
7 People walking through arches. ☐
8 A designer showing a group of people around an installation. ☐

D Watch the video again. Complete the sentences with the best option.

1 What Camille Walala loves most about an outdoor art installation is that it *makes art easier for people to understand and enjoy* / *allows her to be more creative*.

2 Camille has lived in London for *fifteen* / *twenty* years.

3 A woman says Camille Walala's installation looks like a *theme park* / *bouncy castle*.

4 Adam Nathaniel Furman says people think ceramics are something *found in your bathroom and kitchen* / *used to cover buildings*.

5 Ben Evans says *a minority* / *the majority* of London's design community have British passports.

AUTHENTIC ENGLISH

A Work in pairs. Read the sentences from the video. Then choose the correct words to complete the information in the box.

There's ***nowhere quite like*** *it, especially when it comes to design.*

I absolutely love London, it's like an eccentricity that you've got ***nowhere else****.*

There's nowhere else *really in the UK where you can just walk down the street and see exciting things like this every day.*

***nowhere* phrases**

We use *there's nowhere quite like, that you've got nowhere else* and *there's nowhere else where* to express that a place is ***ordinary*** / ***unique***.

We have many other phrases with *nowhere like: nowhere on Earth, … but nowhere more so than …, out of nowhere, go nowhere, be going nowhere fast, in the middle of nowhere, nowhere near* and *nowhere to be found*.

B Write sentences using phrases with *nowhere* about these places.

1 Paris *There's nowhere on earth like Paris for culture.*
2 London ______
3 Dubai ______
4 New York ______
5 Italy ______
6 Brazil ______

C Work in pairs. Tell each other about some of your favorite places (countries, cities, restaurants, stores, museums, etc) and why they are unique.

Art critics

A Work in pairs. Discuss the questions.

1 Do you like modern art? Why/Why not?
2 What do you think about art criticism?

B Watch the video and answer the questions.

1 What does Malcolm like about the painted paper?
2 What does each of the following people think the message of the painted paper is?
   - Amanda
   - Malcolm
   - male customer
3 Whose opinion is most popular among the three of them?
4 What misunderstanding has occurred?

SPEAKING SKILL

A Work in pairs. Look at the underlined expression from the video and answer the questions.

Amanda: The artist is clearly making a comment on …
Sam: I think you're a little confused …
Amanda: Sam … <u>Can you let me finish?</u> Thanks. The artist is clearly making a statement on feelings of isolation …

1 What has happened in the exchange between Sam and Amanda?
2 Why do we use expressions like this when we're speaking?

Read the information in the box. Which of the ways of managing a discussion (1–5) are used in the exchange in Exercise A?

SAM MALCOLM AMANDA HARRY EMILY

B Match the ways of managing a discussion (1–5) with the examples from the video (a–e) below.

Managing a discussion

1 Interrupting: Say something to stop someone speaking so that you can speak instead.
2 Taking the floor: Signal that you are now going to join a debate or discussion.
3 Returning to a point: Indicate that you want to further discuss a point that you previously made.
4 Stopping an interruption: Tell the person who is trying to interrupt that you want to finish your point first.
5 Pre-empting an interruption: Anticipate that someone will interrupt you and briefly state all the points you want to cover before they cut in.

a Well that leads back to my point … without meaning there is no relationship.
b If I could just finish … my main point though is that it doesn't really matter what it is.
c I couldn't agree more … it does evoke some really intense emotions.
d I don't mean to cut you off, Amanda, but I think it's the exact opposite.
e And that's my point exactly. When you are using bold colors like this artist has, you are clearly trying to expose just how superficial those connections are.

C Work in small groups. Discuss one of the following topics. Use the strategies from Exercise B.

- Art in the past and now
- The greatest artist ever
- Different forms of art

SPEAKING HUB

A **PREPARE** You are going to talk about a work of art in a small group. Look at the picture on page 13. Think about what you want to say about the picture and art in general.

B **PRESENT** Work in small groups. Discuss the picture and present your views.

A: I usually tend to prefer landscapes rather than portraits …
B: Can I just stop you there? … The style of painting is what makes it special.
A: Exactly. What I was actually saying was that while I usually prefer landscapes, in this case …

Discuss a work of art

➤ Turn to page 157 to learn how to write a review about a classic book or movie.

Unit 2 Review

VOCABULARY

A Complete the conversations with the words in the box.

groundbreaking	hilarious	repetitive
sensational	tedious	unconventional

1 **A:** That was a really funny movie. I was crying with laughter.
B: Yes, it was ________________.

2 **A:** I thought her performance was amazing.
B: She was ________________. She deserves an Oscar.

3 **A:** Have you read this book? I'm finding it pretty dull.
B: Yeah, it's a little ________________, isn't it?

4 **A:** It was such an innovative musical. I loved it.
B: Me, too. As you say, it was ________________.

5 **A:** Can we turn this off? It's just car chase after car chase.
B: Yeah, it's kind of ________________, isn't it?

6 **A:** Do you like her work? Her pieces are very unusual.
B: She's ________________, but I find her work exciting.

B Complete the sentences with the words in the box. Then choose which ideas help you feel most creative.

bounce	draw	fresh	trust
immerse	run	stimulate	hit

1 Take a break. ________________ yourself in a TV show for 30 minutes.
2 ________________ ideas around with your best friend. Ask them for a ________________ perspective.
3 ________________ inspiration from a piece of music.
4 Whenever you ________________ a wall, take a walk.
5 Drink coffee to ________________ your creativity.
6 Don't think carefully – just ________________ with an idea. ________________ your instincts.

C Match numbers (1–8) to letters (a–h) to form full sentences. Then think of some jobs which match each sentence.

1 You need to be thick-
2 It's a well-
3 You need to be highly
4 Most people won't become world-
5 It's like being self-
6 There are a lot of late-
7 You have to be open-
8 It's a high-

a night shifts, so you'll have an irregular sleeping pattern.
b risk job, so it pays well.
c employed, because you can work from home.
d paid job.
e minded, because things change all the time.
f motivated, because it's competitive.
g skinned to handle the criticism.
h famous, but they still make a living.

GRAMMAR

A Complete the text with the correct form of the verbs in parentheses.

My first role

When I was about ten, I [1] ________________ (*join*) a drama group in a nearby town and they [2] ________________ (*perform*) a show every year. That year, we [3] ________________ (*do*) *Peter Pan*.

We [4] ________________ (*rehearse*) for weeks. I [5] ________________ (*give*) a pretty big role – I [6] ________________ (*play*) Michael, the smallest of the children Peter Pan [7] ________________ (*bring*) to Neverland.

I [8] ________________ (*remember*) how nervous I [9] ________________ (*be*) when we [10] ________________ (*peek*) out from behind the curtain to see the people in the audience.

However, it was worth all the nerves when the audience [11] ________________ (*applaud*) at the end. I [12] ________________ (*feel*) so proud – and I couldn't wait to start practicing for the next show.

B Choose the correct option to complete the sentences.

1 The band did not know they ***would have / were going to be*** the biggest selling rock group this decade.
2 Little did he know, it was this discovery that ***would change / is to have changed*** the experiment completely.
3 This ***was supposed to be / would be*** a dream vacation, but it turned into a nightmare.
4 They ***were supposed to finish / be finished*** in May, but the deadline was pushed back until June.
5 The highway was ***due / meant*** to be completed by now.
6 Carlos had been ***about / set*** to go through airport security when he realized he didn't have his passport.

3 PROGRESS

If there is no struggle, there is no progress.
Frederick Douglass

Blazing a trail at thirty thousand feet.

OBJECTIVES

- make predictions about the future
- use persuasive language to sell something
- discuss progress and society
- evaluate costs and benefits
- discuss renewable energy
- write a persuasive email

Work with a partner. Discuss the questions.

1 Look at the picture. What does it say about progress? What other examples can you think of to illustrate the same idea?
2 Read the quote. What does Douglass mean?
3 How could you measure 'progress':
   - in your own life
   - in your city/country
   - in the world?

3.1 Progressive design

- Make predictions about the future
- Use persuasive language to sell something

V – sustainability; forming verbs from adjectives
G – future structures
P – sounding persuasive
S – listening to identify persuasive techniques

VOCABULARY
Sustainability

A Work in groups. Which of these sustainable / environmentally friendly solutions would most benefit your country?

- recycling
- biodegradable plastic
- electric vehicles
- beach clean-ups
- wind power

B Choose the correct words to complete these statements about sustainability.

1 We will *never* / *soon* run out of **renewable** energy sources like solar and wind power.
2 A sustainable building generates *less* / *more* electricity than it **consumes**.
3 To be carbon-**neutral**, you might *cut down* / *plant* some trees to **offset** the pollution caused by a plane trip.
4 A zero-**emission** factory causes no *air* / *water* pollution.
5 **Over-exploitation** of natural resources will *lead to* / *prevent* the **depletion** of those resources over time.
6 **Biodegradable** materials break down into *harmful* / *harmless* parts which don't **accumulate** in the environment.

C Go to the **Vocabulary Hub** on **page 143**.

D **SPEAK** Work in groups. Discuss the questions.

1 Can ordinary people be carbon-neutral/cause zero emissions in the modern world?
2 Is it worth the effort? Can ordinary people make a difference?

READING

A **SPEAK** Look at the pictures in the article. What might be special or unusual about the buildings?

B **READ FOR GIST** Read the article quickly. Match the names below with the pictures (a–c).

1 Aequorea ___
2 Nautilus Eco-Resort ___
3 The Lilypad ___

C **READ FOR DETAIL** Read the article again. Which project(s) from Exercise B does each statement apply to?

1 Scientists will work there.
2 It takes its shape from the natural world.
3 It will collect its own water.
4 It will use less energy than it generates.
5 The buildings will move up and down.
6 It will move from place to place.
7 It will hold tens of thousands of people.

D **SPEAK** Would you like to live or stay in any of these places? What would be the benefits and drawbacks?

a

GRAMMAR
Future structures

A Look at the underlined sections (1–10) in the article. What time do they refer to?

B **WORK IT OUT** Match the sections (1–10) with the rules in the box (a–f).

Future structures

a We use the future progressive to describe a situation that will be in progress at a particular point in the future (__), or to emphasize that it will cover an extended period of time (__).

b We use the future perfect to describe changes that will be completed before a particular point in the future (__).

c We use the future perfect progressive to focus on the future results of an earlier future process, and/or to measure the length of time of that process (__).

d We can use a modal verb (e.g. *might*, *could*) instead of *will* in these structures (__).

e After words like *if*, *unless*, *when*, *while*, etc, future tenses (e.g. future progressive) usually become present tenses (e.g. present progressive) (__, __).

f Other future structures include *be on the brink/verge of (doing)* (__) and *be about / due / set to (do)* (__, __).

C Go to the **Grammar Hub** on **page 126**.

SPEAKING

SPEAK Work in pairs. Ask and answer the questions about the times in the box.

ten years from now | the end of this lesson | this time next year

1 Where will you be? What will you be doing?
2 What will you have achieved? How will the world have changed?
3 How will you be feeling? Why?

ONE ARCHITECT'S VISION

TO BRING US BACK FROM THE BRINK

The world of 2100 will look considerably different from the world of today. [1]By then, much of the ice around the north and south poles will have melted, according to the Intergovernmental Panel on Climate Change. [2]Sea levels could well have risen by as much as 88 cm. [3]Many of the world's low-lying islands and coastal regions will be disappearing – or will already have disappeared – beneath the rising tides. Millions of people will have lost their homes. In short, [4]we're on the brink of witnessing irrevocable changes to our world.

A visionary Belgian architect, Vincent Callebaut, has an innovative answer to the problem of rising sea levels: The Lilypad, a futuristic-looking city that will drift around the world following ocean currents like a giant ship. If his plans come to fruition, [5]this self-contained city is set to become home to around 50,000 climate refugees.

The Lilypad's design is inspired by the shape of the *Victoria amazonica* lilypad. At its center will be a lake to catch, store and purify rain water, surrounded by three 'mountains'. Thanks to a series of renewable energy sources, this eco-city will produce more energy than it consumes. All its carbon dioxide and other waste will be recycled, making the Lilypad entirely zero-emission.

The Lilypad isn't Callebaut's only attempt to re-think the design of buildings and cities. Back in 2015, he revealed spectacular plans for the world's first underwater skyscrapers, called Aequorea, which will be 500 meters wide, have 250 floors and be capable of holding 20,000 people. These eco-friendly structures will be self-sufficient, as they'll produce all their own energy, heat, food and water. They'll also be made of 100% recycled plastic, collected from the world's oceans.

Each oceanscraper will have a jellyfish-like structure: the entrance will be located at the surface and then the structure will spiral down to depths of 1000 meters. Inside will be homes, offices and workshops, science laboratories, sea farms and fruit and vegetable gardens. Fresh drinking water will be produced using in-depth pressure to separate salt from seawater.

The Aequorea will be moored off the coast of Brazil, rather than in the open ocean. Residents will certainly be glad of the chance to visit the mainland and soak up some much-needed sunshine at the end of each work week – [6]they'll have been breathing processed air and staring out into the deep, dark ocean all week, after all.

b

Mr. Callebaut's latest project, the Nautilus Eco-Resort in the Philippines, takes its name and inspiration from a mollusk, the nautilus. The hotels themselves will also be shaped like seashells, which will rise and fall as they rotate around a central coil. Visitors can expect uninterrupted sunshine throughout the day as the towers follow the course of the sun. Some rooms will even disappear underground [7]when they're not being used. But before you book your ticket, be warned that [8]the resort isn't about to open any time soon – like most of Mr. Callebaut's designs, it's still some way from actually being built.

The Nautilus Eco-Resort aims to be a 'zero-emission, zero-waste, zero-poverty' project, built entirely from reused or recycled materials from the islands. Visitors will also be actively involved with scientists, engineers and ecologists to ensure their experience encourages sustainable progress. So if you do decide to take a luxury vacation there, [9]you won't be spending all your time lounging around by the pool. You'll also get some practical lessons on sustainability [10]while you're collecting garbage from the beach!

c

Glossary

brink (n) the point in time when something very bad or very good is about to happen

irrevocable (adj) impossible to change or stop

moor (v) to stop a ship or boat from moving by fastening it to a place with ropes or by using an anchor

sustainable (adj) using methods that do not harm the environment

visionary (adj) original and showing a lot of imagination

LISTENING

A SPEAK Work in pairs. Read *(Very) Smart Materials*. Discuss why each material mentioned might be useful.

Glossary

smart materials (n) technologically advanced materials with properties (e.g. color, shape, magnetism, etc) that can change in response to stimuli such as light, temperature, pressure or moisture

(VERY) SMART MATERIALS

1

COLOR-CHANGING PAINT:
The roof and walls of a building automatically change color during the day, depending on the temperature.

3

PIEZOELECTRIC SHOES:
Walking in the shoes causes crystals in the soles to change shape, generating an electric current.

2

SHAPE-CHANGING AIRPLANE WINGS:
The wings detect the plane's height (using atmospheric pressure) and change shape automatically.

4

SELF-REPAIRING RUBBER TIRES:
The rubber contains tiny balls of glue. If the tire is damaged, the bal open, glue is released and solidifies, and the holes are repaired.

3.1 **B LISTEN FOR DETAIL** Listen to a conversation about smart materials. Choose the correct options (a, b or c) to answer the questions.

1 What is the woman trying to do?
   a make friendly conversation
   b teach the man something
   c sell something
2 How does the hat work?
   a Its fibers change shape to control air flow.
   b It uses electricity to warm your head.
   c You can adjust its shape based on the weather.
3 What must the man do to keep the hat?
   a write a detailed report about his experiences of wearing it
   b pay $50
   c test it in the rain
4 Why does the woman call her boss?
   a to ask for advice about the jacket
   b to persuade her boss to lower the price
   c to put the man under pressure to buy the jacket

3.1 **C LISTEN FOR TECHNIQUES** Listen again. Which persuasive techniques does the woman use for 1–6? Use the information in the box to help you.

Listening to identify persuasive techniques

People sometimes use tricks to persuade us to do things. When someone is trying to persuade you, listen for these tricks.

Exaggeration: listen for words like *absolutely* and *extremely*.

Leading questions: listen for questions that 'push' you toward a particular answer, including question tags (e.g. *isn't it?*).

Personalization: listen for phrases like *if you imagine* and overuse of *you/your*.

1 biking more frequently ______
2 how the hat works ______
3 testing the hat ______
4 the problem and the solution ______
5 the smart jacket ______
6 paying for the jacket ______

D SPEAK Work in pairs. Discuss the questions.

1 Is it acceptable to use techniques like these to persuade or manipulate other people? In what situations is it OK? When is it unfair?
2 What techniques do you use when you're trying to persuade someone?

PRONUNCIATION
Sounding persuasive

A Listen to the extracts which include the sentences below. How is the woman trying to sound persuasive? Use the information in the box to help you.

1 You just look like a very healthy and athletic person.
2 Yeah, tell me about it!
3 Hmm, I know exactly what you mean.
4 I think you got yourself an excellent deal there, sir. I can see you're a very smart negotiator!
5 You know what? Maybe I can help you out there.
6 But … hmm … maybe … I can offer you … a special price … to thank you for your help.

Sounding persuasive

a Speak fairly quietly (as if you're sharing a secret) and slowly, with a lot of pauses (as if you're thinking of new ideas while speaking).
b Start fast and then slow right down, placing extra stress on all positive words.
c Use slightly exaggerated rising and falling intonation on key words to express emotions.

B SPEAK Work in pairs. Practice saying the sentences in Exercise A as persuasively as possible.

VOCABULARY
Forming verbs from adjectives

A Complete the extracts with the correct form of the verbs in the box.

ensure formalize simplify strengthen tighten warm

1 I bet you can't wait for the weather ______________ up!
2 It's fairly complicated technology, but I'll try ______________ it for you.
3 The fibers in your hat respond to the cold temperature by ______________ up.
4 That ______________ there's no heat loss from your head.
5 As the hat gets wet, the water ______________ the fibers.
6 I just need you to sign this form ______________ our agreement.

B What adjective is each verb from Exercise A formed from?

C Use the affixes in the box to create verbs. The same affix is used for all words in each group. Other spelling changes may also be needed. One group doesn't require any change.

-en -ify en- -ize

1 strong long short
____
2 final visual equal
____
3 empty smooth narrow
____
4 pure solid simple
____
5 danger able large
____

D Complete the advice with the verbs you formed in Exercise C. Sometimes more than one answer is possible.

How to be *persuasive*

1 Don't just offer weak opinions. ______________ your arguments with evidence and examples.
2 Help your potential customers to ______________ themselves using your product.
3 Don't try to persuade everybody at the same time: ______________ your focus to a small group of key people.
4 ______________ complicated explanations to make them easier to understand.
5 ______________ the decision-making process for your customers by removing any barriers that make their decisions harder.
6 Don't speak too quickly. Try to ______________ the pauses between key words.

SPEAKING HUB

A PREPARE Work in pairs. You are going to try to persuade somebody to buy a product made from smart materials. Choose one of the ideas from Listening Exercise A or use your own idea.

B DISCUSS Discuss how your product works and why it's useful.

C PLAN Plan a sales strategy using the persuasion techniques from Listening Exercise C.

D PRESENT Swap partners. Take turns to try to persuade your new partner to buy your product.

E REFLECT Share your experiences with the class. Would you buy your partner's product? Why/Why not?

- Make predictions about the future
- Use persuasive language to sell something

3.2 Better ... or worse?

- Discuss progress and society
- Evaluate costs and benefits

P – stress-shift words
G – negative inversion
V – verb–noun collocations
S – reading to determine costs and benefits

LISTENING

A SPEAK Work in groups. Do you think life is generally getting better or worse for your generation?

3.3 **B LISTEN FOR MAIN IDEA** Listen to the first part of a radio show. Match the people (1–5) with the opinions (a–e).

1 Bob ___
2 Mary ___
3 James ___
4 Callum ___
5 Sonia ___

a I'm more aware of bad things happening than I was.
b The earlier generation didn't have the same financial worries as we do.
c Everything was better when I was younger.
d Young people were more polite in the past.
e I feel bad when I compare myself with others.

C SPEAK Work in pairs and discuss the questions.

1 Do you agree with the interviewees' opinions?
2 What are some possible explanations for their opinions?

3.4 **D LISTEN FOR GIST** Listen to the second part of the radio show. Match the opinions (a–e) in Exercise B with the concepts (1–5).

1 the inequality paradox ___
2 the reminiscence bump ___
3 the them-and-us delusion ___
4 the invisible struggle phenomenon ___
5 the window-on-the-world effect ___

3.4 **E LISTEN FOR DETAIL** Listen to the second part again. Are these sentences true (T) or false (F)? Correct the false sentences.

1 Professor Martinelli believes that life is getting better everywhere. T / F
2 Declinism proves that things really are getting worse. T / F
3 When average levels of well-being improve, it can lead to a rise in declinism. T / F
4 People usually have nostalgia for their youth. T / F
5 We tend to focus on good behavior in groups that we don't belong to. T / F
6 Professor Martinelli's parents never worried about financial problems. T / F
7 Professor Martinelli is optimistic that people will try to prevent global tragedies. T / F

F SPEAK Work in pairs. Discuss the questions.

1 What are your experiences of the five concepts from the radio show?
2 Are you generally optimistic or pessimistic about the near future?

PRONUNCIATION
Stress-shift words

A **Listen to the sentences. Underline the stressed syllables**
5 **in the words in bold.**

1. Despite amazing **progress** in technology and sharp **increases** in living standards, many of us believe our quality of life has actually **decreased**!
2. Let's hear a few **extracts** from those interviews.
3. You feel like a **reject** from society.
4. It's almost as if we **rewrite** the events in our memories.
5. You've simply erased their negative **attributes** and bad **conduct** from your memory.
6. We tend to **attribute** other people's success to luck.
7. That's a major source of inter-generational **conflict**: young adults always **suspect** that earlier generations had it much easier!

B **Underline the stressed syllables in the words in bold.**
6 **Then listen and check.**

1. Why are you always such a **rebel**? Why do you always **rebel** against everything I say?
2. I didn't think I'd like Thai food, but now I'm a **convert**. Your cooking has **converted** me!
3. You need to install an **upgrade** for your computer. When did you last **upgrade** it?
4. I deal with **imports** and **exports** in my job: I **import** raw materials and **export** finished products to customers.
5. I **frequent** this café during the summer, but I'm not really a **frequent** visitor during the rest of the year.

C **Practice saying the sentences with the correct stress.**

GRAMMAR
Negative inversion

A **Complete the extracts from the radio show with one word.**

1. No sooner _____ **an older person gotten on the bus** than we all stood up.
2. Only after they'd all gotten off the bus _____ **I finally sit down.**
3. No way **could I** _____ **afford an apartment.**
4. None of our neighbors had much money, and neither _____ **we.**
5. Not _____ **did I have great friends**, but we also did cool things all the time.
6. By no means _____ **I suggesting** that life is wonderful for everybody everywhere.
7. _____ in a million years **did it occur to me** that my parents were worried about money.

B **WORK IT OUT** **Match the sentences (1–7) in Exercise A with the rules (a–d) in the box.**

> **Negative inversion**
>
> When we want to emphasize a negative element of a sentence (e.g. *never*), we can move it to the beginning and swap the subject and auxiliary verb. This process is called inversion.
>
> **a** When there is no auxiliary verb, we add *do/does/did*. ___ ___ ___
>
> **b** Inversion with *could* is common after phrases like *only after* and *no way*. ___ ___
>
> **c** Inversion is very common in the structure *not only … but also*. ___
>
> **d** After *no sooner*, we need a *than*-clause. ___
>
> We don't use inversion when a negative word/phrase is the subject: *Not one person offered me a seat.* (NOT: ~~did offer~~)

C **Go to the Grammar Hub on page 126.**

D **Complete the sentences so they are true for you.**

1. Under no circumstances would I …
2. Only rarely do I …
3. Not only do I think …

SPEAKING

A **PREPARE** **Work in pairs. Imagine you are on a radio interview about progress. Student A – read the information below. Student B – go to the Communication Hub on page 154.**

B **SPEAK** **Role-play your interview.**

Student A

> You're a radio interviewer. You believe that while people complain about the world today, overall it is actually getting better. Interview Student B about progress. Also give your view on the subject.
>
> Discuss the following areas.
>
> - the impact of technology
> - community
> - quality of life
> - cost of living
> - employment
> - the environment

READING

A PREDICT Work in pairs. Discuss the questions.

1 Look at the pictures and title of the article. What do you think 'voluntourism' might be?

2 What do you think attracts people to these kinds of activities?

3 Why might some voluntary work do more harm than good?

B SKIM Read *Voluntourism: more harm than good?* quickly and check your ideas in Exercise A.

C READ FOR COSTS AND BENEFITS Work in pairs. What are the deep costs and benefits of voluntourism? Use the information in the box to help you.

Reading to determine costs and benefits

When you read a for-and-against, or pro and con, article, it's useful to distinguish between **surface-level** costs/benefits (e.g. obvious, short-term or unimportant ones) and **deep** costs/benefits (e.g. hidden, long-term or highly important ones). When deciding whether you agree with the writer's opinion, focus mainly on the deep costs and benefits.

VOLUNTOURISM

more harm than good?

When Pippa Biddle was a teenager, she went on a school trip to Tanzania, where she and her classmates were tasked with building a library for an orphanage. Lacking even basic construction skills, they did their best and, remarkably, over the course of a week, the building started to take shape. Only later did Pippa learn the truth: every night, a group of professional builders had been carefully undoing and redoing the teenagers' work in order to make the construction structurally sound. The whole project was an illusion: the true purpose wasn't to get help on the building project, but to make the teenagers feel good about themselves.

Welcome to the world of voluntourism, where volunteering meets tourism. Unlike true volunteering, this is paid work – but it's the worker who pays for the privilege. On the surface, voluntourism is a win–win situation. The voluntourist seizes an opportunity to travel to an exotic country and work with real people in authentic locations, while the recipients get free help. But the reality, as Pippa's story brings home to us, is somewhat more complicated.

The main criticism of voluntourism is that it perpetuates the myth that people in some countries need help from wise and generous benefactors in richer countries. The reality, of course, is that these countries have plenty of kind-hearted experts of their own. But of course, most voluntourists aren't even experts: they're typically students looking for a quick adventure, with no valuable skills to offer. At best, their input is frequently a waste of time. At worst, it could do more harm than good, as with Pippa's building experience.

Even worse are stories of fake projects created merely to keep the volunteers busy, regardless of any inherent local need. For example, there are English-language schools in remote communities where the locals neither want nor need to study English.

It's hard to avoid the conclusion that voluntourism is nothing more than an ego-trip: a chance to pretend you're making the world a better place, so you can wow your friends back home with tales of your generosity, your suffering and your profound experience of 'finding yourself'.

But there's another side to volunteerism. While many people do sign up with naïve expectations, they frequently emerge from their experiences with a far deeper understanding. On their return home, they can spread a more positive and realistic image of the countries they visit, and counter rather than perpetuate stereotypes. Finally, many voluntourists go on to become committed life-long volunteers, with their new-found habit of helping others, whether globally or in their own communities.

It's also an oversimplification to claim that voluntourism is always harmful to local communities. Highly-skilled volunteers like doctors, scientists and engineers can indeed bring real benefits. The key is to do so in a spirit of cooperation and mutual respect with local experts, rather than following the 'watch me and learn' approach. Many voluntourism agencies can have a genuinely positive impact both on the volunteers and the communities they serve.

So if you're considering signing up as a voluntourist, seize the initiative and do some research beforehand. Be honest and realistic about your skills and expectations. Above all, never forget that the main beneficiary of your voluntourism adventure will probably be you. With the right mindset, this could well be the most important experience of your life.

D READ FOR DETAIL Work in pairs. Read the article again and discuss the questions.

1. Why did the builders work at night?
2. How did Pippa's building experience 'do more harm than good'?
3. What does the writer mean by 'the right mindset' in the last paragraph?

E SPEAK Work in groups. Do you think voluntourism does more harm than good? Would you consider doing it yourself?

VOCABULARY

Verb–noun collocations

A Choose a verb to complete each pair of verb–noun collocations. Then decide on the best collocation to complete each sentence. Use the information in the box to help you.

> **Verb–noun collocations**
>
> Verb–noun collocations are a good way to build vocabulary. Sometimes these include advanced verbs (e.g. *perpetuate*), but mostly they include very common verbs (e.g. *make, do, take*). Try to underline these as you read in English.

1. Unless you have valuable work experience you'll usually ____do____ ~~*your best*~~ / *more harm than good*.
2. Volunteer organizations should always ________ the *time* / *shape* to train volunteers before a project.
3. A trained English teacher can ________ *benefits* / *home* to a host community.
4. It's vital that voluntourists ________ *the responsibility* / *the opportunity* to understand their host community before and during their visit.
5. Volunteer organizations should not ________ the *myth* / *problem* that their projects are just extended vacations.

B Go to the **Vocabulary Hub** on **page 143**.

C SPEAK Work in pairs. Do you agree with sentences 1–5 in Exercise A? Why/Why not?

SPEAKING HUB

A PREPARE Work in pairs. Imagine you are going to volunteer in another country. Choose one of the following voluntary projects or use your own idea.

- working at an animal sanctuary
- planting trees
- teaching children
- cleaning up trash

B PLAN Create a list of surface-level and deep costs and benefits for:

- you and your partner
- who you are helping
- the world in general.

C DISCUSS Discuss whether the benefits outweigh the costs. How could the costs be reduced? How could the benefits be increased?

D PRESENT Present your plans to the class. Whose ideas would have the best chance of making the world a better place?

Glossary

beneficiary (n) someone who gets an advantage from a situation
illusion (n) a false or wrong belief or idea
mindset (n) a way of thinking about things
orphan (n) a child whose parents have died
perpetuate (v) to make something such as a situation or process continue, especially one that is wrong, unfair or dangerous
profound (adj) used about very strong feelings
recipient (n) someone who receives something

- **Discuss progress and society**
- **Evaluate costs and benefits**

Café Hub

3.3 Sustainability

A – the 'rule of three'   S – maintaining a conversation

Seaweed farming

A Work in small groups. What is being shown in each picture (a–e)?

B Watch the video. Check your ideas to Exercise A and number pictures a–e in the order they appear.

a ☐

b ☐

c ☐

d ☐

e ☐

C Watch the video again. Answer the questions.

1 What have scientists discovered about seaweed?
2 What can seaweed help us do?
3 What are the three countries mentioned in the video?
4 Is the presenter's tone generally positive, negative or neutral?

Glossary

allotment (n) a small piece of land in town you can rent and use for growing vegetables
harvest (v) to pick and collect crops or plants
seaweed (n) a green or brown plant that grows in the sea

AUTHENTIC ENGLISH

A Work in pairs. Read the sentence from the video and the information in the box. What three things doesn't seaweed need?

This doesn't need lots of land space to grow it, it doesn't need awful artificial fertilizers, it doesn't need lots of fresh water.

The 'rule of three'

The 'rule of three' is a rhetorical device we use to express concepts more completely, emphasize our points and increase the memorability of our message. In the 'rule of three', we frequently repeat the same grammatical construction.

B Work in pairs. Complete the sentences using your own ideas and the 'rule of three'.

1 To succeed in life, you need to work hard, you need ___to have passion___ and you need ___to have a role model___.
2 I'm ready to start the day. My face is washed, my ______ and my ______.
3 Maria was the ideal employee – she was always on time, she always ______ and she ______.
4 The current government has ruined the economy, it ______ and it ______.
5 I told the sales clerk I wanted to exchange the item, ______ or ______.
6 I ______. You ______. The whole class ______.

C Compare your sentences with another pair.

D Work in small groups. Write sentences with the 'rule of three' to say what you need to do to learn a language successfully.

Fueling the future

SAM MALCOLM AMANDA HARRY EMILY

A Work in pairs. Discuss the questions.

1 Do you prefer to use public transportation or travel by car? Why?

2 What do you think about policies that ban or limit cars in city centers?

B Watch the video. Are these statements true (T) or false (F)? Correct the false sentences.

1 Malcolm has recently achieved a long-held ambition. *T / F*

2 Amanda understands the appeal of owning a sports car. *T / F*

3 Malcolm believes speed is the main positive of car ownership. *T / F*

4 Amanda says that all new vehicles will be banned from the UK by 2040. *T / F*

5 Amanda thinks that other feasible options besides gas vehicles currently exist. *T / F*

6 Harry thinks alternative fuels will be the norm in the distant future. *T / F*

7 Malcolm is going to let Amanda test drive his car. *T / F*

SPEAKING SKILL

A Watch the video again. Complete the sentences (1–6) from the video.

1 ______________________ coming out for a look at my new wheels?

2 I mean we don't really need them in the city. ______________________?

3 ______________________ Harry? You're a cool young guy … you must like sports cars.

4 Just the other day we were discussing alternative fuels, ______________________?

5 That kind of thing, must be a long way off though, ______________________?

6 ______________________ Malcolm?

B Work in pairs. Look at your answers in Exercise A. What are the speakers doing in each sentence?

1 Malcolm is asking Amanda to give her opinion.

Maintaining a conversation

Inviting people to give their opinion or speak

Ask a direct question (*Would you like to say something here, Andy?*) or invite someone to speak using a statement (*You haven't said anything yet, Maria.*)

Noticing changes in attitude

Respond to body language and facial expressions by asking questions or making statements. (*I can tell you don't agree with me.*)

Question tags

Add these to a statement to make it a question or to request agreement. (*I think we all pretty much agree on this, don't we?*)

Asking questions to get agreement

Ask people directly to agree with you in order to move conversations along. (*Am I right in thinking that's true?*)

C Work in pairs. Choose one of the topics below and try to maintain a conversation for four minutes without any long pauses.

- the environment
- a documentary you watched recently
- public transportation in your country

SPEAKING HUB

A PREPARE Work in a small group. Think about the pros and cons of the sources of energy below.

- wind power
- tidal power
- fossil fuels
- nuclear power
- solar power

B PLAN You are going to discuss which of the energies would be the best for achieving a sustainable future with another group. Plan how you are going to achieve agreement within your group and get all the members of the group to give their opinion.

A: What's your opinion?

B: Tidal power is too expensive compared to other renewable sources.

C DISCUSS Join with another group to discuss the pros and cons of the sources of energy.

D REFLECT As a class decide which arguments were the most convincing and which of the energy sources are necessary for a sustainable future.

Discuss renewable energy

➤ Turn to page 158 to learn how to write a persuasive email about sustainability.

Unit 3 Review

VOCABULARY

A Complete the brochure with the words in the box. There are two extra words that you do not need to use.

accumulate	biodegradable	consume	depletion
emissions	exploitation	neutral	offset	renewable

Want to live a more sustainable life?

Here's how.

1 Stop buying products wrapped in plastic, which ________ in the oceans. Choose products that use ________ packaging instead.

2 Cut down on the energy you ________, and use solar power, wind power or other ________ energy sources if possible.

3 Reduce your ________ of greenhouse gases by walking or biking instead of driving.

4 Become carbon-________ by planting trees to ________ the carbon you generate.

B Complete the sentences with the correct form of the word in parentheses.

1 They want to ________ (*large*) our college by adding a new building.
2 The dirty water is ________ (*pure*) before being released into the sea.
3 If your dinner's cold, you can ________ (*warm*) it up in the microwave.
4 They're ________ (*strong*) the old bridge before it falls down.
5 We didn't bother to ________ (*formal*) our agreement – we trust each other.
6 Some screws are loose on this table. Can you ________ (*tight*) them up?
7 We were winning six-five, but the other team ________ (*equal*) in the last minute.

C Complete the conversation with one verb in each space.

A: I want to [1] ________ the world a better place, but I don't know how. Could you [2] ________ me in the right direction?
B: The only thing that [3] ________ to mind is voluntourism.
A: Good idea! I'll go for it.
B: Well, please don't [4] ________ this personally, but you don't really have any skills to offer. They have strict rules about who they accept.
A: Really? Maybe they'll [5] ________ an exception for me.
B: No, I think you need to [6] ________ the time to research it carefully so you don't end up [7] ________ more harm than good.
A: OK, thanks for the advice. I'll try to [8] ________ it on board.

GRAMMAR

A Find and correct the mistakes in four of the sentences.

1 Fifty years from now, the world will have been changing completely.
2 My life's about getting a lot more complicated.
3 We'll be seeing a lot more of each other when we're neighbors.
4 Call me again at ten – I might have finished by then.
5 I'm on the verge of resigning from my job.
6 Your eyes will hurt after you'll have been studying all night.
7 Prices setting to fall by 10% over the next year.

B Reorder the words to make sentences. The first word is given in bold.

1 **By** / you / do / I / should / means / believe / no / resign
________.
2 **Under** / be / opened / may / circumstances / no / this box
________.
3 **Not** / did / thanked / all the work / you / have / me / once / for / I
________.
4 **Only** / the waiter / our food / three times / we / bring / complained / had / after / did
________.
5 **No** / the laundry / started / had / than / put out / sooner / it / I / to rain
________.
6 **No** / to college / ever / going back / I / way / consider / would
________.
7 **Not** / this hard / since / worked / students / we / have / I / were
________.

4 INTELLIGENCE

I know that I am intelligent because I know that I know nothing.

Socrates

Future choices at the Istituto Italiano Di Tecnologia, Genoa.

OBJECTIVES

- discuss improving the brain
- talk about future technology
- talk about regrets
- discuss intelligence
- recount events
- write a report

Work with a partner. Discuss the questions.

1 Look at the picture. How is it connected to the topic of intelligence?

2 Read the quote. What do you think Socrates means? Do you agree?

3 Would you rather be very intelligent, very strong or very attractive? Why?

4.1 Brain training

- Discuss improving the brain
- Talk about future technology

G conditionals without *if* · V conceptual metaphors · P adding information · S identifying logical fallacies

LISTENING

A Work in pairs. Look at the brain teaser below. Do you know the answer? Go to the **Communication Hub** on **page 149** for more brain teasers.

TODAY'S BRAIN TEASER

David's mother had three children.
The first one was named April.
The second one was named May.
What was the name of the third child?

4.1 **B** **LISTEN FOR GIST** Listen to a radio discussion about ways to increase your brain power. What four methods of boosting brain power are discussed?

1 ______
2 ______
3 ______
4 ______

4.2 **C** **LISTEN AND IDENTIFY** Listen to three extracts from the radio discussion. Whose argument is weaker in each extract? Which type of logical fallacy (a–c) from the box have they used?

Identifying logical fallacies

a **Generalization:** drawing a conclusion about a large group from a very small amount of data.
b **Anecdotal evidence:** using non-scientific personal experience as proof for something.
c **False cause:** claiming a relationship exists between two things when there is no evidence to support this.

1 *Dr. Carter / Amanda* ___
2 *Dr. Carter / Amanda* ___
3 *Dr. Carter / Amanda* ___

D **SPEAK** Work in pairs and discuss the questions.

1 Which of the methods that the speakers discussed do you think can really boost people's brainpower?
2 Do you agree with what Dr. Carter said about Sudoku?
3 Why do you think findings have been inconclusive on some methods?

PRONUNCIATION

Adding information

A Underline the part(s) of these sentences that provide additional information about something.

1 To answer the question, I'm joined today by two experts, Dr. Ramona Carter, a leading neuroscientist, and Amanda Saraha, a life coach and the author of *How to be smarter*.
2 So for example, if you do a lot of Sudoku, the math puzzle where you write the numbers in boxes, it's most likely that you will just become better at playing that game.
3 Recently, we've seen a lot of media stories about super foods, food that you should eat to boost your brain power.

4.3 **B** Listen to the sentences in Exercise A. Draw arrows where the intonation rises or falls.

C **SPEAK** Work in pairs. Give additional information about the underlined words.

1 I like to do some exercise before I start work in the mornings. (give more detail)
2 My friend is definitely one of the smartest people I know. (give more detail)
3 I try to do some meditation because it helps me relax. (define the word)

VOCABULARY
Conceptual metaphors

A Match the sentences (1–6) with the related conceptual metaphor (a–c). Use the information in the box to help you.

> **Conceptual metaphors**
>
> Conceptual metaphors help us to talk about abstract or complex ideas by comparing them with something else. For example, life is frequently compared with a journey, such as in sentences like this:
>
> *She had reached a crossroads. Should she go to college or continue with her job?* (= reached a point when she needed to make an important decision about her life)

1 I spent an hour doing Sudoku. ____
2 She shot down my arguments. ____
3 He has a really fiery temper. ____
4 After I had cooled down, I apologized. ____
5 I've invested a lot of time in brain training. ____
6 I couldn't defend my position. ____

a anger = heat
b argument = war
c time = money

B Read three sentences from the radio show. What do the underlined words and phrases mean?

1 Of course, everyone would like to be more intelligent, but is it really possible? And if so, how can we make ourselves brighter?
2 A team from Cambridge actually tried to shed some light on the impact of brain training games.
3 As Dr. Carter says, we may still be in the dark about the science behind it, but I personally believe that the food we eat has a huge effect on every aspect of our lives.

C SPEAK Identify the conceptual metaphor being used in the questions. Then discuss the questions in pairs.

1 Do you think brain training is a waste of time?
2 What's a good strategy to convince people to buy brain-training products?
3 Do you think intelligent people are usually more hot-tempered?
4 Are you able to stay cool in an argument?

SPEAKING

A Look at the advertisements. Which products would you try? Which would you avoid? Why?

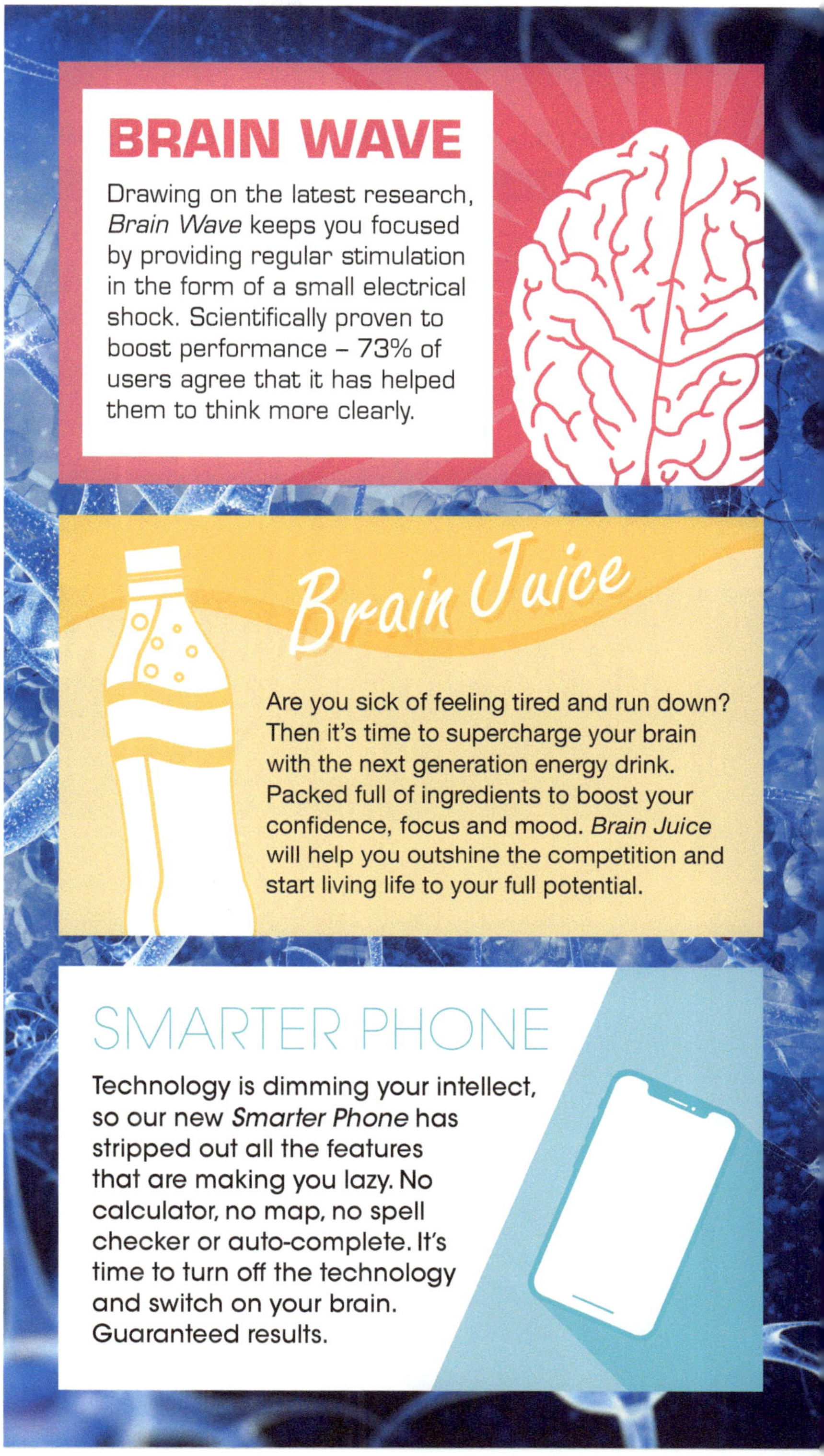

B PRESENT Work in groups. Think of a product or service that you could sell to people who wanted to boost their brain power. Present the product to the class. Which product is the most popular?

C DISCUSS Work in pairs and discuss the questions.

1 Do you believe that it's really possible to make yourself smarter?
2 Should companies be allowed to sell products like the ones in Exercise A? Why/Why not?

READING

A SPEAK Work in pairs. If you could significantly boost your intelligence overnight, would you do it? Why/Why not?

B PREDICT Work in pairs. Look at *Brain augmentation: The key to super intelligence*. In your own words, explain to your partner what you think the article is about.

C READ FOR MAIN IDEA Read the article and complete the table.

	Method of augmentation	Examples of benefits
1		
2		
3		

D READ FOR DETAIL Read the article again and answer the questions.

1 When do scientists predict highly sophisticated robots will be a common sight?

2 How has technology been used to help blind people?

3 What did scientists learn from the research with epilepsy patients?

4 What potential dangers of brain augmentation does the article mention?

E SPEAK Work in pairs and discuss the questions.

1 What was the most surprising thing that you learned from the article?

2 Do you think that the government should control this kind of augmentation?

BRAIN AUGMENTATION:

The key to super intelligence

How far would you go to enhance your own intelligence? Would you implant a chip into your brain? For many scientists around the world, the answer appears to be *yes*. Brain augmentation, enhancing the intelligence of human brains with implants, is a growing area of interest as some predict that super-intelligent cyborgs will be a normal part of everyday life within the next 10 to 20 years.

In fact, experts believe that there are three main approaches to brain augmentation: interfacing with the brain, stimulating the brain and enhancing the brain with implants.

Suppose that a computer could interface with a brain, it could record information, store it, and even use this information for some other purpose – such as sharing it with others. In theory, if people's brains were linked through the internet, they could benefit from each others' knowledge.

Another way of augmenting the brain is by stimulating it in some way – typically with electricity. One goal of stimulation is to produce artificial sensations, such as the sensation of touch or vision. In this case, the main motivation comes from a desire to help repair the brains of people with neurological conditions. For example, in the last couple of years, scientists from *Second Sight* have been able to partially restore the sight of some blind people by implanting a chip into their retinas that sends signals to the brain from a camera. Although these people cannot see, the stimulation of the brain creates pictures in their mind. Right now these are just black and white, pixelated images, but assuming that the technology continues to improve, this could be the beginning of a permanent cure for blindness.

Another goal of stimulating the brain is to improve its function and its capabilities. A recent study led by Dong Song of the University of Southern California looked at the effects of stimulating the brain on memory. Researchers worked with twenty volunteers who were having electrodes implanted into their brains to treat epilepsy. Researchers examined the effects of stimulating the brain through these electrodes during tests that involved either the volunteers' short-term memory or working memory and found that the right kind of stimulation improved short-term memory by 15% and working memory by 25%. Interestingly, unless the right kind of stimulation was provided, the volunteers' memory was actually worse. So, there is clearly a lot of work to be done to understand the right kind of stimulation to provide.

GRAMMAR

Conditionals without *if*

A Underline conditional sentences in the article with the same meaning as sentences (1–6).

1. If a computer could connect to a brain, it could download information and make it available to others. (Paragraph 3)
2. If the technology gets better, it could lead to a cure for blindness. (Paragraph 4)
3. If robots decided to fight against humans, we would have to be smart enough to take them on. (Paragraph 6)
4. If people created successful brain-augmentation implants, we would need to think about the moral implications. (Paragraph 7)
5. If you ask many people about what's happening right now, they will tell you they don't know anything about it. (Paragraph 8)
6. If the government had not allowed this work into augmentation, we would not be developing innovations to assist people with vision problems. (Paragraph 8)

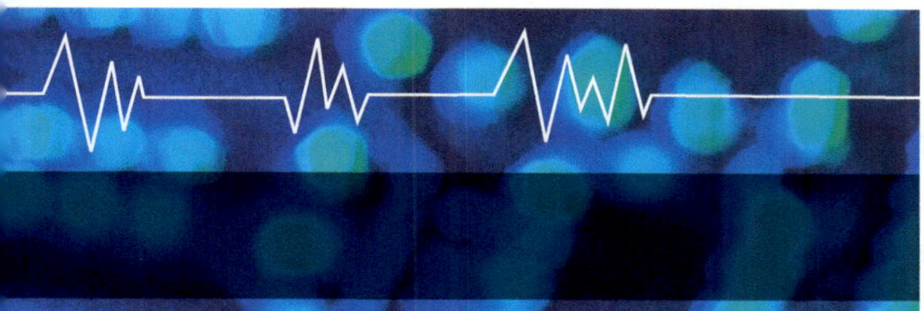

The final approach to augmentation is the most radical, because it involves merging man and machine. The biggest impact is likely to be from implanting a chip into your brain. Bryan Johnson, founder and CEO of neuroscience company Kernel, believes that these chips could be used to help us learn faster, enhance our memories, and provide us with a cognitive boost. *Space X* and *Tesla* are also working on technology to boost the human brain through the company Neuralink. One concern raised is that humans are able to enhance their intelligence, because, should AI turn against humans in the future, we would need to be smart enough to fight back.

Of course, were brain-boosting implants to be successfully developed, they would raise several difficult ethical questions. Would changing people's brains change their personalities? If someone had an implant fitted, would they be at risk of being hacked? Could these super intelligent cyborgs be a danger to the rest of us?

Ask many people about what's happening right now in this field and they will tell you they are completely in the dark. Unfortunately that includes the government, who many feel should be doing more to regulate the technology and ensure that it really is safe. However, had the government banned this kind of research, the technology to help blind people would not be under development.

B Choose the correct words to complete the rules (a–c). Then look at the example sentences you found in Exercise A to complete the rules (d–f).

Conditionals without *if*

We can use inversions to talk about hypothetical situations in formal or literary English:

a *Had*: We use *had* + subject + ***infinitive / past participle / base form***.

b *Should*: We use *should* + subject + ***infinitive / past participle / base form***.

c *Were*: We use *were* + subject + ***infinitive / past participle / base form***.

We can use other words instead of *if*:

d Verbs: *imagine*, ______________

e Present participles: ______________, *presuming, providing, supposing*

- Past participles: *provided*

f We can also make a conditional sentence by starting with an imperative and joining the clauses with ______________.

C Go to the **Grammar Hub** on **page 128**.

D Change the start of these sentences to make conditionals without *if*. Complete the sentences with your own opinions.

1. If people were able to upload information into their brains, …
2. If we ignore the potential danger of AI, …
3. If brain implants were only affordable for the super-rich, …
4. If I were to be offered a brain-boosting implant, …

E Compare your sentences with your partner. Do you agree with your partner's opinions?

SPEAKING HUB

Work in pairs. Student A – go to the **Communication Hub** on **page 150**. Student B – go to the **Communication Hub** on **page 152**. Describe the situations to your partner. Discuss what you would do.

Glossary

cyborg (n) a creature in science fiction stories that is part human and part machine

electrode (n) a small metal or carbon object inside an electrical cell or a battery that electricity flows through. There are two electrodes, one positive and one negative.

neurological (adj) relating to your nervous system or to the diseases that affect it

retina (n) the part at the back of your eye that sends light signals to your brain, where they are changed into images

Discuss improving the brain

Talk about future technology

4.2 Thinking and thought

- Talk about regrets
- Discuss intelligence

G – wishes and regrets
P – adding information or changing the topic
V – science and research; thinking
S – identifying different writing styles

READING

A SPEAK Read *No need to be embarrassed?* Discuss the following questions.

1 Have any of the situations described happened to you?

2 Which stories do you think are the most and least embarrassing?

B Read *The positive side of embarrassment*. What do scientists think is the purpose of embarrassment?

C READ TO IDENTIFY Who is each text written for? What is the purpose of each text?

Text 1 ____________________________

Text 2 ____________________________

D Read both texts again. Find examples of the writing styles (a–e) in the box. Use the information in the box to help you.

Identifying different writing styles

Texts written for a general audience usually use:

a shorter, simpler sentences (including sentences that start with *and*, *but* and *so*)

b idiomatic language (contractions, phrasal verbs, idioms).

Academic papers and articles:

c are objective not personal (no *I*, *you* or *we*, no emotional adjectives)

d use longer, more complex sentences

e use formal language (no contractions or phrasal verbs, but academic vocabulary).

E SPEAK Work in pairs. Do you agree that displaying embarrassment can make a positive impression on others?

NO NEED TO BE EMBARRASSED?

Glossary

buddy (n) (American English) friend

consolation (n) something that makes you feel less unhappy or disappointed

cringeworthy (adj) something that makes you feel embarrassed or ashamed

Psychologists believe that embarrassment should actually be viewed as a positive thing. When we blush or stammer in embarrassment, we are showing that we know that we shouldn't have said or done something and that we don't normally do this kind of thing. In other words, showing we are embarrassed is a kind of non-verbal apology.

Well that's all well and good, but when you're caught red-faced, I don't think that would be any consolation. In light of this research, I thought I'd do some of my own. Now I'm no stranger to embarrassment, but a quick survey revealed embarrassing work stories far worse than mine. Here are some of your most cringeworthy moments.

"Can you even begin to imagine what it's like to walk into a glass door at full speed? Must be painful, right? Now add to that the mortification that it was in front of your new boss. If I hadn't been trying to impress her with my walking-while-emailing skills – like I was a hot-shot political aide on a TV show – I might have noticed the door. But the humiliation doesn't stop there. All of my co-workers were sitting around a conference table on the other side of that glass door. I would have loved to make a good impression. But all I ended up with was wounded pride ... and a broken nose."

"Generally speaking I'm a pretty confident person. I'm great at putting people at ease and keeping conversation going. I just wish I wasn't so absent-minded. Over the years it has caused me infinite amounts of awkwardness. But never more so than just last month. An important client was flying in from Vancouver for an even more important meeting. So I offered to pick him up from the airport. The only problem was by the time he came through the arrivals gate, I had completely forgotten where I'd parked my car. We spent the next two hours wandering aimlessly around various parking lots in the pouring rain. I wish I'd never offered to give him a ride ... and I bet he does, too!"

"This happened five years ago but to this very day the memory still haunts me! The CEO where I used to work sent a (very smug) company-wide email congratulating *himself* on record profit margins. In response I wrote a very rude message making fun of the CEO to my office buddy ... or so I thought. If only I hadn't been in such a rush to have lunch, I might have noticed that I had hit *reply to all* instead of *reply* ... those two little words make a huge difference. My email was sent to every employee in London and Boston. It was only when I came back from lunch and everyone was snickering that it clicked what had happened. I just wanted the ground to swallow me up."

The positive side of embarrassment

The outward signs of embarrassment are well known, and include blushing, gazing downward, turning away and face touching. However, researchers have been attempting to identify the evolutionary purpose of embarrassment.

Several researchers have postulated that embarrassment may help to signal whether humans are willing to develop long-term bonds with each other. For example, Lewis (2008) believes that embarrassment is when individuals make a negative evaluation of their actions, thoughts or feelings because they feel they have not behaved according to social standards.

Feinberg, Willer, Keltner and Dacher (2012) **hypothesised** that embarrassment served several important social functions and **conducted** several **experiments** to test this hypothesis.

In one experiment, **participants** were asked to tell an embarrassing story and then complete a questionnaire that looked at their tendency to be kind. The **findings** indicated that people who showed more embarrassment were more likely to be kinder people. The researchers **concluded** that these people were more 'pro-social' – that is they wanted to be part of the group and not behave in a way that was counter to the social **norms** of the group.

In another experiment, participants witnessed an interaction between a researcher and someone that they thought was another participant (but was actually an actor). The researcher praised the fake participant's performance on a test, and the fake participant either expressed embarrassment or pride. The participants who saw the actor look embarrassed were more likely to think he was trustworthy and want to interact with him. This experiment **demonstrated** that people are more likely to have a positive perception of someone who shows embarrassment. The researchers **speculated** that this was because this person is showing a desire to fit in with the group.

From examining the findings of studies such as these, it appears that the evolutionary purpose of embarrassment was to help identify individuals who would be likely to cooperate with the group. So although embarrassment is widely thought of as a negative emotion, displaying embarrassment most likely makes a positive impression on others.

VOCABULARY
Science and research

A Match the words in bold from the second text with the meanings (1–9).

1 do (an experiment, a study) ____________
2 standard behavior ____________
3 suggest a theory ____________
4 guess ____________
5 people taking part in a study or experiment ____________
6 results ____________
7 test ____________
8 decide ____________
9 show ____________

B Go to the Vocabulary Hub on page 143.

C SPEAK Work in pairs and discuss the questions.

1 Would you like to be a participant in a psychology study?
2 Think of an experiment you've heard about. What did it hypothesize? What were the findings?
3 Is it ethical to conduct a study where you make people feel embarrassed?

GRAMMAR
Wishes and regrets

A WORK IT OUT Look at the underlined sentences in *No need to be embarrassed?* Then choose the correct words to complete the rules.

Wishes and regrets

1 We use *wish* or *if only* + simple ***present*** / ***past*** to wish that the present was different.
2 We use *wish* or *if only* + ***present*** / ***past*** perfect to wish that the past was different.
3 We can use *should (not)* or *ought (not) to* + *have* + *past participle* or *been* + ***present*** / ***past*** participle to talk about regrets.
4 We can use *would* + *love* or *prefer* or *hate* + ***to have*** / ***have*** + *(not)* past participle to talk about regrets.

B Go to the Grammar Hub on page 128.

C Complete the sentences so they are true for you.

1 If only I could …
2 I wish I were …
3 I would have loved to …

SPEAKING

A PREPARE Think of a time when you did something you regret. You can use the list of ideas on page 150 of the Communication Hub or your own ideas. What happened? What do you wish had happened differently?

B DISCUSS Tell your partner about what happened. Listen to your partner and ask questions.

LISTENING

A SPEAK Work in pairs. Look at the pictures. Discuss which of the following gives people the biggest advantage in life. Give reasons for your choice.

- Money
- Intelligence
- Supportive family
- Good health

4.4 **B LISTEN FOR MAIN IDEA** You are going to listen to part of a debate about whether being highly intelligent gives people an advantage in life. What are the speaker's three main points?

1 ______________________
2 ______________________
3 ______________________

4.4 **C LISTEN FOR SPECIFIC INFORMATION** Listen again and answer the questions.

1 What is the 'nutty professor' stereotype?
2 What mistakes do intelligent people frequently make at social events?
3 What do intelligent people sometimes do to preserve their reputation?

D SPEAK Work in pairs. Can you think of any counter-arguments or challenges to the three points in Exercise B? Present them to your partner. Use the phrases below to help you.

First of all, the speaker claimed that … but …
In addition, the speaker stated that …
The speaker also mentioned the fact that …

E SPEAK Work in pairs and discuss the questions.

1 Do you know any intelligent people who behave in the ways that the speaker described?
2 Do you think the speaker has a convincing argument? Why/Why not?
3 The speaker says that intelligence and happiness don't necessarily come together. Do you agree?

VOCABULARY
Thinking

A Complete the questions (1–8) with the correct form of a word or phrase in the box.

absent-minded common sense curious eccentric eureka moment overthink troubleshoot wishful thinking

1 Are you good at ______________ or do you find it difficult to find and fix problems and faults?
2 Do you sometimes think about the same thing over and over again? Are you ______________ things?
3 Do you solve problems with sudden bursts of inspiration, like a ______________?
4 Do you like to take things apart? Are you ______________ about how things work?
5 Do you make time in the day to organize work? Or does it seem like ______________ ______________ to sit down and plan things?
6 Do you forget where you leave things? Are you ______________?
7 Are you a practical person? Or do you lack ______________?
8 Would you describe yourself as fairly conventional and similar to most people? Or are you a little ______________?

B Go to the **Vocabulary Hub** on **page 144**.

C SPEAK Work in pairs. Ask and answer the questions in Exercise A. Then decide if your partner is a genius.

PRONUNCIATION

Adding information or changing the topic

.5 **A** Listen again to the beginning of the debate. Draw arrows to show whether the intonation is rising (↗), falling (↘) or fall-rising (↘↗) at the end of the underlined words/phrases.

Thank you very much. It's an honor to speak against the motion tonight. [1], ( ) it's easy to see why so many people believe being intelligent makes your life better. [2]After all, ( ) we see intelligent people thriving at school. We see them getting into the colleges they want. We see them graduating with good academic certifications. And [3]on top of that, ( ) we see the importance the world gives to certifications.

So, it may seem strange for me to stand here and argue that intelligent people aren't necessarily at an advantage in life. [4]However, ( ) that is exactly what I'll do. [5]In fact, ( ) there are several clear disadvantages in having a superior intellect.

B SPEAK Work in pairs. Read the dialogues, focusing on the intonation of the underlined words and phrases. Then continue them with your own ideas.

1 **A:** I read that highly-intelligent people frequently like to spend time alone.
B: On top of that, they find it really hard to make friends.

2 **A:** Are you going to watch the debate on intelligence on TV tonight?
B: Yes, I'm planning to. By the way, do you want to go to a debate?

3 **A:** Einstein has been voted the most intelligent person ever.
B: Really? Incidentally, how did you do on your exam?

SPEAKING HUB

A PREPARE Work in groups. Read the motion below and decide whether you will argue for or against it.

Motion: Highly intelligent people should be educated separately.

Order of debate

1. Presentation in support of the motion.
2. Challenge to this presentation.
3. Presentation against the motion.
4. Challenge to this presentation.

B PLAN Decide on the roles each team member will have. Brainstorm arguments to support your position. Try to anticipate the arguments the other team will make, and prepare counter-arguments to them.

C DISCUSS Hold the debate. Follow the order given in Exercise A.

D REFLECT Discuss the following questions:

- How successful was the debate?
- What was your real opinion about the motion?
- Is it difficult to argue for a point of view you don't really agree with?

- Talk about regrets
- Discuss intelligence

Café Hub

4.3 Life-changing tech

A – *straight out of* S – recounting events

Sound and vision

a

b

A Work in pairs. Look at pictures a and b and discuss the questions.

1 In picture a, is each half of the circle the same shade of red?

2 In picture b, are the rectangles the same shade of blue?

Turn to **page 154** to check your answers.

B 4.6 Listen to two short pieces of music. What colors do they make you think of? Why? Turn to page 153 to check your answers.

C Watch the video about an artist. Complete the sentence with the best option.

Neil Haribsson has …

1 partial color blindness in which it is difficult to distinguish between blue and yellow, violet and red, and blue and green.

2 slight color blindness in which it is difficult to distinguish between red, green, brown and orange.

3 total color blindness in which colors are seen as black and white.

Glossary

implant (v) to put an organ, group of cells, or device into the body in a medical operation

sensor (n) a piece of equipment that reacts to physical changes such as the amount of heat or light that exists somewhere

skull (n) the bony case which contains the brain

D Watch the video again. Complete the summary.

Neil Harbisson, an [1] ________, has never been able to see color. He was [2] ________ about color because people always refer to it. He wanted to be able to [3] ________ color rather than to alter his sight. A team of doctors and [4] ________ helped him create an electronic device. This is made up of a color sensor and a [5] ________. The sensor picks up [6] ________ frequencies and the chip [7] ________ the frequency into a sound. Each color creates a different [8] ________.

AUTHENTIC ENGLISH

A Read the sentence from the video and the information in the box. Why do you think Neil's electronic device is compared to something from science fiction?

*With the help of a team of engineers and doctors he created something **straight out of** science fiction.*

straight out of

You use *straight out of* to say that something is similar in type to something else. This structure is frequently used to compare the thing we are describing to an imagined or fictional scenario.

B Work in pairs. Complete the sentences in an interesting way.

1 The scenery in Ireland is stunning – straight out of *a travel brochure*.

2 The band is really like *The Beatles*. They sound like something straight out of ________.

3 Himari saw snow for the first time that winter. It was like something straight out of ________.

4 The town has spectacular old buildings, a beautiful lake and no roads. It's straight out of ________.

5 My bag had been stolen, it was pouring rain and I couldn't speak the language. It was straight out of ________.

6 The climb to the summit was long and difficult. It was like something straight out of ________.

C Join with another pair. Compare your answers to Exercise B.

Hearing colors

A Work in pairs. Discuss the following questions.

1 What gadgets or devices do you use?
2 Are there any new gadgets or devices you want to buy?
3 Have you ever been to a technology fair or exhibition? Why/Why not?

B Watch the video. Are these sentences true (T), false (F) or not given (NG)?

1 Harry is out sick from work. *T / F / NG*
2 The café was very busy in the morning. *T / F / NG*
3 Emily was about to leave the Tech Fair when a woman approached her. *T / F / NG*
4 The device looked like headphones. *T / F / NG*
5 The first thing that Emily saw on the screen was a red square. *T / F / NG*
6 Emily agrees that Sam should go to the Tech Fair. *T / F / NG*

SPEAKING SKILL

A Work in pairs. Put the following sentences from the video in the order they are spoken.

- [ ] Well, I was at this big Health Tech Fair earlier today, right?
- [ ] But hang on, I'll get to that.
- [ ] Tell me about it. I've had rather a strange one myself.
- [ ] [The woman] asked me to step inside a large box. So I did.
- [ ] [I'm] thinking about heading out when all of the sudden, this woman stops me.
- [ ] Overall it was a strange but unforgettable experience.
- [ ] I was just about to ask her what it was when she slammed the door on me!
- [ ] So I'm standing there saying 'Excuse me … what's going on' and thinking what on earth have I got myself into.

SAM MALCOLM AMANDA HARRY EMILY

B Match the sentences from the video (1–8) with the strategies (a–d) in the box.

Recounting events

We frequently recount events. To do this effectively we use a number of strategies.

a signaling the start of a story. For example, ___
b giving the background to a story. For example, ___
c evaluating parts of a story. For example, ___, ___
d sequencing events in a story. For example, ___, ___, ___, ___

SPEAKING HUB

A PLAN You are going to tell an interesting anecdote to a partner. You can choose one of the following topics or use your own idea.

- a strange coincidence
- a great event
- an unforgettable trip

B PREPARE Write notes on how you are going to sequence the events in your anecdote.

C DISCUSS Work in pairs. Tell your anecdote. Change roles.

So I'm thinking to myself this is like something straight out of a Hollywood movie.

D REFLECT Work with a new partner and retell them your previous partner's anecdote.

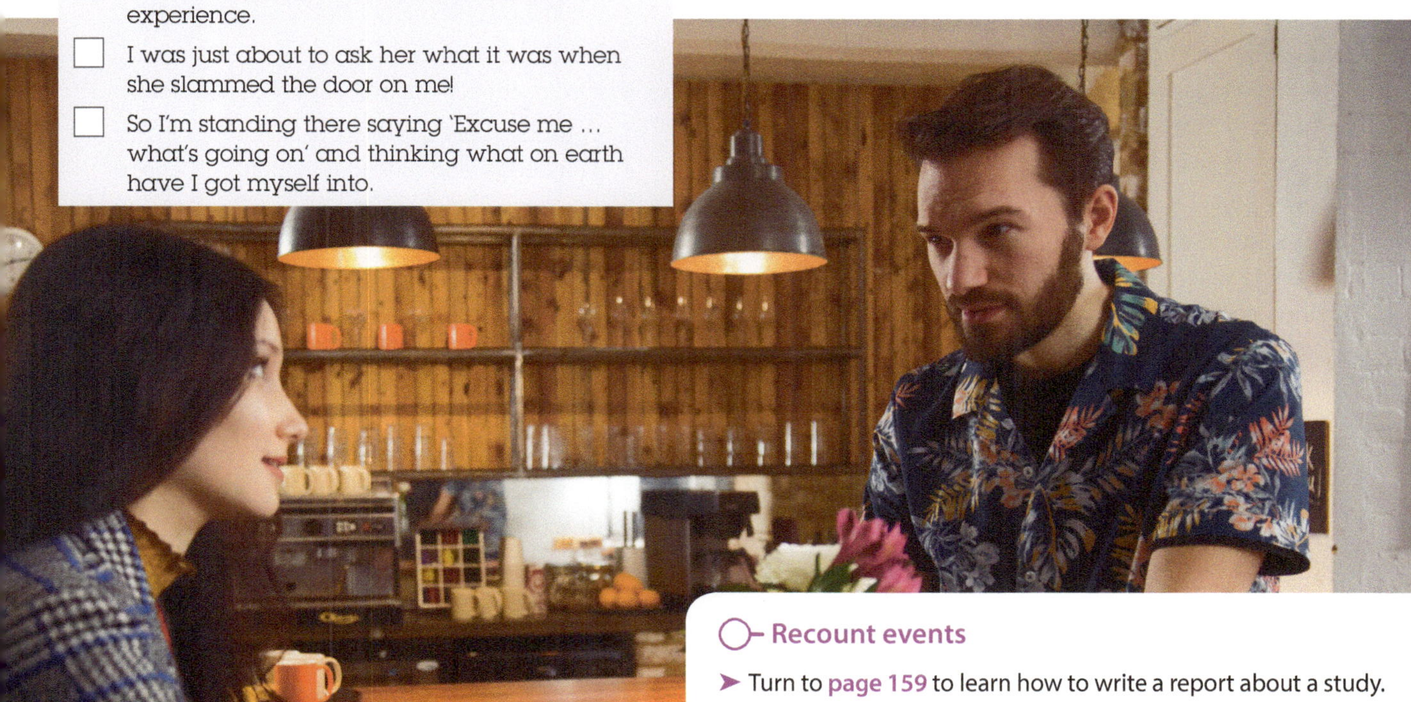

Recount events

➤ Turn to page 159 to learn how to write a report about a study.

Unit 4 Review

VOCABULARY

A **Identify the conceptual metaphor in each sentence. Do you agree with the sentences?**

1. If you're not learning something, you're wasting your time.
2. Don't show that you're bright or people will expect big things.
3. Always keep moving, but never go backwards.
4. Invest in your friendships above all else.
5. If you want to win an argument, attack first and attack hard.
6. Keep people in the dark about your goals until you succeed.

B **Replace the underlined words in the article with the words in the box. You may need to change the tense of the words.**

conclude	conduct	demonstrate	experiment	findings	hypothesize	participants	speculate	the norm

Pavlovian responses

One of the most famous psychological [1]studies was [2]done by Ivan Pavlov, where the [3]subjects were dogs. Pavlov observed that all dogs naturally salivated whenever they saw food, so he [4]decided this was not a behavior they had to learn.

However, he noticed that his dogs also salivated when his assistant, who frequently fed the dogs, walked into the room. Pavlov [5]guessed that the dogs had learned to associate his assistant with food.

He [6]theorized that the dogs could learn to associate a stimulus with food and would salivate when exposed to this stimulus even when no food was present. He rang a bell whenever he fed his dogs, so that this became [7]typical for them.

After several sessions, he rang the bell when no food was present and his dogs salivated. His [8]results [9]showed that dogs could learn an automatic response to a stimulus.

C **Match the sentences (1–8) with the sentences (a–h) that have the same meanings.**

1. You're great at troubleshooting.
2. You frequently overthink things.
3. You can be a little absent-minded.
4. You have no common sense.
5. You're a little eccentric.
6. You frequently engage in wishful thinking.
7. You're naturally curious about everything.
8. You frequently have eureka moments.

a. You don't have conventional tastes.
b. You have sudden instances of inspiration.
c. You like learning about things and how they work.
d. You are pretty forgetful.
e. You're not always realistic when you think about future events or situations.
f. You have a tendency to spend too much time considering an issue.
g. You don't understand how to do basic things.
h. You're good at analyzing and solving problems.

GRAMMAR

A **Rewrite the beginning of the sentences using the words in parentheses. Then complete the sentences with your own ideas.**

1. If all vehicles were automated … (*Were*)
   ____
2. If companies started selling robots to do the housework … (*Should*)
   ____
3. If schools employed robot teachers … (*Imagine*)
   ____
4. If humans could marry robots … (*Supposing*)
   ____
5. If factories hadn't started using robots … (*Had*)
   ____
6. If robots develop conscious thought … (*Suppose*)
   ____

B **Choose the correct words to complete the sentences.**

1. Jim wishes he ***is* / *were*** better at sports.
2. If only I ***can* / *could*** speak three languages.
3. She would love ***have* / *to have*** a better memory.
4. Tina and Bill wish they ***could save* / *had saved*** more money as they can't afford their mortgage this month.
5. We should ***not eat* / *not have eaten*** so much junk food when we were younger.
6. If only I ***have* / *had*** traveled more.
7. My brother ought to ***spend* / *have spent*** more time with our parents while they were visiting.
8. I wish I ***can* / *could*** cook.

5 GAMES

> We do not stop playing because we grow old; we grow old because we stop playing.
>
> Benjamin Franklin

Generation games – a grandma and granddaughter play.

OBJECTIVES

- discuss problem-solving tasks
- discuss gaming and game design
- identify generalizations
- discuss ideas for solving a challenge
- plan a fundraising event
- write a formal report

Work with a partner. Discuss the questions.

1. Look at the picture and read the quote. Why do you think people stop playing games? How does this make us 'grow old'?
2. What games did you like when you were younger? Did you stop playing these games? Why?
3. What games do you like now? Will you keep playing these games when you are older? Will you start any new games?

5.1 21st century games

- Discuss problem-solving tasks
- Discuss gaming and game design

G the passive voice V competition and cooperation P expressing disbelief S understanding colloquial asides

LISTENING

A SPEAK Read about escape rooms. Do they exist in your country? Are they popular? Why/Why not?

5.1 **B LISTEN FOR GIST** Listen to a conversation between three friends, Lin, Joe and Olga, in an escape room. The conversation is in three parts. Answer the same three questions after each part.

1 Which objects from the pictures did they mention for the first time?
2 Which problem(s) are they trying to solve in this part?
3 What do you think will happen next?

ESCAPE ROOMS

An escape room is a game where a group of people try to escape from a locked room, for example by finding hidden objects, solving clues and working as a team. The idea came from TV shows and computer games with similar problem-solving activities. Escape rooms started in Japan in 2007 and quickly spread around the world. They are popular with children (as venues for birthday parties) and adults (for team-building exercises). There are now over 2,800 escape room venues worldwide.

5.1 **C LISTEN FOR DETAIL** Listen to the whole conversation again. Choose the correct options (a, b or c) to answer the questions.

1 Apart from the metal bar, why can't they get the key out?
  a The cylinder is too deep to reach the bottom.
  b They're worried about breaking the cylinder.
  c The cylinder is too narrow for their arms.
2 How many of the friends have read the instructions?
  a one
  b two
  c three
3 Why can't they use the vase to transfer the oil?
  a It's full of water.
  b It's too big.
  c It can't be moved.
4 Why didn't they notice the message before?
  a The room was too bright.
  b They didn't look in the right direction.
  c They couldn't open the drawer.
5 Why does Joe want to keep playing?
  a He's having too much fun.
  b He's sure they've found all the clues.
  c He thinks people will laugh at him.
6 Why was the towel necessary?
  a Because they needed an accurate measurement.
  b Because the ball was too slippery to hold.
  c Because they needed to weigh it on the scale.

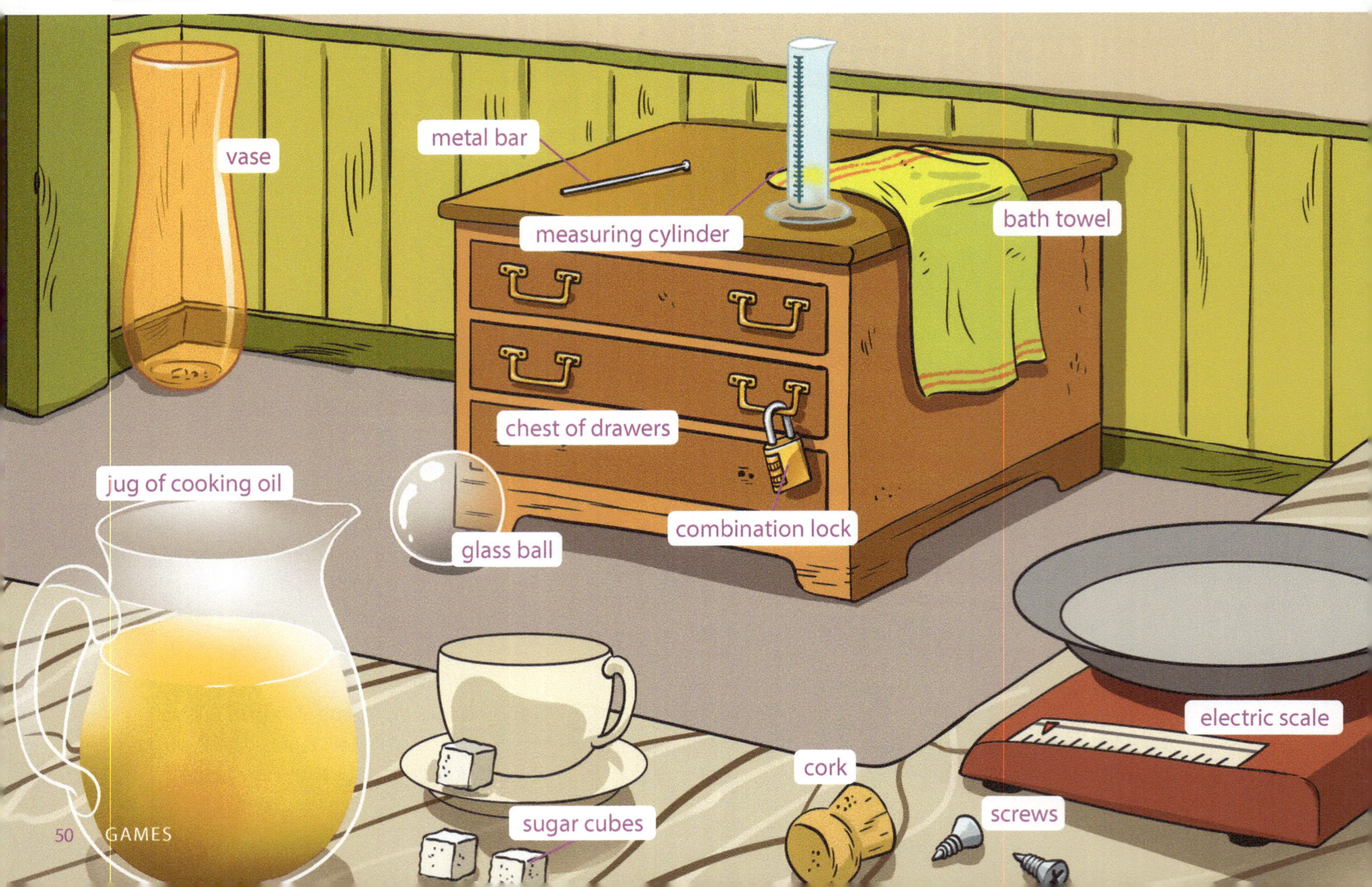

D SPEAK Work in pairs and discuss the questions.

1 How could they have escaped more quickly?
2 Do you think you would have solved all the puzzles?
3 How long would it have taken you to escape from the room?

GRAMMAR
The passive voice

A Look at these sentences from the conversation. Complete the second sentence so that it is in the passive voice.

1 OK, so they've locked us in.
OK, so, *we've been locked in.*
2 Somebody's probably listening to us right now!
__________ right now!
3 Somebody must have written it in fluorescent paint.
__________ in fluorescent paint.
4 They should have given us more clues.
__________ more clues.
5 If we give up now, my friends will make fun of me for weeks.
If we give up now, __________ for weeks.
6 I can't think when somebody's shouting at me!
I can't think when __________!

B Match the sentences (1–5) with the rules (a–d).

The passive voice

a In the structure *make sb do sth*, you need to add *to* in the passive voice (e.g. ___).
b You can make the passive voice from *-ing* forms (e.g. ___) and infinitives (e.g. ___).
c The *get*-passive voice (*get* + past participle) is somewhat informal. Use it to describe unexpected/unwanted events (e.g. ___). It's also useful for distinguishing actions (e.g. *to get married*) from states (e.g. *to be married*).
d Use the causative passive voice (*have/get* + something + past participle) to focus on the person who organizes/pays for a service (e.g. ___) or is the victim of a crime (e.g. *I had my car stolen*).

1 We'll get thrown out if anything gets broken!
2 I don't remember being given any instructions.
3 We were made to sign a form at the front desk.
4 I think the cylinder needs to be filled with water.
5 You need to get your eyes tested!

C Go to the **Grammar Hub** on **page 130**.

D SPEAK Work in pairs. Ask and answer questions about these topics.

- a way you like/don't like being treated
- a time when you were made to do something
- something you've had done recently/you need to get done soon
- a time when you got lost/stuck/delayed, etc

A: I hate being treated like a child.
B: Really? When do you get treated like that? Who by?

PRONUNCIATION
Expressing disbelief

A 5.2 Match the extracts from the conversation (1–7) with the responses (a–g). Then listen to check.

1 It's at the bottom of this measuring cylinder.
2 Try pulling it really hard.
3 I wondered what that form was.
4 Should we give up?
5 Something metal? Aha! Two screws.
6 You did it! We're free!
7 There's something in the jug!

a Screws? What are we supposed to do with them?
b Didn't you read it?
c Give up? No way!
d Seriously? That's cheating!
e Yeah right! There's nothing there apart from the oil.
f Really? That was easy!
g Are you joking? We still need to remove the metal bar.

B 5.3 Listen and decide in which sentence (a or b) the speaker is expressing disbelief.

1 ___ 2 ___ 3 ___ 4 ___

C SPEAK Work in pairs. Take turns to talk about something surprising you did this month. Express disbelief at your partner's statements.

A: I volunteered to teach in India.
B: Really? India? No way!

SPEAKING

DISCUSS Work in small groups. Imagine the room you're in now is an escape room. What clues might help you to escape? Where might those clues be hidden? Express disbelief at each other's suggestions.

READING

A SKIM Look at the picture and the title of the blog post. What do you think urban games are? Skim the blog post to check.

B READ FOR GIST Read the blog post. Which game (a–d) …

1 isn't only played in cities? ___
2 teaches you about a place while you play? ___
3 has more viewers than live players? ___
4 has players who stand out from the crowd? ___
5 can be confusing to play? ___
6 takes advantage of a weakness in technology? ___

a Hidden Bonds
b Geocaching
c Pac Manhattan
d Poznan Beyond Time

URBAN GAMES TURN CITIES INTO PLAYGROUNDS

Glossary

encapsulate (v) to express something in a short clear form that gives the most important facts or ideas
gobble (v) to eat something quickly and usually noisily

It's 6 am and I'm sitting on Trafalgar Square, feeling apprehensive. [1]What on Earth have I let myself in for? The square is virtually empty but I have the distinct feeling I'm being watched by thousands of curious eyes. I receive an SMS: 'Follow the man with the striped umbrella. Don't let him see you.' I spot the man in the distance, jump to my feet and set off in hot pursuit, heart pounding.

I'm playing *Hidden Bonds*, one of the new generation of urban games that are taking off in cities around the world. Urban games encapsulate the best elements of computer games and transfer them to the real world, adding social and physical dimensions to activities that would otherwise involve sitting alone for hours in a darkened room – [2]something I'm all too familiar with!

Urban games originated from a game called *Geocaching*, which uses GPS devices to create virtual treasure hunts. Players are given the GPS coordinates of special boxes called caches, which could be hidden anywhere in the world. Part of the challenge comes from the limitations of GPS, which is only accurate to within a dozen or so meters, so you need to use your eyes. After locating a cache, you win the prize inside – but you must replace it with an appropriate prize for the next player. [3]Sounds amazing, right? … If you're into trudging around muddy fields disoriented and in the middle of nowhere!

One of the best-known modern urban games is *Pac Manhattan*, a version of the arcade game *Pac Man*, played out on the bustling, grid-like streets of New York. [4]How cool is that? Players dressed up as brightly-colored characters from the game race around city blocks, gobbling up virtual 'dots' as they go – and trying to **outmaneuver rival** players to avoid being caught.

Luckily, some urban games are played at a more moderate pace. Visitors to Poznan in Poland can choose from a range of treasure-hunt games to explore the city, while solving clues about the city's cultural heritage and history. For example, in *Poznan Beyond Time*, players embark on a time-traveling adventure to save the world. All you need is a printed game sheet … and some good walking shoes – [5]as I learned through experience!

Then there are games played out for an online audience – which brings me back to *Hidden Bonds*. It's fairly complicated, but in a nutshell, there are four teams, each represented by five 'agents' on the streets of London. The objective is to **cooperate** with your **allies** to **overcome** rival agents, by sending a Bluetooth message to their phone before they can send one to yours. Problem is, the agents have no idea who the other agents are and who's just a normal passer-by, which can lead to some embarrassing moments, [6]I can tell you! The agents receive instructions on their cell phones from 'spymasters', who **coordinate** the players' movements based on the votes of hundreds of 'team members' watching the game live online. The team with the last remaining agent **prevails**.

At a rough estimate, I'd say I've played *Hidden Bonds* as an online team member about 50 times – [7]yeah, sad, I know. **Collaborating** with hundreds of strangers is surprisingly satisfying, but playing live is altogether more exhilarating, especially when you come face-to-face with a rival agent. I managed to catch four opponents before getting caught myself mid-afternoon. Only later did I realize that I'd walked over 20 kilometers in the process! [8]Pretty impressive, right? I'd do it again tomorrow if I could, but there's a seven-month waiting list to participate again as an agent. [9]Just my luck, huh?

C UNDERSTAND ASIDES Look at the asides (1–9) underlined in the blog post. Then answer the questions (a–f). Use the information in the box to help you.

Understanding colloquial asides

Colloquial asides are informal phrases that comment on other information in the text (e.g. *Not bad, huh?*). They frequently take the form of questions or exclamations and they make a text feel more chatty, personal and friendly.

Asides can reveal the writer's personality and attitudes. However, watch out for irony, where the writer means the opposite of what they've written.

Which aside(s) …

a express(es) genuine enthusiasm? ___ ___
b is/are likely to be irony? ___
c suggest(s) the writer feels guilty about their lifestyle? ___ ___
d show(s) how the writer felt at the beginning? ___
e suggest(s) the writer frequently describes frustrations in their blog posts? ___
f hint(s) at problems the writer experienced while playing? ___ ___

D SPEAK Work in pairs and discuss the questions.

1. Which games from the blog post would you like to play? Why?
2. Which would you not want to play? Why?
3. Can you think of any dangers or weaknesses of urban games?
4. Why do you think games like this have become more popular?

VOCABULARY

Competition and cooperation

A Match the words in bold in the blog post with the definitions.

1 ______________ (v) working in partnership
2 ______________ (n) people on the same side as you
3 ______________ (v) wins (e.g. after a long contest)
4 ______________ (v) organize people working together
5 ______________ (v) beat another player or solve a problem
6 ______________ (n) a person competing against you
7 ______________ (v) help/support others

B Go to the **Vocabulary Hub** on **page 144**.

C SPEAK Work in groups and discuss the questions.

1. Do you prefer games that involve overcoming rivals or cooperating with allies? Think of examples.
2. Think of examples of sports or games where you have to outsmart, outmaneuver, outplay or outrun your opponents.

SPEAKING HUB

A PLAN Work in pairs. Create an urban game for your town/city. Use ideas from the blog post and your own ideas.

B DISCUSS Present your ideas to another pair. Ask and answer questions about how your game ideas will work in practice.

C PREPARE Choose one game idea to develop more fully as a group. Write some simple rules or instructions for your game.

D PRESENT Present your ideas to the class. Which games would you most like to play? Why?

- Discuss problem-solving tasks
- Discuss gaming and game design

5.2 Serious gaming

- Identify generalizations
- Discuss ideas for solving a challenge

G – passive reporting structures
P – *-ate* words
V – reporting verbs; motivation and manipulation
S – distinguishing generalizations from preferred solutions

LISTENING

A SPEAK Work in pairs. Read *The Food Truck problem.* Discuss two or three possible solutions.

B Work in small groups. You are going to think of a solution for three more puzzles. Go to the **Communication Hub** on **page 151**.

5.4 **C LISTEN FOR SOLUTIONS** Listen to the presentation on Game Theory. What are the correct answers to the puzzles? Use the information in the box to help you.

> **Distinguishing generalizations from preferred solutions**
>
> A speaker frequently presents his or her preferred solution to a problem or puzzle, alongside obvious but problematic solutions or generalizations. Frequently, the generalization is discussed first, before the speaker's preferred solution.
>
> Use the following techniques to distinguish the preferred solution.
>
> - Pay attention to the order in which the speaker presents solutions. Preferred solutions may be presented later.
> - Listen for phrases that signal a generalization (e.g. *it seems obvious, you might expect, according to conventional wisdom*).
> - Listen for solutions presented with questioning intonation. This may indicate the speaker does not believe this is the correct answer.
> - Listen for attitude words like adverbs which can show that the speaker has a skeptical or cautious attitude to a solution (e.g. *presumably, allegedly*).

5.4 **D LISTEN FOR DETAIL** Listen again. Are these sentences true (T) or false (F)? Correct the false sentences.

1. In puzzle A neither participant is likely to win any money. *T / F*
2. Game Theory uses scientific models to find solutions. *T / F*
3. The favorite in talent shows is rarely eliminated in reality. *T / F*
4. The food truck owner in C has no good reason to move. *T / F*
5. The new network would double the amount of traffic. *T / F*

PRONUNCIATION

-ate words

5.5 **A** The suffix *-ate* has two pronunciations. Listen to the extracts from the presentation on Game Theory. Complete the table with the words in the box.

accurate appropriate complicated cooperate eliminated fascinating

/eɪt/	/ət/

B SPEAK Work in groups . Discuss the following questions.

- Do you prefer games where you have to cooperate with others rather than compete individually?
- What is the most fascinating sporting event you've ever watched?
- Do you prefer playing simple or complicated games?

PUZZLE C:
THE FOOD TRUCK PROBLEM

You decide to open a food truck business.
There's already one other food truck in town, which always parks in the town center (point C).
Where's the best place to park your food truck? You can negotiate with the other food truck owner, if you wish.

VOCABULARY
Reporting verbs

A **Replace the underlined words in each sentence with the correct form of the verbs in the box.**

acknowledge assert conclude
imply instruct urge

1 If you share the money, you're saying indirectly that you're willing to cooperate.
2 It's important to say (although it makes my argument weaker) that this strategy doesn't always work.
3 You might decide after thinking carefully that voting for her would be a waste.
4 So I'd strongly advise you to resist the temptation to vote tactically.
5 You should give instructions to the other truck to move to point D.
6 She can simply state as a fact that she's staying in her prime spot.

B **Go to the Vocabulary Hub on page 144.**

C **SPEAK Complete the sentences with your own ideas. Then discuss your sentences with a partner.**

- I firmly believe that …
- I'm not sure whether …
- I'm great at …
- Maybe if I'd done … I might not have …
- You really must …

D **Swap partners and report what your previous partner said using reporting verbs.**

GRAMMAR
Passive reporting structures

A **Complete the sentences so they mean the same as the passive voice sentences with *It*.**

1 **It** can be assumed that your opponent is having the same thoughts.
Your opponent can be ______________________ having the same thoughts.
2 **It** is said that Game Theory is one of the hardest branches of mathematics.
Game Theory is ______________________ one of the hardest branches of mathematics.
3 **It**'s rumored that sports coaches have been experimenting with Game Theory.
Sports coaches ______________________ have been experimenting with Game Theory.
4 **It**'s expected that she'll win by a landslide.
______________________ to win by a landslide.
5 **It**'s reported that this type of thing has happened many times in real life.
This type of thing ______________________ happened many times in real life.

B **WORK IT OUT Complete the rules about passive reporting structures with information from Exercise A.**

Passive reporting structures

Reporting verbs can be used with passive voice structures when we want to introduce a widely held opinion or fact. There are two main ways of doing this.

- __________ + passive voice + __________ clause
- __________ + passive voice + infinitive

Some verbs commonly used with these structures are:
__________, __________, __________, __________ and __________.

C **Go to the Grammar Hub on page 130.**

D **SPEAK Work in pairs and discuss the questions.**

1 When is it useful to use the passive voice to report speech/thoughts?
2 Why do you think 'to rumor' has no active voice form?
3 What's the advantage of using the structure with an infinitive?

SPEAKING

DISCUSS Work in pairs to think of examples of how Game Theory might be used in sports, business, etc. Use the structure with an infinitive to report generalizations, expectations and assumptions.

The best time to make an investment is assumed to be when the price is low, but if everyone has the same idea at the same time, then …

READING

A SPEAK What tricks do smartphone games use to keep people playing again and again? Try to think of other situations where these tricks are used.

B SKIM Read *Gamification: treading the line between motivation and manipulation*. Are any situations from Exercise A mentioned?

C READ FOR DETAIL Read the article again. According to the article, are these sentences true (T) or false (F)? Correct the false sentences.

1 Many companies are not yet aware of the potential of gamification. *T / F*
2 Virtual prizes can still be highly motivating. *T / F*
3 The majority of people are aware that gamification has been used on them at some point. *T / F*
4 The major benefit of gamification for charities is that it increases financial donations. *T / F*
5 Gamification is used to help people recover from injuries. *T / F*
6 A brand new interactive show is being developed by a production company. *T / F*
7 Gamification sometimes encourages people to behave in a way that isn't right. *T / F*
8 The personality of workers may affect how motivating gamification techniques are. *T / F*

D Work in pairs. Look at the two quotes from Christabel Maware and Lisa Tanaka in the article. Which speaker do you agree with most? Why?

VOCABULARY

Motivation and manipulation

A Match numbers (1–7) with letters (a–g) to form full sentences. Then check by looking for the underlined phrases in the article.

1 As a result of marketing tricks, customers **went**
2 Getting into the college **spurred**
3 People don't mind working hard if you can **tap**
4 If people know ***why*** they're doing something, they'll be more **inclined** …
5 Gamification can make people **act against** …
6 We offered virtual prizes to **coax** …
7 The online store is designed to **steer** people …

a **to** spend time doing it properly.
b people **into** giving us their data.
c **me on** to study harder for the exams.
d **toward** the most expensive products.
e **nuts for** the new product.
f **their best interests**.
g **into** their natural desire to do a good job.

B Look at the complete sentences in Exercise A. Decide whether the phrases in bold are related to motivation or manipulation.

C Go to the **Vocabulary Hub** on **page 145**.

D SPEAK Work in pairs. Think of examples from your own experience of each verb in Exercise A. Tell your partner your examples.

My friend tried to coax me into editing her dissertation for her.

SPEAKING HUB

A PREPARE Work in small groups. Choose one of the following challenges, or a similar idea, to solve with your group.

- How to motivate children to read/write more
- How to encourage people to pick up trash

B PLAN Discuss ideas for solving your challenge, using Game Theory and/or gamification techniques.

C PRESENT Present your challenge and solution to the class. Ask and answer questions about how it will work in practice.

D REFLECT Discuss with the class. Which solutions have a chance of becoming popular? Could they make money?

GAMIFICATION

treading the line between MOTIVATION and MANIPULATION

Hitting the treadmill before work, ploughing through deadlines, and finding time to study in the evenings. Maybe these aren't the sort of activities you'd necessarily associate with fun. Yet a glut of apps, websites and online communities that place game-like experiences right at the center of motivation might give you pause for thought. None of this is news for many commercial and public organizations which are already **tapping into** gamification – the application of elements from gameplay psychology to everyday tasks.

Gamification is about more than creating new games for non-gaming contexts. At its heart lies an understanding of the powerful principles that underlie gameplay, the elements that make it so compelling to so many: gratification, competition and rewards. Games increase engagement. Giving people rewards even virtual ones releases dopamine, the feel-good hormone. This leads them to associate that activity or behavior with positive emotions. And that's frequently enough to **spur them on** to repeat it.

The applications of this are diverse: **steering commuters toward** the stairs over the escalator on the Odenplan subway in Sweden by turning them into a giant piano staircase or promoting good learning habits and classroom behavior by giving students 'experience points'. It's highly likely you've experienced gamification yourself, although you probably didn't realize it.

So how can this benefit us? Gamification has made inroads into both the not-for-profit and health sectors. For charities, its greatest potential lies not in fundraising but in fostering a sense of community. If volunteers feel part of an engaged community, they are more **inclined to** stay. Furthermore, they can be incentivized to recruit others or blog about a cause through rewards.

Gamification can also be integrated directly into grassroots campaigning. Hopelab's Zamzee, a physical activity program for families, uses child engagement with technology to improve health. It guides younger users toward doing more physical activity through an activity sensor and a 'physical points' reward system. More specialized healthcare like physical rehabilitation is using and trialing similar approaches. The Medical Interactive Recovery System (Mira) uses a camera to track a patient's physiotherapy movements and translate them into actions within a video game.

As well as bringing fun to areas where it might be wanting, gamification promises to take fun to the next level in traditional entertainment. Younger and more technologically-savvy viewers may crave an immersive experience, being able to participate in a TV show rather than simply view it. Well, now they can have both their needs for compelling stories and recognition or rewards for their gaming achievements, met at the same time. For example, the popular sci-fi TV show, *Defiance,* by Universal Cable Productions, allowed viewers to shape the plot of television episodes through their actions in an accompanying game.

Some are cautious about gamification, precisely because of its power and how widely it is being used. 'If it can help change our behavior, it can also manipulate us to **act against** our best interests', warns technology lecturer and game designer Christabel Maware. 'I can see it being used very cynically to exploit consumers and employees.' Some companies and organizations have already been called out. For example, a ride-sharing app was criticized for supposedly encouraging drivers to drive further without breaks.

And even where gamification is encouraging 'healthy' competition or making a mundane but necessary work task more appealing, there are concerns around work freedom and surveillance. While leader boards and badges can keep us motivated, having our performance and potentially complex interactions monitored, graded and immediately reported back on by machines sounds more dystopian. 'Simply, not everyone is going to **go nuts for** badges at work', says a Recruitment Manager for AdTech Analytics. For workers who are more introverted or prefer to work privately, this kind of surveillance might be unwelcome and demotivating.

As Lisa Tanaka, founder and CEO of creative agency Gamified International puts it, 'On balance gamification can bring some very positive benefits to many sectors. This stuff works, our brains really are hard-wired for rewards and fun is addictive. We're already being **coaxed into** doing all kinds of things. But with such a powerful tool, there's a pressing need now for companies to be socially responsible in how they use it.'

Glossary

crave (v) to want something very much and in a way that is very hard to control
incentivize (v) to give someone a reason for wanting to do something
grassroots (adj) relating to or involving ordinary people, especially in politics
plough (v) to finish something that takes a long time and is difficult or boring
recognition (n) praise, respect or admiration

- Identify generalizations
- Discuss ideas for solving a challenge

Would you risk it?

A Work in pairs. What do you think is happening in the pictures (a and b) from the video?

B 00.00–01.00 Watch the first part of a video about an experiment. Answer the questions.

1 What happens if the coin lands on heads?
2 What happens if the coin lands on tails?

Glossary

flip (v) to turn over quickly or to make something turn over
heads (n) the side of a coin that has a picture of a head on it
scenario (n) a situation that could possibly happen
tails (n) the side of a coin that does not have a picture of a person on it

C 01.00–01.30 Watch the second part of the video. Choose the best option (a, b or c) to complete the sentence.

In this situation most people …

a take a risk and maybe win an extra ten pounds or nothing.
b choose the safe option and take fifteen pounds.
c risk it for the chance to win an extra five pounds.

D 01.30–02.20 Work in pairs. Watch the third part of the video and complete the sentences with the correct option.

1 In the second scenario you are given *ten* / *twenty* pounds.
2 You have to choose to accept a safe loss of *five* / *ten* pounds or take a risk.
3 You flip a coin. If it comes up heads, you don't lose anything, but if it comes up tails, you lose *five* / *ten* pounds.

E 02.20–03.27 Watch the last part of the video. What do most people do in the second scenario? Why?

AUTHENTIC ENGLISH

A Work in pairs. Read the sentence from the video and the information in the box. What word has been left out of the sentence?

Would you choose the safe option and get an extra five pounds or take a risk and maybe win an extra ten or nothing?

Ellipsis

Ellipsis is the practice of leaving a word or words out of a sentence when they are not necessary for understanding it. In spoken English, unstressed words are frequently left out at the beginning of sentences if the meaning remains clear.

B Work in pairs. Match the questions (1–6) with the replies (a–f). Then cross out any words which can be omitted from each question and reply.

1 Did you enjoy your vacation?
2 Are you ready yet?
3 Is your dad any better?
4 Are you coming out with us tonight?
5 Did you have any luck with the tickets for the Beyoncé concert?
6 I'm sorry, are you talking to me?

a I'm almost ready. I'm just putting on my makeup.
b Yes, I was asking if you're doing anything nice on the weekend.
c Yes, thanks. He should be out on the weekend.
d No, they were all sold out. It's a shame, really.
e I'm afraid, I can't. I have to work late.
f It was absolutely amazing! Just got back, actually.

C Work in pairs. Take it turns to ask each other short questions from Exercise B and reply with your own short answers.

How sure are you?

A Work in pairs. Look at the picture.

1 What board games are popular in your country?
2 Do you ever play them?

B Watch the video. Answer the questions.

1 If Sam and Amanda go in a counter-clockwise direction, which category do they land on?
2 Why does Amanda think Geography is the better option?
3 How does Sam feel about Amanda's strategy?
4 How does Malcolm indicate the correct answer to Sam and Amanda?
5 How does Amanda suggest making the game more interesting?
6 Why doesn't Emily want to take the risk?
7 What's the question Emily and Harry have to answer?
8 What's Malcolm's answer? Is he correct?

SPEAKING SKILL

A Work in pairs. Look at the underlined expression from the video and answer the questions.

1 What is Harry doing?
2 Why do we do this when we're speaking?

Sam: Don't you think it's better to play it safe and go for your strongest categories first … you know … try and build up a lead?
Harry: <u>That sounds like a solid strategy to me</u>.

SAM MALCOLM AMANDA HARRY EMILY

B Look at the information in the box. Decide which strategy (a or b) is being used in the exchanges (1–4) from the video.

> **Building relationships**
>
> We can build relationships using the following strategies.
>
> **a** Agreeing with the other person by adding on to what they have said.
>
> **b** Relating to what the other person has said by evaluating or commenting.

1 Sam: I'm thinking we should go for Geography.
Amanda: Totally … I absolutely hate Geography … it's better to try and get it out of the way earlier.

2 Emily: Ah, good – this is quite hard, I think.
Sam: That is quite tricky.

3 Sam: OK, it can only be one of two countries …
Amanda: … either Finland or Norway.

4 Emily: I mean sport hardly looks like it would be Malcolm's strongest category.
Harry: I guess not but he is smart.

C Work in small groups. Give your opinions on one of the following topics. Use the strategies from Exercise B to build a positive rapport.

- your favorite board game
- your favorite type of movie
- your favorite type of book

SPEAKING HUB

A PLAN Work in small groups. You are going to plan a fundraising event for a local charity. Decide on one of the following.

a dinner   a board game evening   a yoga class
a bake off   a fashion show   a quiz

B PREPARE Individually think about the preparations for the event. Consider the following points.

- space
- logistics
- timing
- cost

C PRESENT Work in small groups. Decide on a course of action for the event. Try to build up positive relationships and create a consensus.

A: We could hold a banquet dinner at the town hall.
B: Great idea! It could go on all evening.

Plan a fundraising event

➤ Turn to page 160 to learn how to write a formal report about gamification.

Unit 5 Review

VOCABULARY

A Complete the instructions with the correct form of a word in the box.

ally collaborate cooperate coordinate overcome prevail rival

Bike clash

The game involves outmaneuvering players on [1]_______________ teams by racing around the city on bikes. Each team has four players, who [2]_______________ with each other, and a 'boss', who [3]_______________ their movements. By [4]_______________ with their [5]_______________, players solve puzzles to identify the times and locations of 'clashes', where they try to [6]_______________ their rivals. When a clash begins, the team with the most players wins a 'trophy'. Any teams that have been outnumbered lose a player. At the end, the team with the most trophies [7]_______________.

B Choose the correct word to complete each sentence.

1 Stores are laid out to ***discourage / steer / trigger*** customers toward expensive items.
2 Salespeople try to manipulate us by ***coaxing / dissuading / exploiting*** us into spending more than we intended.
3 Loyalty cards can make people ***act / spur / tempt*** against their best interests.
4 My sister ***spurred / influenced / dissuaded*** me on to enter the race.
5 I wasn't ***exploited / inclined / influenced*** to go, but you've persuaded me.
6 Advertising can ***tap / tempt / influence*** into people's emotional needs.

C Complete the definitions with the words in the box.

discourage dissuade exploit influence manipulate motivate tempt trigger

1 If you _______________ somebody, you encourage them to want to do something.
2 If you _______________ somebody, you use tricks to convince them do something.
3 If you _______________ somebody from doing something, you persuade them not to do it.
4 If you _______________ somebody from doing something, you encourage them not to do it.
5 If you _______________ somebody, you take advantage of their kindness or naivety.
6 If you _______________ somebody, you offer them something that's hard to resist.
7 If you _______________ somebody's behavior, you change it, maybe without the person noticing.
8 If your actions _______________ a response, they cause it to happen automatically.

GRAMMAR

A Rewrite the sentences so they start or end with the words in parentheses.

1 Somebody must have moved my car. (*my*)
_______________.
2 You can always rely on Leo. (*Leo*)
_______________.
3 I'm worried about somebody seeing me. (*seen*)
_______________.
4 They made us leave our phones outside. (*we*)
_______________.
5 Somebody's going to fix my car. (*I'm*)
_______________.
6 It was nice of them to invite us. (*invited*)
_______________.
7 How did somebody break the vase? (*broken*)
_______________?

B Put the words into the correct order to make sentences.

1 good / considered / my proposal / be / to / enough / wasn't
_______________.
2 to / anyone / to the party / expected / hardly / was / come
_______________.
3 have / reported / is / hundreds of complaints / received / to / the company
_______________.
4 going / at / been / alleged / have / the time / to / the driver / is / too fast
_______________.
5 planning / is / a new hospital / to build / rumored / to / the city council / be
_______________.
6 been / the kidnappers / have / is / the letter / by / to / believed / written
_______________.

6 DISCOVERIES

Unearthing the past in Huara Rajada, Northern Peru.

> The real voyage of discovery consists not in seeking new landscapes, but in having new eyes.
>
> Marcel Proust

OBJECTIVES

- speculate and make deductions about the past
- plan an amazing journey
- discuss rewarding jobs
- give a presentation about someone you admire
- plan and perform an interview
- write an expository essay

Work with a partner. Discuss the questions.

1 Look at the picture. What do discoveries like this tell us? Are they important? Why/Why not?

2 Read the quote. What does Proust mean? Do you agree?

3 What do you think has been the greatest discovery ever? Give reasons for your answer.

6.1 Challenging journeys

- Speculate and make deductions about the past
- Plan an amazing journey

V – journeys and adventures; three-part phrasal verbs
P – showing your attitude
G – past modals of speculation and deduction
S – prediction strategies for reading

READING

A SPEAK Work in pairs. Do you know any famous explorers? What did they do?

B PREDICT Look at the title and the pictures in the article. Read the information in the box and answer questions a and b.

> **Prediction strategies for reading**
>
> Use the prediction cycle to help you predict the content of a text:
>
> - Make predictions about the content of the text.
>   - **a** What information will be included?
>   - **b** What questions will it answer?
> - Read part of the text to find out if your predictions were correct or not.
>   - **c** Were your predictions correct?
>   - **d** What information supported or challenged your predictions?

C SKIM Read *The disappearance of Percy Fawcett*. Answer questions c and d in the box in Exercise B.

D READ FOR DETAIL Complete the table with evidence for and against each theory in the article.

	For
1	
2	
3	
	Against
1	
2	
3	

E SPEAK Work in groups. Which theory do you think is the most likely explanation for what happened? Why?

THE DISAPPEARANCE OF PERCY FAWCETT

In the age of **long-haul** flights and travel **off the beaten path**, many now consider themselves seasoned **globetrotters**. However, there was a time when traveling to the far corners of the world was both dangerous and rare.

This was true in January 1925 when accomplished British explorer Percy Fawcett **embarked on** his latest expedition, hoping to find an ancient city in the jungle, the Lost City of Z.

Despite previous failed attempts to find it, he was still convinced that a large city that was 'more ancient than the oldest Egyptian discoveries' lay **at the heart of** the Amazon. On April 20th, his group departed from the Brazilian city of Cuiabá and headed for the jungle.

On May 29th, Fawcett sent a letter to his wife telling her that they were about to enter **uncharted territory**. They were never heard from again.

So what happened to Fawcett and his party? This remains one of the world's greatest unsolved mysteries and has inspired a lot of speculation. Here are three possible explanations.

1 THEY WERE KILLED BY INDIGENOUS PEOPLE

Some people believe that Fawcett and his companions must have been killed by an indigenous tribe. While journalist David Grann was retracing Fawcett's journey in 2005, he met with a tribe called the Kalapalo. They told him that they had heard stories from their grandparents about explorers coming to their territory and ignoring warnings not to walk through territory belonging to another tribe because this tribe was hostile to intruders. The Kalapalo tribe believe that it is highly likely Fawcett and his companions were killed by this other tribe. However, no bones have ever been found.

2 THEY DIED OF NATURAL CAUSES: EXHAUSTION, STARVATION OR ILLNESS

According to Henry Costin, a man who accompanied Fawcett on several of his previous expeditions, Fawcett was always friendly and respectful toward the tribes he met, so he couldn't have been killed by them.

Costin believed that there was a distinct possibility, given the scale of the expedition and the **impenetrable** terrain, that Fawcett and his companions died from exhaustion, or lack of food when their **provisions** ran out. Alternatively, given that several explorers at the time died from tropical diseases, they may well have succumbed to illness in the jungle.

3 THEY STAYED IN THE JUNGLE

After studying Fawcett's private papers, television director Misha Williams came up with an alternative theory. She believed that Fawcett had become disillusioned with life in Europe and may have decided to establish a commune in the jungle and live a simpler life.

However, many people point out that this theory doesn't make a lot of sense, because Fawcett had a wife and two children, so he couldn't have deliberately abandoned them. Similarly, he could have found the Lost City of Z and decided to stay. In recent years, archaeological discoveries have shown that Fawcett might have been right after all.

Researchers have found the ruins of huge cities in the Amazon that may well have been home to thousands of people. Did he finally find what he was looking for?

Glossary

disillusioned (adj) disappointed because you have discovered that someone or something is not as good as you had believed

starvation (n) a situation in which a person or animal suffers or dies because they do not have enough to eat

succumb (v) to become very sick or to die from a disease

intruder (n) someone who enters a place where he or she is not allowed to go

retrace (v) to go along the same path or route that someone else has gone along previously

seasoned (adj) experienced in a particular activity or job

VOCABULARY

Journeys and adventures

A Scan the article again. Complete the definitions with the words in bold.

1 ________ (n) supply of food, drink, equipment, etc for a journey
2 ________ (adj) impossible to move through or enter
3 ________ (v) begin
4 ________ (n phr) places not covered by maps
5 ________ (n) middle of
6 ________ (n) frequent international travelers
7 ________ (adj) long distance
8 ________ (phr) away from frequently visited places

B Go to the **Vocabulary Hub** on **page 145**.

C **SPEAK** Work in pairs. Tell your partner about an adventurous journey you've been on or heard about.

GRAMMAR

Past modals of speculation and deduction

A Look at the underlined sentences in the article. Complete the rules with the words in the box.

adjective adverb can't/couldn't could/might/may may well must

Past modals of speculation and deduction

1 We use ________ + *have* + past participle for things we believe logically happened.
2 We use ________ + *have* + past participle for things we think are likely to have happened.
3 We use ________ + *have* + past participle for things we think possibly happened.
4 We use ________ + *have* + past participle to say something was not logically possible.
5 We can use phrases that start with *There's a/an* + ________ + noun + (*that*) ... to speculate.
6 We can use phrases that start with *It's* + ________ + adjective (*that*) ... to speculate.

B Go to the **Grammar Hub** on **page 132**.

C **SPEAK** Work in pairs. Discuss these theories about Percy Fawcett's disappearance.

1 They were attacked by wild animals.
2 Rival explorers killed them.
3 They were killed by a natural disaster.
4 They decided to join one of the tribes.

SPEAKING

A **DISCUSS** Work in small groups. Group A – go to the **Communication Hub** on **page 153**. Group B – go to the **Communication Hub** on **page 155**.

B **PRESENT** Work with someone from the other group. Tell him or her about the historical mystery you read about.

VOCABULARY
Three-part phrasal verbs

A Work in pairs. Read *Seven reasons to go traveling*. Discuss which you think is the best reason to go traveling.

B Find nine three-part phrasal verbs in the article. Use the information in the box to help you.

1 ______________________
2 ______________________
3 ______________________
4 ______________________
5 ______________________
6 ______________________
7 ______________________
8 ______________________
9 ______________________

Three-part phrasal verbs

Phrasal verbs are common in informal English.

Most phrasal verbs only have two parts (for example, *sit down*, *turn up*). However, there are also three-part phrasal verbs which contain a verb + a particle + a preposition (for example, *look up to*).

C Choose the correct options to complete the rules. Use the examples in Exercise B to help you decide.

1 Most three-part phrasal verbs are ***separable / inseparable***.
2 The particle and the preposition ***can / can't*** be separated.
3 Some three-part phrasal verbs can take an object after the ***verb / particle***.

D Complete the sentences with a three-part phrasal verb from Exercise B. Use the hint in parentheses to help you.

1 It's important to ______________ (*research*) a place before you visit it.
2 If you ______________ (*experience*) problems on a trip, it makes it more of an adventure.
3 ______________ (*moving away from*) the crowds is more interesting than going sightseeing.
4 I don't think I ______________ (*be interested in*) traveling to another country by myself.
5 I ______________ (*remember*) my childhood vacations with fondness.
6 Travel is a great way to help people to ______________ (*stop thinking about*) work or study.
7 You should always ______________ (*review and practice*) your language skills before a trip.
8 You should always pack in advance rather than only ______________ (*eventually do*) it the night before you leave.

E Work in pairs. Discuss whether you agree or disagree with the sentences in Exercise D.

F **SPEAK** Work in small groups. Which reasons from the article do you think are the most worthwhile? Why? Think of three more reasons to go traveling.

Seven reasons TO GO TRAVELING

1 Because you are up for an adventure. Challenge yourself with something that pushes you outside your comfort zone. See how you react when you come up against obstacles.

2 Because you want to find out about the world. You can read about different countries and cultures, but nothing compares to being there and seeing it for yourself.

3 Because you want to learn the language. If you really want to brush up on your language skills, you need to travel to where the language is spoken.

4 Because you want to learn about yourself. Getting away from home and work means you have time to reflect on your life and decide if you want to make any changes.

5 Because you need to recharge your batteries. If you find it hard to keep yourself away from work, traveling can help you switch off from all the things you need to do and get some well-earned rest.

6 Because you want to celebrate a special occasion with friends or family. Travel can create precious memories that you can look back on together.

7 Because you always wanted to. Don't keep putting it off or you'll never get around to it!

LISTENING

A PREDICT Work in pairs. You are going to listen to a discussion about travel challenges on a radio program. What do you think a travel challenge is?

.1 **B LISTEN FOR GIST** Listen to the radio program. Answer the following questions.

1 What is a travel challenge?

______

2 How many examples of travel challenges does Kyle give?

______

3 What reasons other than to be different does Kyle give for people doing these challenges?

______

4 What does the presenter think you need to do a trip like Adam Leyton's?

______

5 What does Kyle admire about Daniel Tunnard?

______

6 What is Kyle's most vital piece of advice for someone doing a travel challenge?

______

.1 **C LISTEN FOR DETAIL** Listen again. What is the significance of the following numbers?

1 24	______	5 41	______
2 12	______	6 140	______
3 22	______	7 14	______
4 900	______	8 55	______

D SPEAK Work in pairs. Discuss the questions.

1 Do you agree that these kinds of travel challenges are becoming more popular?
2 Which of the three travel challenges sounds the most interesting to you?
3 Would you donate money to help someone pay for his or her trip?
4 Would you rather go on a normal vacation or try a travel challenge?

PRONUNCIATION
Showing your attitude

6.2 **A** Listen to these extracts from the radio program. Match each extract (1–4) with the speaker's attitudes to what they say (a–d).

a certain that what they say is true ___
b believes what they say is a generalization or approximation ___
c believes that what they say is an important point ___
d unsure that something is true ___

6.3 **B** Work in pairs. Draw arrows to predict whether the intonation rises (↗), falls (↘) or fall-rises (↘↗) on the underlined attitude words. Then listen to check.

1 Allegedly, ( ) you need to be very careful backpacking in some areas of that country.
2 On the whole, ( ) I think it's better to travel alone than with a group of friends.
3 The question is, ( ) do you have the luxury of taking time out from work.
4 Surely, ( ) it can't be that much fun visiting a lot of countries in a short span of time.

C SPEAK Work in pairs. Discuss the questions using words, phrases and intonation to show your attitude.

1 Which countries would you like to visit and why?
2 Should people travel more within their own countries before they go to another country?
3 Do you think taking time out to go traveling can help your career?

SPEAKING HUB

A PREPARE Work in small groups. You have entered a competition to win sponsorship for a trip to another country. To win, you must come up with an original travel challenge. Think of an idea to enter into the competition and prepare to present this idea to your class. Think about:

- how you will travel.
- where you will travel.
- what your goal will be.
- what the budget will be.
- how you will publicize the trip.

B PRESENT Present your idea to the class. Listen to the other groups' ideas.

C DISCUSS Vote on the most interesting idea.

- Speculate and make deductions about the past
- Plan an amazing journey

6.2 Inquisitive minds

- Discuss rewarding jobs
- Give a presentation about someone you admire

G – *-ing* and infinitive forms
P – pauses and pitch in presentations
V – binomial expressions
S – writing notes while listening

READING

A SPEAK Work in pairs. Rank the following qualities in order of how important they are in journalism. Give reasons for your answer.

___ passion
___ curiosity
___ integrity
___ courage
___ determination

B READ FOR MAIN IDEA Read *Chase down your story*. What is the purpose of the article?

1 To give advice to journalism students.
2 To share life lessons which the writer has learned from journalism.
3 To evaluate the importance of journalism in the 21st century.

C READ FOR DETAIL Read the article again. Match the questions (1–6) with the sections (a–d). Sections may be chosen more than once.

Which section of the article …

1 acknowledges a misconception the writer had? ___
2 highlights the difference between news in the past compared to now? ___
3 mentions an event which changed the writer's approach to learning? ___
4 describes a characteristic which the writer admires? ___
5 emphasizes the importance of personal experience? ___
6 mentions discovering lessons by accident when looking for help? ___

D SPEAK Work in pairs. Discuss the questions.

1 Which do you think is the most useful piece of advice? Which do you think is the least useful? Why?
2 Have you ever learned anything from work or study that you could apply to your personal life?

Chase down your story

a Finding stories

Ever wondered how journalists find the stories worth telling? Over my first year at a bona fide national newspaper, I learned the hard way that getting the 'scoop' – being the first to report an exciting or important newsworthy story – was easier said than done. So I asked some of my more experienced colleagues to pass on their tricks of the trade. But what I soon discovered was that their advice could be applied not only to my job, but also to my personal life.

b Be curious

As journalists, we're paid to be curious. The number one suggestion I got was to have an inquisitive mind: figure out what matters, and which stories will inspire, move or make us laugh. It is not enough to report facts these days. But if something sparks your curiosity, the chances are other people will be interested, too.

There was the time I met a woman who mentioned she was thinking about moving to a remote Pacific island for a year. A whole year away from family, friends … the internet! I had so many questions – and it was no surprise it made a great story, too.

In every conversation I have now, I think about what I can ask and what I can learn. Everybody has something they can teach you. It also helps to ask yourself questions about your own life: Why am I doing what I'm doing? What do I hope to achieve?

c Local is global

Writers have a great imagination. But, as I learned from my colleagues, that can sometimes have a downside. It can keep us looking toward the horizon, craving uncharted territory. Fresh out of college, I pictured myself jetting off to parts unknown to break the next big story. While there is much to be said for this, articles don't need to be exotic or even big news to catch a reader's attention. More often than not, we find that we write best when we write what we know. This second lesson is possibly one of the hardest to learn as a new writer.

GRAMMAR

-ing and infinitive forms

A Choose the correct form of the verbs to complete the sentences.

1. She was thinking about ***moving*** / ***to move*** to a remote Pacific island for a year.
2. It is time to acknowledge how vital it is ***staying*** / ***to stay*** on course.
3. It's all too easy for details ***slipping*** / ***to slip*** through the cracks.
4. Articles don't need to be exotic ***catching*** / ***to catch*** a reader's attention.
5. It is not enough ***reporting*** / ***to report*** facts these days.
6. Ever wondered how journalists find the stories worth ***telling*** / ***to tell***?

B Scan the article again and check your answers to Exercise A.

Most of the greatest reporters have cut their teeth reporting on local news, whether that's uncovering home-grown corruption and injustice or just telling human-interest stories. What I've come to realize is that these stories often have a global reach because we have the same emotions, interests and concerns the world over. This has led me to believe – that while we must not be inward looking – appreciating what is right in front of us can be just as rewarding as looking further afield.

d Follow up

We are living in a world that is always on, where consumers can access massive amounts of content and expect instant gratification. In comparison to only five or ten years ago, we are so concerned with the beginning of the story that the middle and end have fallen by the wayside. It's all too easy for details to slip through the cracks and for stories, which should be huge, to be all but forgotten by the next news cycle.

And here lies the last tip, get to the conclusion of your story. Don't get distracted. Many of the finest journalists in history were renowned for their tenacity – their innate ability to chase down the facts in the face of seemingly indomitable odds.

This is a quality to aspire to in life. It is time to acknowledge how vital it is to stay on course, not to allow yourself to be side-tracked by modern distractions and the illusion of endless choice. See things through to their conclusion: whether that's the project you're working on or the sport you're learning. And it applies to people too – valuing and caring for the friends and networks you have is as important as growing them.

Glossary

cut your teeth on (phr) to get your first experience in a particular job by doing something

tenacity (n) the behavior of being very determined and unwilling to stop when trying to achieve something

C Match the examples in Exercise A to the rules in the box.

-*ing* and infinitive forms

We use the *-ing* form:

a after prepositions ____________

b after expressions such as *it's no good …, it's not worth …, there's no point in …, have a good time/difficulty/fun/problems …* ____________

We use the infinitive:

c after adjectives ____________

d after nouns ____________

e after quantifiers ____________

f after the word *time* ____________

D Go to the **Grammar Hub** on **page 132**.

SPEAKING

Work in pairs. Look at the pictures of people with different jobs below.

Student A: Compare the two pictures. Say what qualities and skills people need for these jobs and why people choose to do these jobs.

Student B: Which job would you most like to do and why?

LISTENING

A **PREDICT** Work in pairs. Look at the infographic of events in a famous inventor's life. Can you guess who it is?

B Read the information in the box and look at the notes table.

Writing notes while listening

When you need to take effective notes, you can use the Cornell system. It involves the following five stages:

Stage 1 Notes: Write notes in the note-taking column. Focus on main ideas. Use bullet points and abbreviations.

Stage 2 Questions: Write questions about your notes in the column on the left. (e.g. *Is this still true today?, What does inhalation mean?*)

Stage 3 Summarize: Read your notes and questions. Then write a summary of what you learned.

Stage 4 Reflect: Think about what you have written. (e.g. *Overall, do you agree with the speaker?*)

Stage 5 Review and recall: Review your notes. Cover the second column and answer the questions in the first.

6.4 **C** **LISTEN TO WRITE NOTES** Listen to a presentation about an inventor. Follow the method in Stage 1 in the box. Write notes in the table as you listen.

Questions	Notes
Summary	

D **REFLECT** Read your notes. Follow Stage 2 in the box. Write questions in the table.

E **SUMMARIZE** Follow Stage 3 from the box. Write a summary of your notes in the table. Use the questions in the box to help you.

F **REVIEW** Compare your notes and questions with your partner. Are they similar? Can your partner answer any of your questions?

G **SPEAK** Work in pairs. If you were an inventor what type of invention would you focus on?

- inventions that save lives
- everyday products that fix common problems
- niche products for rich people

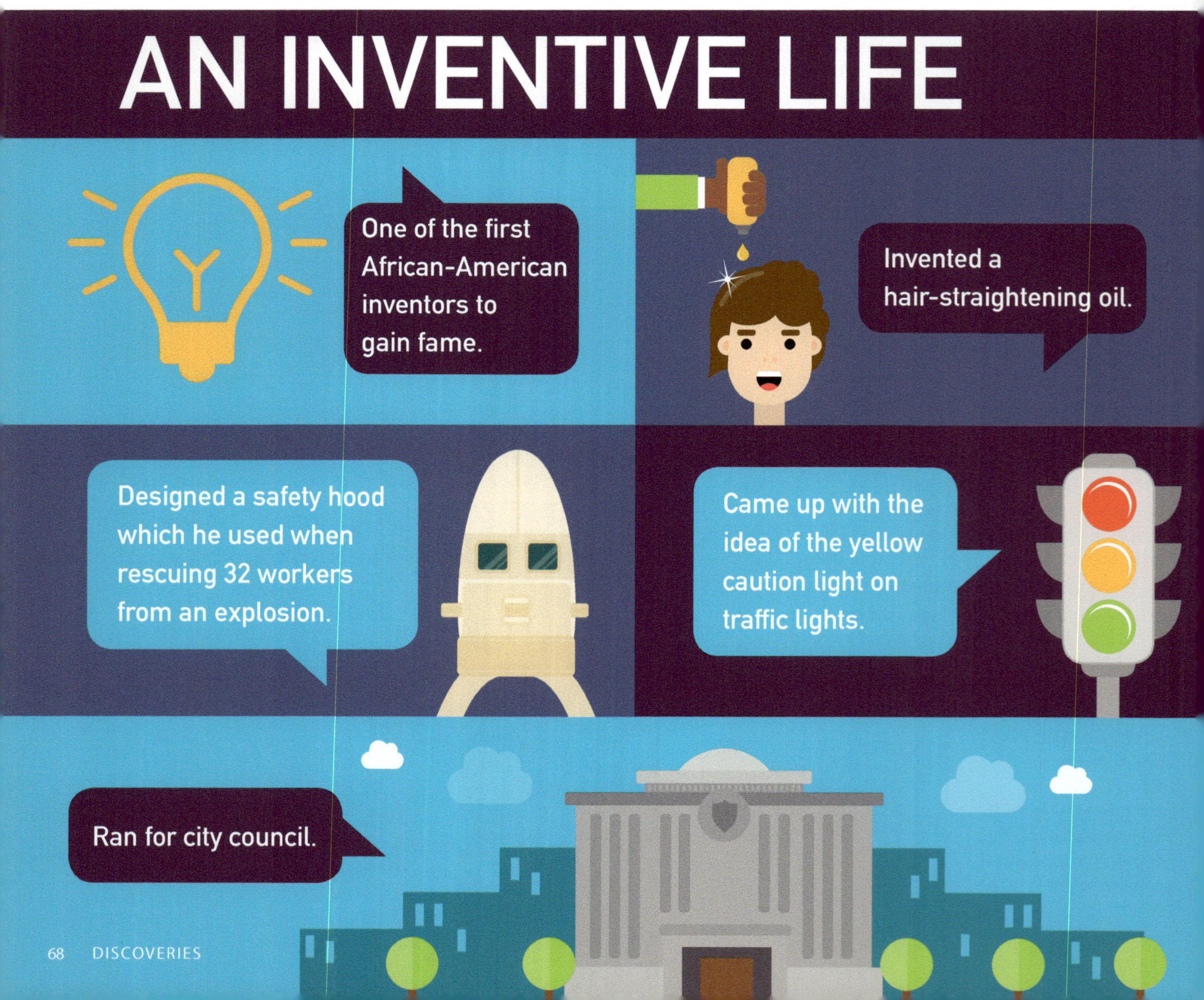

VOCABULARY
Binomial expressions

A Match the binomials in bold (1–10) with their definitions (a–j). Use the information in the box to help you.

Binomial expressions

A binomial expression is two words (nouns, verbs, adjectives or adverbs) joined by words like *and, or, but, by* and *to*.

The two words can:

- be antonyms (*give and take*)
- be synonyms (*peace and quiet*)
- use the same word twice (*back to back*)
- use words that start with the same sound (*black and blue*)
- use words that sound similar (*here and there*).

When a binomial expression is a compound adjective used before a noun it is generally hyphenated (a *happy-go-lucky* person).

1 In my opinion, he's **far and away** one of America's greatest inventors.
2 He was soon selling it **far and wide**.
3 It was truly a **life-or-death** situation.
4 Morgan and his brother Frank raced to the scene and went in **side by side**.
5 They soon re-emerged **safe and sound** with survivors.
6 Morgan's fame began to spread **slowly but surely**.
7 **By and large**, in the early 1920s, American roads were dangerous places.
8 **Time after time** there were stories of injuries and fatalities in traffic accidents.
9 But he also put his **heart and soul** into the community.
10 While his life was a classic **rags-to-riches** story.

a generally
b all of one's energy and passion
c repeatedly
d by a very large amount
e next to each other
f from poor to wealthy
g unharmed and not in danger
h in many different places
i potentially fatal
j gradually

B Go to the Vocabulary Hub on page 145.

C SPEAK Work in pairs. Complete the sentences with your own ideas. Then share your ideas with your partner.

1 ______________________ is **far and away** the greatest invention.
2 I always put my **heart and soul** into ______________________.
3 When I was younger, I couldn't ______________________. Then **slowly but surely**, I learned how.

PRONUNCIATION
Pauses and pitch in presentations

6.5 **A** Listen to the first part of the presentation again and mark any pauses with (/).

Today, I'd like to talk about someone who I particularly admire. In my opinion, he's far and away one of America's greatest inventors. His innovations have fixed everyday problems but also probably saved thousands of lives. In addition, he was one of the first African-American inventors to gain public recognition for his work. His name was Garrett Morgan and he was a prolific inventor and entrepreneur who lived between 1877 and 1963. And while you may not all know his name, you're likely to have experienced his innovations.

One of Morgan's early successes was actually an accident. He was repairing a sewing machine in his store when he noticed that some oil he was using had straightened the hairs on a cloth.

B Work in pairs. Turn to the audio script on page 172 and practice reading the presentation about Garrett Morgan. Focus on pauses and pitch.

SPEAKING HUB

A THINK You are going to give a presentation about someone you admire. Choose someone who made a big difference to the world by:

- leading social change
- challenging the status quo
- inventing or discovering something important.

B PREPARE Write a short presentation to tell your classmates about this person. Focus on:

- the life of the person you are talking about
- the main achievements of the person you are talking about
- a big problem the person solved.

C PRESENT Give your presentation.

D DISCUSS Listen to your classmates' presentations. Which of the people do you want to learn more about? Why?

Discuss rewarding jobs
Give a presentation about someone you admire

6.3 World of knowledge

A– engaging listeners S– conducting an interview

Connecting with nature

a

b

c

A Work in pairs. Look at the pictures (a–c) and discuss these questions.

1 What are they?

2 How might they be connected?

B Watch the video. Check your answers to Exercise A.

Glossary

assemble (v) to build something by joining parts together
countless (adj) very many
tangled (adj) twisted into an untidy mass
vaporize (v) to turn from a solid or liquid state into gas

C Watch the video again. Are the sentences true (T) or false (F) according to the video? Correct the false sentences.

1 An oak tree is made up of only carbon, nitrogen, oxygen and hydrogen. *T / F*

2 The carbon atom in the acorn was created inside a star billions of years ago. *T / F*

3 The carbon atom in the acorn has formed part of the earth for two billion years. *T / F*

4 The carbon atom in the acorn got into some ancient oak tree through the action of photosynthesis. *T / F*

5 In billions of years, when the sun dies and the earth is vaporized, all atoms will die. *T / F*

D Watch the video again. Complete the sentences.

1 When atoms react and ________________ they make up everything in the Universe.

2 Many different types of plants, trees and animals make up the ________________ of a forest.

3 When you understand that everything is made of atoms, a forest doesn't seem like such a ________________ place.

4 An atom in an acorn has spent many years in ________________.

5 Life is only a ________________ home of the atoms that make up the universe.

AUTHENTIC ENGLISH

A Work in pairs. Read the sentence from the video and the information in the box. Which device has been used to engage listeners?

So life is just a temporary home for the immortal elements that build up the universe.

Engaging listeners

Brian Cox is a very engaging speaker. He uses a number of strategies to engage listeners.

- Summarizing information, for example, *So, when you look at it like that it's really not that complicated at all.*
- Repetition of certain words such as *billions* to emphasize a point.
- Dynamic words such as *thrown back out* and *vaporize.*

B Go to the transcript on page 154. Underline examples of the strategies from the box that Brian Cox uses to engage listeners.

C Write a short speech on a topic that you're passionate about. Use strategies to engage your listeners.

D Work in pairs. Read your speech to your partner. Try to be as engaging and passionate as possible.

Getting answers

SAM MALCOLM AMANDA HARRY EMILY

A Work in pairs. Discuss the questions.

1 Do you ever watch documentaries about science? Why/Why not?

2 Should we try to make science more accessible than it is now?

3 Are there any cons to simplifying science for a wider audience?

B Watch the video. Were any of the things you discussed in Exercise A mentioned?

C Watch the video again. Complete the sentences with one to three words.

1 Amanda is interviewing Veronica about ______________________.

2 Malcolm tells Sam that Veronica is one of the country's ______________________.

3 Veronica says she saw Brian Cox ____________.

4 Since being inspired by Brian Cox, Veronica has been ______________________.

5 Malcolm comments that Veronica's book is at the top of the ______________________.

SPEAKING SKILL

A Work in pairs. Complete the line from the video. Why has Amanda asked her question in this way?

> Professor Matos, ______________________ respond to accusations that your book is under-researched?

B Look at the information in the box. Match the questions (1–5) with the types (a–e).

Conducting an interview

a **Direct questions** are asked in order to make a point about a situation or to point out something for consideration. For example, ___

b **Indirect questions** are used when we want to be more polite. We use an introductory phrase followed by the question itself in a positive sentence structure. For example, ___

c **Negative questions** can ask for confirmation of our opinions or make invitations or suggestions. For example, ___

d **Tag questions** can either be 'real' questions where we want to know the answer or simply ask for agreement when we already know the answer. For example, ___

e **Rhetorical questions** are often statements given in question format in order to make a point about a situation. For example, ___

1 Why don't you go over and introduce yourself?

2 It builds on some of the theories set out by Professor Brian Cox, doesn't it?

3 I hope you don't mind me asking, why did you decide to write a book?

4 Can I quote you on that?

5 Did I dumb down the science a little for the masses?

C Work in pairs. Think of one more example for each of the question types (1–5) in Exercise B.

SPEAKING HUB

A **PLAN** Work in pairs. Student A: Imagine you are a journalist for a website. Look at the bullet points and prepare a list of questions to ask Veronica Matos.

Student B: Imagine you are Veronica Matos. You are going to be interviewed. Plan what you are going to say using the bullet points.

- when you first became interested in science
- your book
- your future career plans
- advice to young people

B **DISCUSS** Work in pairs. Perform your role-play.

A: What advice would you give to teenagers who want a career in science?

B: Decide early which area of science you want to work in. There are hundreds and hundreds of different career paths.

Plan and perform an interview

➤ Turn to page 161 to learn how to write an expository essay about space exploration.

Unit 6 Review

VOCABULARY

A Choose the correct words to complete the sentences.

1. Airlines keep introducing new long-haul flights to tempt today's *globetrotters* / *distance travelers*.
2. You *embargo* / *embark* from Santiago, Chile, to fly direct to Easter Island.
3. Fourteen of the world's highest *summits* / *culminations* are in the Himalayas.
4. It takes several hours of trekking through *ragged terraces* / *impenetrable terrain* to reach Waimea.
5. Manaus is the closest city to the *heart* / *heat* of the Amazon.
6. Siberia still has a lot of *unchartered* / *uncharted* territory.
7. You can quickly get off the beaten *path* / *road* in the outback in Australia.

B Complete the three-part phrasal verbs with the correct preposition.

1. I use language learning apps to **brush up** ________ my vocabulary.
2. I'd like to **find out** ________ volunteering.
3. Playing video games helps me **switch off** ________ the stress of the day.
4. I frequently **look back** ________ the vacations I took with my parents as a child.
5. I keep meaning to visit my grandparents, but I never **get around** ________ it.
6. I **am up** ________ a camping trip.
7. Whenever I suggest somewhere to go, my family **come up** ________ objections.
8. I don't like staycations. I want to **get away** ________ the area where I live for a vacation.

C Match numbers (1–10) to letters (a–j) to form full sentences.

1. I looked far and
2. She amazes me time after
3. Slowly but
4. She's far and
5. He always puts his heart and
6. They always work side by
7. It was a matter of life
8. It's a real rags-to-
9. By and
10. She returned safe and

a surely he taught himself how to do it.
b riches story, because he was born into a very poor family.
c soul into everything he does.
d wide, but I couldn't find it.
e large, I don't read biographies, but his story was fascinating.
f time with her ideas.
g away the most important scientist working today.
h side, which is really sweet.
i sound from her adventures.
j or death at one point, but he survived.

GRAMMAR

A Complete the text using *can't have*, *could have*, *couldn't have*, *may/might well have*, *might have*, *must have* and the verbs in parentheses.

In 1900, three men mysteriously disappeared from the lighthouse where they were working on a remote island in Scotland. Initially, newspapers contained implausible explanations such as that they [1] ________________ (*kill*) by ghosts or they [2] ________________ (*capture*) by foreign spies. However, a later investigation concluded that they [3] ________________ (*not abduct*), because there were no signs of a struggle.

The investigation found a lot of damage had been done to one of the landing stages and that the kind of damage indicated that this [4] ________________ (*cause*) by large waves during a storm. Therefore, it's possible that the men were securing boxes on the landing stage in bad weather and the investigators believed that they [5] ________________ (*sweep*) into the sea by strong waves. Normally, one man should have stayed behind to man the lighthouse, but he [6] ________________ (*go*) to the landing stage to warn his colleagues of the approaching waves.

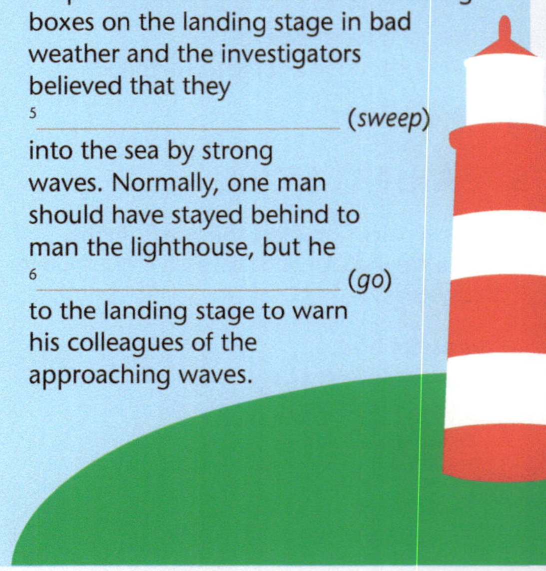

B Choose the correct words to complete the sentences. Then decide if you agree or disagree with each sentence.

1. In my country, schools have problems *encouraging* / *to encourage* children to study science.
2. It's not worth *studying* / *to study* the arts at school because it's not useful for work.
3. It's impossible *making* / *to make* history interesting for school children.
4. It's time *introducing* / *to introduce* more practical subjects into the school curriculum.
5. Schools need to teach computer programming *helping* / *to help* students get jobs in the future.

7 EXTREMES

> Courage is resistance to fear, mastery of fear – not absence of fear.
>
> Mark Twain

Stepping over the abyss in Mondsee, Austria.

OBJECTIVES

- describe reactions to extreme experiences
- describe extreme situations and achievements
- discuss extreme jobs
- deal with difficult interview questions
- tell a story about an exciting journey
- write a cover letter

Work with a partner. Discuss the questions.

1 Look at the picture. Why do people put themselves in extreme situations? When do you think this is a positive thing? When is it negative?

2 Look at the quote. How can we resist fear? Is it possible to master fear? Think of examples.

3 Do you prefer extreme experiences or safe/predictable ones? Why? What does it depend on?

7.1 Beyond the limits

- Describe reactions to extreme experiences
- Describe extreme situations and achievements

G *it* clefting **V** feelings **P** intonation in question tags **S** identifying causation

READING

A PREDICT Work in pairs. Look at the picture. Discuss the questions.

1 What do you think the story is going to be about?

2 Have you ever been somewhere like this? If so, how did you feel? If not, how do you think you would feel?

3 Why do you think some people choose to put themselves in dangerous situations?

B SKIM Read *Into the abyss*. What different emotions does the writer go through on her journey? Were any the same as your answers to Exercise A?

C READ FOR DETAIL Read *Into the abyss again*. Six sentences have been removed from the story. Choose from the sentences (a–g) the one which fits each blank. There is one extra sentence which you do not need to use.

a It was his lack of words that finally allowed me to shake off the morning's nerves.

b It was myself who I was really trying to convince.

c It was that murky half-light, before the night gives in to the dawn, which I now watched.

d It is hard to describe moments like these.

e It is in situations like this that it occurs to me how often I put my life in the hands of complete strangers.

f It was reaching the summit that was my ultimate goal.

g It was just as Batsal disappeared over a rise that I lost my footing.

D INFER MEANING Work in pairs. Decide which of the words in bold from the story match the meanings (1–5).

1 ______________ (n) fear of something bad that might happen or that is going to happen

2 ______________ (n) a feeling of sadness and of being without hope

3 ______________ (n) a feeling of extreme excitement and happiness

4 ______________ (adj) relaxed and pleasant because shared with friends or friendly people

5 ______________ (adj) very serious, and not smiling or friendly

E SPEAK Work in groups. Think of a time when you felt one of the emotions from Exercise D. Tell your group about your experience. Mention the following points.

- when you felt this way
- the reason(s) for feeling the emotion

GRAMMAR

it clefting

A Find a sentence in Reading Exercise C that means the same as the one below. What is different about the version in the article? What is the focus in each sentence? Use the information in the box to help you.

I was really trying to convince myself.

> ***it* clefting**
>
> We can use *it* clefting to focus attention on part of a sentence (e.g. the subject, an object, a time clause, a *because*-clause, infinitive, etc).
>
> *My ultimate goal was reaching the summit. → It was reaching the summit that was my ultimate goal.*

B Rewrite the remaining sentences in Reading Exercise C so they don't use *it* clefting.

a ____________________________

b *I was really trying to convince myself.*

c ____________________________

d ____________________________

e ____________________________

f *My ultimate goal was reaching the summit.*

g ____________________________

C Go to the Grammar Hub on page 134.

D SPEAK Work in pairs and complete the sentences so they are true for you.

1 It was because I wanted to … that I …

2 It's not … that's important …

3 It wasn't until …

SPEAKING

DISCUSS Work in pairs. Can you think of a time when you felt a mix of emotions? Use the questions to help you.

1 What was the situation?

2 How did you feel?

3 What happened?

INTO THE ABYSS

1 ___ I had arrived early at the café and now sat waiting at a formica table, tentatively sipping the strongest coffee I had ever tasted. The bitterness was cloying, my hands shaking, but a 6 am start meant that rocket fuel was what I needed. The front door burst open, my coffee spilling across the table. The light struggling through the smeared glass door was blocked out by the silhouette of a man. He paused there in the doorway for a second. Though I couldn't see his face, I knew he was watching me.

He crossed the café in two strides. A weathered face forced itself into a half smile. 'Carla?' 'Yes. Batsal?'. A curt nod and then, 'If we are going, we go now, before the weather turns.'

I shouldered my pack and we set off down the pot-holed street beneath the shuttered-up houses and the tangle of electricity cables dangling menacingly low above us. 'Where is everyone?' He gestured a few meters ahead where a teenage boy was struggling to kick-start a motorcycle, way past its prime, into life. The boy, who was almost certainly Batsal's son, glanced at me shyly and stepped aside as his father took hold of the motorcycle. With a swift movement the engine roared. Batsal jerked his head at the seat behind him.

We were off. Hurtling down the road and then out toward the distant mountains. 2 ___ I've been conned, ripped off and outright robbed during my travels even by friendly-faced guides. Batsal was different though … I found his **dour** demeanor weirdly reassuring. 3 ___

Maybe I was feeling too calm as we set off on foot up a narrow trail. My mind didn't dwell on the terrifying exposure of the route or the crevasses that seemed to plunge down into the depths of the earth. Instead I let my gaze calmly return to the untouched snow of the peaks which glistened in the low sun. We climbed in **companionable** silence for an hour or so. Up and over some boulders the size of cars.

4 ___ A small lapse in concentration. I found myself on my back skidding toward the edge. The boulder felt smooth. I watched in panic as my hands and feet flailed, trying to get ahold of something, anything. My legs were disappearing into the abyss. I thought of my family. Then time slowed, my focus narrowed and I gripped the rock. As I held on I found myself in a place I'd never been, somewhere between **dread** and calm.

A searing pain jolted through me as I was yanked by my arm. I twisted my neck to see Batsal retreating up the boulder, dragging me behind him like a rag doll. He pulled me to my feet. The question in his eyes. 'I can continue on,' I replied. 5 ___ And my shoulder throbbed in protest.

We scrambled upward for five more hours over loose shale. The air was thinning out – every breath was labored. But something of that strange calmness remained. When we reached a ledge, we stopped. I looked again over at the peaks that seemed no closer than they had at sunrise. 'OK, but let me see it more fully before we turn back.' With one last effort I pulled myself up onto the ridge above the ledge and looked out over the perfect vista. 6 ___ The sheer **exhilaration** but also **melancholy** of a journey's end. After ten minutes, we began our descent. My heart thumping.

Glossary

gesture (v) a movement that communicates a feeling or instruction

skid (v) to slide across the ground in an uncontrolled way

weathered (adj) appearance changed because of the effects of wind, rain, etc

VOCABULARY

Feelings

A Match the quotes (1–10) with the adjectives in the box. How do the people feel?

courageous devastated disgusted frustrated grumpy humbled hysterical indifferent resilient superior

1 'I feel bad because there's nothing I can do about my situation.' ____
2 'I was overwhelmed by our local community's kindness and generosity.' ____
3 'I lost control of my emotions and started shaking and crying.' ____
4 'I feel terrible because I've lost all hope.' ____
5 'When I'm in a bad mood, I'm not very nice to other people.' ____
6 'You can do what you like. I really don't mind.' ____
7 'When other people do stupid things, it makes me feel better about myself!' ____
8 'I know it's dangerous, but I won't let my fear stop me.' ____
9 'When things go wrong, I just have to pick myself up and continue on.' ____
10 'I'm so angry! It makes me feel sick.' ____

B Go to the **Vocabulary Hub** on **page 146**.

C SPEAK Work in pairs. Think of examples of situations where people feel the ten emotions in Exercise A. Share your ideas with the class.

LISTENING

A SPEAK Work in pairs and discuss the questions.

1 What morning TV shows are there in your country?
2 What type of news stories are discussed on them?

7.1 **B LISTEN FOR SPECIFIC INFORMATION** Listen to part of a TV show, *The Breakfast Show*. Decide if the statements are true (T), false (F) or not given (NG).

1 Arjun didn't see the accident happening. ____
2 The other driver helped Arjun to move the car. ____
3 The car that Arjun lifted weighed over 1,500 kg. ____
4 Professor Ivănescu thinks Arjun has extremely unusual powers. ____
5 Tony (the announcer) doesn't think he'd ever be able to lift the car. ____
6 Arjun used hysterical strength. ____
7 Whenever our muscles hurt, it means we're damaging them. ____
8 The bicyclist suffered permanent injuries. ____

7.1 **C LISTEN FOR CAUSATION** Listen again. Which pairs of events are examples of correlation (a)? Which are examples of causation (b)? Use the information in the box to help you.

Identifying causation

It's important to distinguish between ***correlation*** (= two or more things happen at about the same time) and ***causation*** (= one thing causes another thing to happen).
Common ways of signaling causation include:

- linking expressions (e.g. *as a result of, due to, thanks to, that's why*).
- conditionals (e.g. *If X hadn't happened, Y might not have happened*).
- past perfect in time clauses (e.g. *After I'd done X, Y happened*) rather than simple past (e.g. *After I did X, Y happened*).

1 Arjun wasn't paying attention to the other vehicles. The car ran over a bicycle. *a / b*
2 The driver freed the bicyclist. Arjun put the car down. *a / b*
3 They used a cell phone. A spark caused the car to explode. *a / b*
4 Arjun was brave. The bicyclist wasn't seriously injured. *a / b*
5 Arjun's back hurts now. He lifted the car. *a / b*
6 Tony was unable to lift the car. His muscles hurt. *a / b*
7 The adrenaline wore off. Arjun felt extreme pain. *a / b*
8 Athletes feel stressed. They can break world records. *a / b*
9 The bicyclist survived. She spent a few weeks in the hospital. *a / b*

D SPEAK Work in groups. Discuss the questions.

1 How do you think you would react in an extreme situation like the one Arjun described?
2 Have you heard of any examples of people doing amazing things in extreme situations? What happened?

PRONUNCIATION

Intonation in question tags

A Complete the extracts from *The Breakfast Show* with the correct question tag. Then listen to check.

1 So the car could have exploded at any second, ______________?

2 I mean, you're a big guy, ______________?

3 It's weird, ______________?

4 I mean, a car weighs, what, a ton and a half, ______________?

5 So that's what helped Arjun, then, ______________?

6 We can't harness this strength in everyday life, ______________?

7 I'm just a normal guy, ______________?

8 Anyway, let's have a break now, ______________?

B Listen again. Try to copy the intonation.

C **SPEAK** Work in small groups and discuss the extreme human abilities shown in pictures 1–5. Use question tags to ask questions, make suggestions, check assumptions and invite agreement.

Should we start with this one? It's bungee jumping, isn't it?

SPEAKING HUB

A **PLAN** You are going to conduct a daytime TV interview about examples of extreme achievements. Work in groups of three. Use pictures 1–5 to help you.

Student A: You are the **interviewee**. You can talk about a real experience from your life, or you can invent the details.

Student B: You are an **expert** (e.g. a college professor). You have been invited to explain Student A's abilities/ achievements. You can use your real knowledge or invent details.

Student C: You are the **interviewer**. It's your job to make the interviewee and the expert feel comfortable, and to make the TV show entertaining for the audience at home.

B **PRACTICE** Practice your interview. Try to use the vocabulary, grammar and pronunciation from this lesson in your interviews.

C **PRESENT** Act out your interview for the class.

D **REFLECT** Which of the interviews was the most believable? Which was the most entertaining?

3

4

5

- Describe reactions to extreme experiences
- Describe extreme situations and achievements

- Discuss extreme jobs
- Deal with difficult interview questions

G – *what* clefting and *all* clefting
P – *any* and *really*
V – polysemy; intensifiers
S – understanding reference within texts

READING

A SPEAK Work in pairs. Look at the pictures. Why do people choose to work in such extreme places?

B READ FOR MAIN IDEA Read *Risky business*. Match the statements (1–6) with the workplaces (a–c).

1 It's dangerous if you go up too fast. ___
2 The weather may prevent you from working. ___
3 You'll need to work at least half a year. ___
4 You'll earn a lot of money. ___
5 It's hard to get a job there. ___
6 It takes over a week to get home. ___

a The Antarctic
b At extreme heights
c Under the ocean

C READ FOR REFERENCES What do the reference devices (1–10) in the article refer to? Use the information in the box to help you.

1	______	6	______
2	______	7	______
3	______	8	______
4	______	9	______
5	______	10	______

Understanding reference within texts

Reference devices (e.g. pronouns, articles, contrast linkers, comparatives) link different parts of a text.

Anaphoric reference: refers back to something mentioned earlier in the text.

Cataphoric reference: refers forward to something mentioned later in the text.

Exophoric reference: refers to things outside the text, e.g. *you* (the reader), *they* (people in general).

D SPEAK Work in pairs and discuss the questions. Do any of the jobs in the article appeal to you? Which would you hate?

RISKY BUSINESS

[1]They say over half of us are doing jobs that we don't care about, and a further 16% actively hate our jobs. If you're **sick** of the nine-to-five, here are some of the more extreme places where you can actually make a living.

ANTARCTICA

Unfortunately, it's not exactly easy – or cheap – to visit Antarctica as a tourist. So if you really want to go, what you should do is get a long-term job, not a summer or spring break job: no employer is going to pay your airfare if you're planning to stay for less than six months.

There are scientific jobs for biologists, glaciologists, geologists, meteorologists, oceanologists, and so on. Trouble is, there's plenty of **competition** for them, with hundreds of applicants for each vacancy. Your best chance of **landing** [2]one is to be a well-qualified specialist already, ideally with a doctorate or two.

There are also a few support jobs for engineers, technicians, divers, radio operators, etc. Just be warned: you'll spend most of your time on the base, where you'll quickly get bored with the same faces every day. Due to the extreme weather, it's usually too dangerous (or too expensive) to venture out into the wilderness for some sightseeing.

AT EXTREME HEIGHTS

For [3]those of us who get dizzy at the thought of standing on a chair, the prospect of climbing up a radio mast, wind turbine or skyscraper is the stuff of our worst nightmares. But for [4]the lucky few who have no fear of heights, there are plenty of career opportunities.

[5]It's not especially glamorous, but the easiest way to make a career at heights is as a window cleaner. You can literally start at the bottom – all you'll need is a ladder and a bucket – and gradually work your way up to office blocks and skyscrapers.

A [6]more lucrative career for real-life 'high-climbers' is as a tower climber. These brave people spend their time 100 to 150 meters above the ground, inspecting cellular phone towers for damage, changing light bulbs, replacing cables, etc. One of the biggest challenges is that they need to work in all **conditions**, including the cold, the wind and the rain, all of which add to the level of danger. The [7]one exception is thunderstorms, which tower climbers steer well clear of.

ON THE OCEAN FLOOR

[8]It's one of the most bizarre careers imaginable. [9]These people do construction, maintenance and demolition work 300 meters or more beneath the ocean's surface. To survive the extreme **pressure** at such depths, they spend weeks or months at a time living in tiny pressurized containers, either deep underwater or inside pressure tanks on board ships. Welcome to the world of the saturation diver.

Breathing pressurized air causes inert gases to dissolve in your blood and body tissues. If you were to release the pressure suddenly, by coming to the surface, the bubbles formed would quickly kill you. To avoid this, saturation divers spend several hours building up to the necessary pressure, saturating their bodies with inert gases. At the end of their work, they spend as much as eleven days de-pressurizing, before finally returning to normal life.

Saturation divers carry out essential work for some of the world's richest businesses, so [10]it's no surprise to find that they're extremely well-paid. However, before sending off your **application**, you need to consider how you'd feel about spending months in a tiny metal container with your co-workers, constantly aware that the failure of a single pressure valve would mean certain death.

Glossary

lucrative (adj) bringing a lot of money
venture (v) to go somewhere unpleasant, dangerous or exciting

VOCABULARY
Polysemy

A Choose the correct definition of the words in bold from *Risky business*. Use the context in the article and the information in the box to help you.

Polysemy

Polysemy is where a word has two or more related meanings. Sometimes different meanings have different grammatical properties (e.g. countable/uncountable).

1 sick
- **a** feel unwell
- **b** bored or tired of something

2 competition
- **a** rivalry
- **b** a contest

3 to land
- **a** bring a plane down
- **b** get something you want

4 condition(s)
- **a** weather
- **b** an important part of a contract

5 pressure
- **a** a feeling of too much work
- **b** a 'pushing' force

6 application
- **a** a way of using something
- **b** a document stating why you want a job

B In which pair of meanings from Exercise A is one meaning countable and the other uncountable? In which pair is one meaning always plural?

C Go to the Vocabulary Hub on page 146.

GRAMMAR
what clefting and *all* clefting

A Complete the rules with examples from the article.

***what* clefting and *all* clefting**

Form: *what/all* + FIRST FOCUS + *is/was* + SECOND FOCUS

Example: *What you need to succeed is mental strength.*

We can use *what* clefting to focus attention on two different parts of a sentence by keeping them separate.

1 You should get a long-term job. → ____________

All clefting has the extra meaning of *only*.

2 You'll only need a ladder and bucket. → ____________

B Go to the Grammar Hub on page 134.

SPEAKING

DISCUSS Work in pairs. Think about the advantages and disadvantages of the jobs in the article. Your partner is planning to apply for one of the jobs. Give your partner advice using *what* clefting and *all* clefting.

LISTENING

A SPEAK Work in pairs. Have you ever had a stressful job interview? What happened?

B Read *Extreme job interviews*. Rank the questions in order from hardest to easiest (1–7).

7.3 **C LISTEN FOR DETAIL** Listen to a recruitment specialist giving advice about the questions below. For each question, write notes on the dos and don'ts for job interviewees.

7.4 **D LISTEN FOR GIST** Now listen to some extracts from an interview for a job as a marketing designer. Does Oscar (the interviewee) follow the recruitment specialist's advice for each question?

EXTREME job interviews

These days, recruiters are going to extremes to sort the best from the rest. The following questions, all taken from real job interviews, have no correct answer. But they are designed to show how you cope with stress and how creative you are. They might also reveal the real 'you' behind the business suit and the polished résumé.

- *What would you take with you to a desert island and why?*
- *If you could be any dinosaur, which dinosaur would you be?*
- *What's your biggest weakness?*
- *Name four uses for a stapler, without the staples.*
- *How many square meters of pizza are eaten in the US each year?*
- *What's the most interesting thing about you that we wouldn't learn from your résumé?*
- *How would your worst enemy describe you?*

7.4 **E LISTEN FOR DETAIL** Listen again. Choose the correct options (a, b or c) to answer the questions.

1 How would Oscar feel on a desert island?
a lonely b inspired c upset

2 What would be Oscar's priority as a dinosaur?
a pleasure b beauty c safety

3 How does Oscar feel at the end of each day?
a relieved b disappointed c exhausted

4 Which one of the following is NOT mentioned as a use for a stapler?
a tissue-holder b child's toy c doorstop

5 How many pizzas does Oscar think a typical American eats each year?
a 12 b 144 c 300

6 How does Oscar feel about taking care of his brothers and sisters?
a grateful b frustrated c proud

7 How does Oscar feel about people who don't like him?
a grumpy b indifferent c superior

F SPEAK Work in pairs. Ask and answer the questions from *Extreme job interviews*.

VOCABULARY
Intensifiers

A Complete the sentences from the interview with intensifiers in the box. Sometimes more than one answer is possible.

altogether immensely noticeably outright practically radically relatively remarkably somewhat utterly

1 I find writing poetry ________ calming.
2 I'd be ________ devastated if I couldn't record my ideas on paper.
3 Compared to the ground, the sky would be a ________ good place.
4 I tend to be ________ disorganized.
5 I learned some ________ simple techniques, and I've improved ________ since then.
6 I'm not ________ sure how typical I am.
7 I'm not ________ different from the average American …
8 It was usually ________ impossible to study.
9 I'm not the sort of person who has ________ enemies.

B Work in pairs. Complete the sentences with an intensifier from Exercise A.

1 ________ means 'to a huge extent'.
2 ________ is mainly used before negative adjectives and adverbs.
3 ________ means 'compared to other things'.
4 ________ means 'a little'.
5 ________ means 'so much that it's obvious or easy to see'.
6 ________ is frequently used in negative sentences, especially with 'sure'.
7 ________ is often used before nouns with a negative meaning.
8 ________ means 'not really 100%, but as good as 100%'.
9 ________ is often used before 'different'.

C Go to the **Vocabulary Hub** on **page 146**.

D SPEAK Work in small groups. Offer advice for preparing for and coping with extreme job interviews. Use intensifiers in your advice.

PRONUNCIATION
any and *really*

7.5 **A** Listen to the extracts from the recruitment specialist's advice. Underline *any* and *really* when they are stressed.

1 Almost any other answer is much better …
2 So don't just say any old number that pops into your head.
3 … on a desert island, without any other people …
4 … would really get my creative juices flowing.
5 … the sense of freedom would be really exhilarating.
6 It's been really challenging …

7.6 **B** Listen and underline the sentence (a or b) in which *really* or *any* is stressed.

1 a The interview was really difficult.
  b The interview was really impossible.
2 a Don't say anything!
  b Don't say anything!
3 a Her house was really dirty.
  b Her house was really dirty.
4 a Any questions can be answered.
  b Any questions can be answered.

SPEAKING HUB

A PLAN Work in groups of three. You are going to interview several candidates for a job. First, decide what the job is, what exactly it involves and what sort of candidate you are looking for. Then plan four or five extreme questions for your interview. Use the ideas below or your own ideas.

- If you could be any …, what would you be?
- Name four uses for a …
- How many … could you fit inside this room?
- How would … describe you?

B PREPARE Discuss what would be a 'good' or 'bad' answer for each of your questions, bearing in mind the type of candidate you are looking for.

C INTERVIEW Interview two candidates from other groups. At the end of each interview, provide feedback on what the candidate did well/badly and give advice on how to improve.

D DISCUSS Work in your original groups to choose the best candidate for your job. Make sure you justify your choice. Share your decision and reasoning with the class.

Discuss extreme jobs
Deal with difficult interview questions

7.3 Push your limits

A – fronting S – changing and recycling topics

Driving on the edge

A Work in pairs. Look at the picture and discuss the questions.

1 Where do you think this is?

2 What do you think it would be like to be a bus driver in these mountains?

B Watch the video. Check your answers to Exercise A.

Glossary

abrasive (adj) having a rough surface
canyon (n) a long deep valley with steep sides made of rock
maze (n) a set of small streets, roads, paths, etc that it is easy to get lost in
slope (n) a surface or piece of land that has one end higher than the other end

C Watch the video again. Complete the sentences with between one and three words.

1 The mountains of Northern Peru consist of a network of ________________, basic roads and deep canyons.

2 Glorioso is considered a ________________ among some of the villagers in Huancabamba.

3 The truck tires need to be changed after ten weeks because the roads here are so ________________.

4 Annually, over a ________________ people die on the mountain roads of Peru.

5 The passengers on the bus are not ________________.

6 The secret to a long ________________ as a Peruvian bus driver is to take your time.

AUTHENTIC ENGLISH

A Work in pairs. Read the information in the box. Complete the sentence from the video.

And that's ________________ to a long career as a Peruvian bus driver – taking the mountains at their own pace.

Fronting

Fronting involves moving information to the front of a sentence, often to give it emphasis. It is often used in informal spoken English, for example, *Really good it was – best movie I've seen for ages.*

Whole clauses can be fronted, for example, *Why they decided to buy that house, I couldn't tell you.*

B Work in pairs. Rewrite the sentences to create emphasis. Begin each sentence with the underlined word.

1 I'll never know <u>why</u> Maria married Tony.
____

2 He didn't know <u>whether</u> he'd gotten the job or not.
____

3 I'll be there <u>in</u> about twenty minutes.
____

4 It cost me <u>three</u> hundred dollars.
____

5 I just don't know <u>how</u> you put up with your boss.
____

6 It started to snow <u>all</u> of a sudden.
____

7 It must have cost <u>an</u> absolute fortune.
____

8 An old woman sat quietly <u>in</u> the corner.
____

C Compare your sentences in Exercise B with another pair.

Hello from the Andes

A Work in pairs. Discuss the questions.

1 Do you prefer traveling with other people or on your own? Why?

2 Do you know anybody who has visited many countries? What motivates them to travel?

B Watch the video. Who calls Sam and where are they?

C Watch the video again. Answer the questions.

1 Who did Fred meet by chance?

____

2 What does Fred's meeting make Sam think of?

____

3 What does Fred say about the condition of the bus?

____

4 What could Fred see when he looked out of the window?

____

5 What did Fred find comforting?

____

6 What does Sam suggest doing when Fred returns?

____

SPEAKING SKILL

A What is the purpose of the phrases in bold in each of the examples from the video?

1 Sorry, not very good signal out here. **So where was I?** Oh yes …

2 **I tell you what** when you're back from the Andes, let's go out for dinner.

SAM

MALCOLM

AMANDA

HARRY

EMILY

B Work in pairs. Underline the words and phrases which are used to change or recycle topics in the extracts below.

1 I had just arrived in Lima and guess who I ran into?

2 Well, funny you should ask. I had a bit of an adventure getting to my adventure.

3 That reminds me of the time when I was in Spain and bumped into my next door neighbor.

4 Well, yeah … made worse by the fact it was quite an old bus.

5 For sure … which brings me back to what I was saying … Daniel suggested I come with him on a trek.

Changing and recycling topics

We use many different set phrases to try to steer conversations toward the topics we wish to talk about.

We can use them to recycle a topic we were speaking about, for example, *as I was saying*. We can also use them to change topic, for example, *that's like the time when*.

SPEAKING HUB

A PREPARE Student A: you are going to describe your exciting journey to your partner. However, your partner is going to try to distract you and talk about himself/herself.

Student B: you are going to listen to your partner describing a journey. However, you are not very interested in what your partner has to say and you want to talk about yourself and your experiences.

B PRESENT Perform your conversation. Change roles.

A: Why I'd decided to drive through the wilderness alone, I couldn't tell you.

B: Speaking of which, I'm going camping in the wilderness next month.

C REFLECT Work in small groups. Perform and listen to each other's conversations again. Give feedback using the points below.

- use of language
- pronunciation
- fluency
- interaction

Tell a story about an exciting journey

➤ Turn to page 162 to learn how to write a cover letter for a dream job.

Unit 7 Review

VOCABULARY

A Match numbers (1–10) to letters (a–j) to form full sentences.

1 I'm frustrated because I
2 I thought she was so courageous
3 I became hysterical
4 I always get grumpy
5 I'm fairly resilient
6 They were disgusted by
7 As a child, I was indifferent
8 I try to be humble
9 I felt devastated about
10 He acted superior

a when I'm tired.
b to my classmates' bad behavior.
c about my success when I meet strangers.
d when she chased away the burglars.
e can't do anything to help.
f losing all that work.
g around the others, as if he were the best player.
h and couldn't calm down for a long time.
i the condition he left the apartment in.
j so I'm sure I'll get over this setback.

B Complete the sentences with the correct form of the words in the box. Use each word twice.

sick competition condition application

1 Unfortunately your _______________ for the job hasn't been successful.
2 We can't go out in these _______________! We'll get wet!
3 I'm _______________ of his excuses. He's just lazy!
4 The product can be used in a number of ways – it has many _______________.
5 I enter a lot of _______________ but I never win.
6 There's a lot of _______________ for each place on the course.
7 I find an early night helps if you are feeling _______________.
8 You can go out on _______________ that you're home by 10 pm.

C Put the lines (a–h) in order so that they form a paragraph.

___ a long periods – the world-record free-diver, Herbert Nitsch, can go an utterly
___ b dangerous changes of pressure. Nitsch's record of 253 meters was spoiled
___ c different from normal deep-sea diving, because the divers have practically
___ d easy compared to the challenge of coping with immensely
___ e somewhat by the medical problems he suffered as a result.
___ f Free diving is radically
___ g incredible nine minutes without breathing. But holding your breath is relatively
___ h no equipment. It involves holding your breath for remarkably

GRAMMAR

A Complete the sentences with words from the box. Each word can be used more than once.

is was until that not because who it

1 It was _______________ I was scared _______________ I decided not to climb the cliff.
2 It's _______________ adrenaline that I'm looking for; it _______________ a sense of flow.
3 It wasn't _______________ I reached the top _______________ I realized how high the cliff was.
4 When I said 'Stop being stupid', it was _______________ you I was talking to; _______________ was James I was talking to.
5 It _______________ at that moment _______________ I realized I was no longer afraid.
6 It _______________ to impress my friends _______________ I tried to lift the car.
7 It's you _______________ is causing most of the delays, _______________ us!

B Find and correct the mistakes in five of the sentences.

1 All what I'm trying to say is you should be careful.
____
2 What you should avoid to do is to pretend you don't have any weaknesses.
____
3 What I did was stretched my arms to calm my nerves.
____
4 All I remember is staring out into the abyss and feeling sick.
____
5 What happened next was that some people call an ambulance.
____
6 All they did was watch TV.
____

Hello from the Andes

SAM

MALCOLM

AMANDA

HARRY

EMILY

A Work in pairs. Discuss the questions.

1 Do you prefer traveling with other people or on your own? Why?

2 Do you know anybody who has visited many countries? What motivates them to travel?

B Watch the video. Who calls Sam and where are they?

C Watch the video again. Answer the questions.

1 What did Fred meet by chance?

____

2 What does Fred's meeting make Sam think of?

____

3 What does Fred say about the condition of the bus?

____

4 What could Fred see when he looked out of the window?

____

5 What did Fred find comforting?

____

6 What does Sam suggest doing when Fred returns?

____

SPEAKING SKILL

A What is the purpose of the phrases in bold in each of the examples from the video?

1 Sorry, not very good signal out here. **So where was I?** Oh yes …

2 **I tell you what** when you're back from the Andes, let's go out for dinner.

B Work in pairs. Underline the words and phrases which are used to change or recycle topics in the extracts below.

1 I had just arrived in Lima and guess who I ran into?

2 Well, funny you should ask. I had a bit of an adventure getting to my adventure.

3 That reminds me of the time when I was in Spain and bumped into my next door neighbor.

4 Well, yeah … made worse by the fact it was quite an old bus.

5 For sure … which brings me back to what I was saying … Daniel suggested I come with him on a trek.

Changing and recycling topics

We use many different set phrases to try to steer conversations toward the topics we wish to talk about.

We can use them to recycle a topic we were speaking about, for example, *as I was saying*. We can also use them to change topic, for example, *that's like the time when*.

SPEAKING HUB

A PREPARE Student A: you are going to describe your exciting journey to your partner. However, your partner is going to try to distract you and talk about himself/herself.

Student B: you are going to listen to your partner describing a journey. However, you are not very interested in what your partner has to say and you want to talk about yourself and your experiences.

B PRESENT Perform your conversation. Change roles.

A: Why I'd decided to drive through the wilderness alone, I couldn't tell you.

B: Speaking of which, I'm going camping in the wilderness next month.

C REFLECT Work in small groups. Perform and listen to each other's conversations again. Give feedback using the points below.

- use of language
- pronunciation
- fluency
- interaction

Tell a story about an exciting journey

➤ Turn to **page 162** to learn how to write a cover letter for a dream job.

Unit 7 Review

VOCABULARY

A Match numbers (1–10) to letters (a–j) to form full sentences.

1 I'm frustrated because I
2 I thought she was so courageous
3 I became hysterical
4 I always get grumpy
5 I'm fairly resilient
6 They were disgusted by
7 As a child, I was indifferent
8 I try to be humble
9 I felt devastated about
10 He acted superior

a when I'm tired.
b to my classmates' bad behavior.
c about my success when I meet strangers.
d when she chased away the burglars.
e can't do anything to help.
f losing all that work.
g around the others, as if he were the best player.
h and couldn't calm down for a long time.
i the condition he left the apartment in.
j so I'm sure I'll get over this setback.

B Complete the sentences with the correct form of the words in the box. Use each word twice.

sick competition condition application

1 Unfortunately your ______________ for the job hasn't been successful.
2 We can't go out in these ______________! We'll get wet!
3 I'm ______________ of his excuses. He's just lazy!
4 The product can be used in a number of ways – it has many ______________.
5 I enter a lot of ______________ but I never win.
6 There's a lot of ______________ for each place on the course.
7 I find an early night helps if you are feeling ______________.
8 You can go out on ______________ that you're home by 10 pm.

C Put the lines (a–h) in order so that they form a paragraph.

___ **a** long periods – the world-record free-diver, Herbert Nitsch, can go an utterly
___ **b** dangerous changes of pressure. Nitsch's record of 253 meters was spoiled
___ **c** different from normal deep-sea diving, because the divers have practically
___ **d** easy compared to the challenge of coping with immensely
___ **e** somewhat by the medical problems he suffered as a result.
___ **f** Free diving is radically
___ **g** incredible nine minutes without breathing. But holding your breath is relatively
___ **h** no equipment. It involves holding your breath for remarkably

GRAMMAR

A Complete the sentences with words from the box. Each word can be used more than once.

is was until that not because who it

1 It was ______________ I was scared ______________ I decided not to climb the cliff.
2 It's ______________ adrenaline that I'm looking for; it ______________ a sense of flow.
3 It wasn't ______________ I reached the top ______________ I realized how high the cliff was.
4 When I said 'Stop being stupid', it was ______________ you I was talking to; ______________ was James I was talking to.
5 It ______________ at that moment ______________ I realized I was no longer afraid.
6 It ______________ to impress my friends ______________ I tried to lift the car.
7 It's you ______________ is causing most of the delays, ______________ us!

B Find and correct the mistakes in five of the sentences.

1 All what I'm trying to say is you should be careful.
____
2 What you should avoid to do is to pretend you don't have any weaknesses.
____
3 What I did was stretched my arms to calm my nerves.
____
4 All I remember is staring out into the abyss and feeling sick.
____
5 What happened next was that some people call an ambulance.
____
6 All they did was watch TV.
____

8 WELL-BEING

> The part can never be well, unless the whole is well.
>
> Plato

Sunset swimming washes away the day's cares.

OBJECTIVES

- discuss wellness treatments
- talk about health and technology
- talk about sports psychology
- discuss nutrition and fitness
- explain and give instructions about a process
- write a summary

Work with a partner. Discuss the questions.

1. Look at the picture. Do you often swim in lakes, rivers or the sea? How is it different from swimming in a pool?
2. Read the quote. What does Plato mean? Do you agree?
3. Do you think it's easy for people to stay healthy these days? Why/Why not?

8.1 Health and wellness

- Discuss wellness treatments
- Talk about health and technology

G – adjective clauses with complex relative pronouns
P – building suspense
V – health problems
S – identifying writers' opinions

VOCABULARY
Health problems

A Work in pairs. Discuss the questions. Try to write down five words for each question.

1. Name five parts of the body connected to the five senses.
2. Name five joints.
3. Name five parts of the body that people have more than two of.
4. Name five parts of the body that can be used as verbs.

B Work in pairs. Match the words in bold in 1–9 with the definitions (a–i).

1. **fracture** a rib/your leg
2. **dislocate** your shoulder/thumb
3. a **sore** throat/back
4. **pull** a muscle
5. **sprain** your ankle/your wrist
6. **inflamed** joint/skin
7. skin **rash**
8. fast/slow **heart rate**
9. high/low **blood pressure**

a the force at which the blood flows through the body
b twist (a joint)
c the speed that your heart beats
d break or crack (a bone)
e painful
f force a joint out of its socket
g red and swollen
h red spots on the skin
i overstretch or tear

C Go to the **Vocabulary Hub** on **page 147**.

D SPEAK Work in pairs. What can people do to avoid having the health problems in Exercise B? What can people do if they have these problems?

READING

A SPEAK Work in pairs. Have you ever tried any wellness treatments (e.g. a massage, a sauna, a spa)? Did you enjoy them? Did they have any lasting benefits?

B READ FOR MAIN IDEA Read *From forest bathing to halotherapy*.

Which treatments are good for …

1. your lungs?
2. your heart?
3. reducing stress?
4. your skin?
5. insomnia?

C READ TO IDENTIFY OPINIONS Work in pairs. Read the article again and discuss the questions. Use the information in the box to help you.

1. What is the writer's attitude to the things she is writing about? Find examples of three types of language which show her attitude.
2. What is the purpose of this article? Is it mainly written to inform, entertain or persuade?

Identifying writers' opinions

Writers can choose particular words and phrases to show their opinion of a topic.

- Adverbs can show a positive attitude (*interestingly, surprisingly, intriguingly*), a negative attitude (*disappointingly, infuriatingly, predictably*) or a skeptical or cautious attitude (*supposedly, allegedly, presumably*).
- Different structures can be used to show writers believe something is true (*it is good for the heart*), they have a neutral stance about reported information (*it is said/thought to be good for the heart*) or they are uncertain or even skeptical (*it is supposed/meant/claimed to be good for the heart*).
- Writers can also use colloquial asides, including tag questions and rhetorical questions (*sounds fascinating, doesn't it?*) to comment on information. They can use humor, sarcasm and irony to show a skeptical attitude.

D SPEAK Work in pairs. Do you agree with the writer's attitude to the treatments? Why/Why not?

SPEAKING

DISCUSS Work in groups. Discuss the questions.

1. Why do some people prefer alternative treatments to conventional medicine?
2. Should doctors be allowed to recommend wellness treatments and alternative medicine?
3. Should companies be allowed to offer scientifically unproven wellness treatments?

FROM FOREST BATHING TO HALOTHERAPY: THE FIVE LATEST WELLNESS TRENDS

Know your 'sound lounger' from your carbon dioxide bath with our guide to the latest and not-so-greatest spa innovations.

'Wellness' is all the rage these days, but we've noticed that some therapies doing the rounds at hotel spas right now sound suspiciously basic. Surely oxygen therapy is just breathing, right? Decide for yourself, as we explore a few of the more interesting treatments we've spotted on spa menus around the world.

Forest bathing or 'going for a walk'

Forest bathing is based on the Japanese practice of *Shinrin-yoku*. That may sound like some sort of elaborately mystical ritual, but in fact involves simply 'being in the forest'. You might call it walking, or even sitting, in, you know, a forest. The practice is supposed to exercise the mind as well as reduce stress by bringing you back to nature. Possibly eager to jazz up the concept, The Mayflower Grace Hotel in Connecticut has put together a forest-bathing package that involves 90 minutes of skin-cleansing treatments, using plant-derived lactic acid and exfoliators made with peat enzymes and berries. Finally, a 'plant hydrosol ionizing mist' supposedly boosts your lymphatic system with a 'stimulating breeze'.

Carbon dioxide dry bath or 'sitting in a bag'

Does lying fully clothed on a bed while wrapped in a bag of carbon dioxide sound fun? Didn't think so, but in the Czech Republic it's all the rage. In the west of the country – an area known for its natural gas – you can have a large bag wrapped around you all the way from your toes to under your arms and watch it slowly inflate with CO_2. The treatment is meant to slow your heart rate, reduce your blood pressure and improve circulation, but this happens by the gas seeping into your clothes and skin – that thought would put most people's blood pressure up, not down.

So Sound lounger or 'napping and listening to music'

Yes, Tibetan singing bowl therapy has been around for centuries, but it's now been upgraded for the digital age. The So Sound lounger is meant to help you relax by, well, sitting in a lounger and listening to music. Revolutionary stuff. You're supposed to be able to take a 'therapeutic nap' while the lounger sends musical vibrations through your body … A little like an airport massage chair, maybe?

Halotherapy or 'a salty room'

Halotherapy is actually a fancy name for salt therapy. In a natural setting, this treatment would mean sitting in a salt cave and breathing in the dry, salty air, which is supposed to be good for respiratory and skin conditions. Now hotels are replicating salt caves; the Windsor Arms Hotel in Toronto has created a room filled with salt and negative ions that has darkened ambient lighting to replicate natural salt caves found in Europe. Supposedly this also helps strengthen the immune system, among other health benefits.

Oxygen therapy or 'breathing'

Oxygen therapy is supposed to help with headaches, depression and sleep deprivation by – that's right – breathing oxygen. It involves being hooked up to a machine, sticking some tubes up your nose and, well, breathing.

Glossary

circulation (n) the continuous movement of blood around your body
lymphatic (adj) relating to the body's liquid lymph, or involved in moving lymph around your body
mystical (adj) relating to or involving mysterious religious or spiritual powers
nap (v) to sleep for a short period of time, usually during the day
ritual (n) a formal ceremony

LISTENING

A SPEAK Work in pairs. Discuss the questions.

1. Do you own any gadgets that monitor your health? If so, how often do you use them?
2. What are some of the benefits and drawbacks of these devices?

8.1 **B LISTEN FOR GIST** Listen to a conversation between friends discussing technology to help you stay healthy and answer the questions.

1. What kinds of health data can be provided by the devices they talk about?

   ____

2. What four devices do they talk about?

   ______________ ______________

   ______________ ______________

8.1 **C LISTEN FOR DETAIL** Listen again and answer the questions.

1. Why are they talking about wellness technology?

   ____

2. Why do Cheryl and Luke think that wellness technology is a good idea?

   ____

3. Why is Jake uncertain?

   ____

D DISCUSS Work in pairs. Discuss the questions.

1. Would you use any of the devices the speakers discussed? Why/Why not?
2. Do you think it's useful for people to collect data about their health?

GRAMMAR

Adjective clauses with complex relative pronouns

A Read the extracts from the conversation. Underline the adjective clauses and circle the relative pronouns.

1. Wellness technology is technology with which we can improve our health and well-being.
2. I've just read several news stories about people whose lives may have been saved because their smart watch alerted them to a problem.
3. I'm meeting the person [who is] writing the article with me for lunch today.
4. It's basically a thermometer which a smartphone can be attached to.
5. This device has an automated diagnosis feature where it checks the symptoms of the person to whom it's attached against a database.

B Complete the rules (1–6) with the words in the box and the example sentences from Exercise A. You may use the words in the box more than once.

informal formal whereby whom whose

Adjective clauses with complex relative pronouns

Advanced relative pronouns

1 Use ______________ to add information about someone's possessions.

2 Use ______________ to add information about a method (mainly used in formal English).

3 Use ______________ to add information about a person where they are the object of the clause (mainly used in formal English).

Prepositions and relative pronouns

4 In ______________ English, prepositions usually come at the end of the adjective clause.

Example: ______________

5 In ______________ English, prepositions come before the relative pronoun.

Examples: ______________
and ______________

Reduced adjective clauses

6 In ______________ English, we can often omit *who*, *that* or *which* in adjective clauses – and in adjective clauses that use *be*, we can leave out the pronoun + the part of *be*.

Example: ______________

C Complete the sentences with the correct relative pronoun. Add a preposition if needed.

1 The device ______________ I'm most interested is something that helps me eat healthfully.

2 Wellness devices are the technology ______________ people will be able to extend their lives.

3 Companies need to develop security systems ______________ it's impossible for hackers to gain access to users' private health data.

4 I don't understand people ______________ first thought when they are sick is to look up their symptoms online rather than go to the doctor.

5 The people ______________ wellness technology will make the biggest difference are older people.

D SPEAK Work in pairs. Do you agree with the sentences in Exercise C?

E Go to the Grammar Hub on page 136.

PRONUNCIATION
Building suspense

8.2 **A** Listen to the example sentences from the conversation. Underline the word where the speaker changes pitch.

1 So check out my brand new smart watch!

2 You'll never guess what … I've just been commissioned to write an article about wellness technology.

3 For example, on this smart watch take this handy heart rate tracker.

4 And if you forget, it starts flashing red.

B Complete the sentences so they are true for you.

1 The app I use most on my phone is …

2 The person I send most messages to is …

3 In one of the messages I received recently, someone said …

C Work in pairs. Present the information in Exercise B to your partner. Use pitch and pauses to build suspense.

SPEAKING HUB

A PLAN Work in groups. Imagine that you work for a technology start up. Your group needs to think of a health and wellness product idea and pitch it to potential investors. Discuss your ideas and think about the following questions.

- Will your idea help prevent health problems, encourage healthy behavior or help people who are already sick?
- What problem do people have that your idea could help to solve?
- Is your idea for a device, an app or a service?
- Who is the target market for your idea?
- How will you make it easy for users to use your product or service?
- What are the benefits for users of your product or service?

B PREPARE Prepare a presentation about your idea. Think of ways to sell the idea to your classmates.

C PRESENT Present your idea to the class. Then as a class, vote on the best idea.

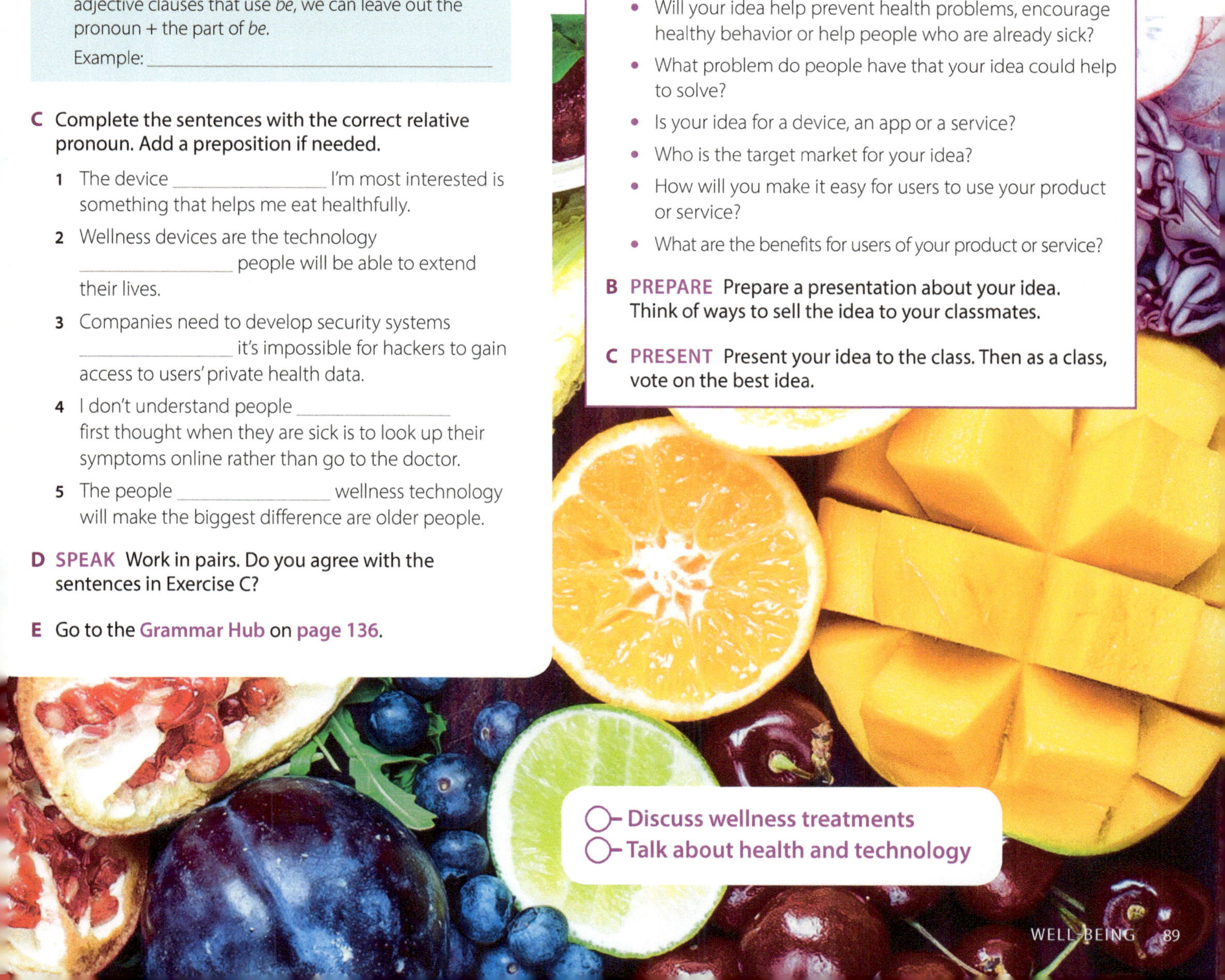

- Discuss wellness treatments
- Talk about health and technology

8.2 Sports and wellness

- Talk about sports psychology
- Discuss nutrition and fitness

G – pronouns and determiners
P – pronunciation of idioms
V – idioms; describing taste
S – understanding speech with background noise

LISTENING

A SPEAK Work in pairs. Discuss the questions.

1 Do you know any players or teams that use a sports psychologist?

2 How do sports psychologists help athletes?

8.3 **B LISTEN FOR GIST** Listen to the first part of a podcast about sports psychology. What are the two training techniques the sports psychologist mentions?

8.3 **C LISTEN FOR DETAIL** Listen again and answer the questions.

1 What example situation does Professor Rohan Kumar give for using therapy?

2 How do Professor Kumar's positive thinking techniques help athletes?

8.4 **D LISTEN WITH NOISE** Listen to the second part of the podcast. Some parts are fairly hard to hear because of background noise. Which two main sports psychology techniques does the interviewee use in her training sessions? Use the strategies in the box to help you.

1 ______________________

2 ______________________

Understanding speech with background noise

If there's a lot of background noise and you can't ask the speaker to repeat what he or she said:

- use the context of the situation to help you. Remember that you don't need to understand every word that is spoken to get the gist of what somebody is saying. Use your knowledge of the topic to help fill in the blanks.
- remember that speakers stress the most important words, so these words should be easier to hear. Use this information plus the context to help make intelligent guesses about what the people are saying.

8.4 **E LISTEN FOR DETAIL** Listen to the second part of the podcast again and answer the questions.

1 What problem had the soccer team been facing?

____

2 What kind of coaching style does she say many players won't accept?

____

3 What kind of coaching style does Bill prefer?

____

F SPEAK Work in pairs and discuss the questions.

1 Do you think sports psychologists are important?

2 Which techniques do you think would be most helpful for you when playing sports?

3 How difficult did you find it to understand what the speaker was saying when there was background noise?

VOCABULARY

Idioms

A Look at the three groups of idioms (1–12). Complete the headings for each group with the words in the box.

body sports food

______________ idioms

1 My <u>gut feeling</u> is we'll lose the game.

2 Their striker <u>was head and shoulders above</u> the rest of us.

3 <u>Keep an eye out for</u> John – we're supposed to meet him at the stadium.

4 ______________________

______________ idioms

5 It wasn't a big problem, but he was really <u>making a meal of it</u>.

6 He says he knows Ronaldo, but you have to <u>take what he says with a grain of salt</u>.

7 What she said about coaching <u>gave me food for thought</u>.

8 ______________________

______________ idioms

9 The other athletes are really good. I think she's <u>out of her league</u>.

10 I can't win, so I think it's time to <u>throw in the towel</u>.

11 I thought I'd finished my part of the work, but then they suddenly <u>moved the goal posts</u>.

12 ______________________

B Put the underlined idioms below into the correct group in Exercise A.

- They have times when they doubt their abilities or <u>get cold feet</u> because they're anxious about competing.
- It's all about staying calm and focused, so they can <u>give it their best shot</u>.
- I need someone to nag me and tell me to up my game, but I know that's <u>not everyone's cup of tea</u>.

C Match the underlined idioms (1–12) in Exercise A with the meanings (a–l).

- **a** something to think about carefully ____
- **b** change the rules or goals ____
- **c** watch for ____
- **d** feel nervous ____
- **e** make something seem more important or serious than it really is ____
- **f** decide to give up ____
- **g** lack the required ability or knowledge ____
- **h** much better than ____
- **i** be skeptical about something as it may not be accurate or true ____
- **j** to have an instinctive feeling about ____
- **k** try your hardest ____
- **l** not something that everyone likes ____

D SPEAK **Work in pairs and discuss the questions.**

1. Do you usually have a gut feeling about who will win a sports game?
2. Have you ever felt out of your league playing a game or sport?
3. Do you keep an eye out for new trends in fitness and nutrition?
4. What kinds of sports are not your cup of tea?
5. Do you know anyone who is head and shoulders above the rest at a sport?

PRONUNCIATION

Pronunciation of idioms

8.5 **A** **Listen to the sentences. Circle the prominent words in the underlined idioms.**

1. I had a gut feeling.
2. It's time to throw in the towel.
3. He was really making a meal of it.
4. Keep an eye out for the others.
5. You have to take what she says with a grain of salt.

B **Complete the advice for sports players with your own ideas.**

1. If you feel that someone is out of your league, remember, …
2. If you have cold feet, …
3. You should always keep an eye out for …
4. If you want to give something your best shot, …
5. If your opponent is making a meal of something, …
6. Take it with a grain of salt if …

C **Work in pairs. Read the sentences you wrote in Exercise B to your partner. Do you agree with your partner's advice?**

SPEAKING

A **Work in groups. Rank the following in order of how important they are for success in sports.**

- coaching
- diet and nutrition
- insights from technology
- natural ability
- physical fitness
- sports psychology
- training facilities

B DISCUSS **Work in groups and discuss the questions.**

1. Could students benefit from using sports psychology techniques? How?
2. Could people at work benefit from using sports psychology techniques? How?

C **Share your ideas with another group.**

READING

A SPEAK Work in pairs. What kind of diet should an athlete have?

B SKIM Read *Should athletes go gluten-free?* about someone trying out a diet. Which foods did the writer eat? Which did the writer have to avoid?

C READ FOR DETAIL Read the article again and answer the questions.

1 Why did he decide to try this diet?
2 What problems did he experience?
3 What was his conclusion about the effectiveness of the diet?

D Work in pairs and discuss the questions.

1 Have you tried a gluten-free diet?
2 Would you like to try a gluten-free diet? Why/Why not?
3 Would might be the advantages and disadvantages?

Should athletes go *gluten-free*?

For those who are gluten intolerant, a diet that is gluten-free is a necessity rather than a choice. But there are some who may be motivated to try this diet for other reasons. When tennis player Novak Djokovic became world number one, he credited going gluten-free as the reason for his success. Some athletes have followed suit and switched to a gluten-free diet and some are already swearing by its effects. So, I'm going gluten-free for two weeks to see if it makes me a better soccer player.

DAY 1 Going gluten-free means no bread and no cereal, so I had nice **tangy** grapefruit for breakfast. Then for lunch, I had a big salad full of nice **crisp** lettuce and **crunchy** carrots. I was briefly impressed by how healthy I was being. But then I worked out in the afternoon, and was suddenly ravenous.

DAY 2 I was overjoyed when I saw the gluten-free section of my local grocery store stuffed full of packets of bread, pasta, cakes, and cookies – all long lost friends! [1]I put several in my basket. Then I added some more packages just in case. At home, I made myself my first sandwich for two days. Disappointingly, the bread was incredibly dry and incredibly **bland**.

DAY 3 [2]I'd been planning to have grapefruit some days and melon some days, but I was so hungry today that I had both. However, the grapefruit tasted **sour**, so I decided to try one of my gluten-free cupcakes instead. It didn't look that **appetizing** but it was actually pretty good – **moist**, unlike the bread, and with very sweet, **sticky** icing. Relieved that I had found some comfort food, I had two more before lunch.

DAY 4 A revelation! Maybe the gluten-free bread would be passable as toast? I spread a generous amount of honey on top. Maybe too much because it was a little **soggy** – but it actually tasted OK. A relief, because I didn't want a grapefruit or melon for breakfast again.

DAY 5 For variety, I decided to try some probiotic food – food rich in healthy bacteria that are said to be good for gut health. I'd been told kefir, a fermented milk drink, is a good way to kick things off. It looked like milk, but it smelled interesting – slightly **cheesy** but also vinegary. Tentatively, I poured some into a glass. It had a **creamy** texture, but it was also a little **gritty**. And it tasted like a slightly **acidic**, **fizzy** glass of milk. I'd found something else I could have for breakfast!

DAY 6 A Japanese friend had warned me that natto – another probiotic food made from fermented soy beans – is somewhat of an acquired taste. I could see what she meant right away. It looked **slimy** and had a very **pungent** aroma – almost like burned tires. I think the beans actually had a pretty **mild** taste, but the smell was so strong that it was hard to tell. [3]I couldn't eat much, so I reached for some gluten-free cakes instead, which I ate with some kombucha, a sweetened tea that looked a little **murky**. Despite the **cloudy** appearance it was nice, although it didn't exactly taste like tea.

DAY 7 I met some friends for a game of soccer. The jury was still out as to whether the diet had had any effect. Unfortunately, there wasn't much to see. I hadn't morphed into an overnight soccer sensation. So, is going gluten-free better for sports performance? It seems highly unlikely. And if you do need to go gluten-free, you should work with a sports nutritionist to create a diet to suit your training needs.

Glossary

appetizing (adj) appetizing food smells or looks very good
morph (v) to change from one thing into another by small and interconnected steps
overjoyed (adj) extremely happy
the jury is still out (phr) used for saying that people have not yet decided what they think about someone or something

GRAMMAR
Pronouns and determiners

A Look at the sentence from the article *Should athletes go gluten-free?* Which of the underlined words in the sentence is followed by a noun? What does the word not followed by a noun refer to?

Some athletes have followed suit and switched to a gluten-free diet and some are already swearing by its effects.

B Choose the best words to complete the rules.

Pronouns and determiners

Words such as *this*, *these*, *many*, *several* and *some* can be used as both pronouns and determiners. To understand whether the word is being used as a pronoun or determiner, we need to look at the context.

1. Pronouns ***are / are not*** followed by a noun. They are used in place of a noun. We need to use the context to understand what the pronoun refers to.
2. Determiners ***are / are not*** followed by a noun. They are used to say which thing or how many things are being talked about.

C Look at the underlined sentences (1–3) in the article in *Should athletes go gluten-free?* For each sentence, decide which words are pronouns and which are determiners. Then decide which nouns the pronouns refer to.

D Go to the **Grammar Hub** on **page 136**.

VOCABULARY
Describing taste

A Complete the table with the words in bold from *Should athletes go gluten-free?* Some words can go into more than one category.

Look	Smell	Taste	Texture

B Go to the **Vocabulary Hub** on **page 147**.

C **SPEAK** Work in pairs. Discuss the questions.

1. Describe a food you have eaten because you wanted to be healthy. Did it have any effect?
2. Describe a food you have eaten from another country. Did you like it?
3. Describe the most unusual thing you have ever eaten. Would you recommend it to other people?

SPEAKING HUB

A **PREPARE** Work in small groups. Imagine you are a fitness instructor or personal trainer. You are pitching your services to a famous athlete. To win the pitch, you need to create the best plan to help him or her prepare for an important competition. First decide what kind of athlete you are pitching to.

B **PLAN** Create a plan to help the athlete. Use the questions to help you.

- What are the best mental techniques to help him or her prepare for the competition?
- What should he or she do to prepare physically?
- What is the best diet for him or her to follow?

C **PRESENT** Present your plan to the class.

D **DISCUSS** Discuss the plans with the class. Which plan was the best?

Talk about sports psychology
Discuss nutrition and fitness

8.3 Health hacks

A– reformulating S– repairing misunderstandings

Is it good for you?

A Work in pairs. Look at the picture and discuss the questions.

1 Are these foods healthy? Why?

2 Would you eat the food shown in the picture? Why/Why not?

B Read the terms below. Now watch a video about food packaging. Check (✓) the terms you see or hear.

☐ source of fiber	☐ high in iron
☐ high in vitamins	☐ low in salt
☐ high in vitamin D	☐ source of calcium
☐ gluten free	☐ good
☐ low in calories	☐ 100% natural
☐ OK for veggies	☐ high fiber
☐ nature is power	☐ high in Omega 3
☐ organic	☐ no refined sugars
☐ no added nonsense	☐ veggie-friendly
☐ low sugar	☐ no added salt

Glossary

back up (phrasal verb) to show that an explanation or belief is probably true

bend the rules (phrase) to allow something that is not normally allowed

dupe (v) to trick someone into believing something that is not true or something that is stupid or illegal

manipulate (v) to influence someone or to control something in a smart or dishonest way

tricks of the trade (phrase) quick and effective methods used by experienced people in a particular profession

C Watch the video again. Complete the summary.

A normal grocery store has thousands of products with [1] ________________ information. Food producers cannot make health [2] ________________ about products unless they can support them with [3] ________________.

However, they often manipulate the [4] ________________ to make their foods appear healthier. People generally only notice certain [5] ________________ when food shopping.

Some terms such as 'good' and 'natural' are [6] ________________ and can be used without any evidence of health [7] ________________.

Glossary

veggie(s) (n, slang) (British) = **vegetarian(s)** (n) (American)

AUTHENTIC ENGLISH

A Work in pairs. Read the sentences from the video and the information in the box. Which of Babita's words has Richard reformulated?

Babita: *So, we're being duped, we're being fooled, are we?*

Richard: *Well, we're being manipulated.*

Reformulating

We reformulate when we want to express that we don't necessarily agree with what another person has said or with their point of view. We frequently reformulate by using *well* and then the same structure the other person has used.

B Match the sentences (1–6) with the replies (a–f).

1 New York's the greatest city in the world.

2 They're definitely lying to us, aren't they?

3 What they're doing is illegal.

4 All health claims on food have to be backed up with scientific evidence.

5 You hated the movie then?

6 So, Maria doesn't want to come to the party then?

a Well, they're not being completely honest.

b Well, they're definitely bending the rules.

c Well, some have to be backed up with evidence.

d Well, it's certainly the most exciting.

e Well, she wants to come but she's working really late.

f Well, I didn't like it very much.

C Work in pairs. Write responses to the sentences.

1 I bet the movie was amazing, wasn't it?

2 What they're doing is immoral.

3 The apartment's filthy.

D Work in pairs. Practice the exchanges you wrote in Exercise C.

SAM MALCOLM AMANDA HARRY EMILY

Healthy display

A Work in pairs. Discuss the questions.

1 Where do you get recipes from?

2 Are you good at following recipes or do you prefer to improvise?

B Watch the video. Complete the recipe.

Amanda's
HEALTHY BROWNIE RECIPE

INGREDIENTS

One [1] ________________ of coconut oil
Two egg whites
[2] ________________ yogurt
small amount of sugar
[3] ________________ cocoa powder
[4] ________________ flour
[5] ________________ of dark chocolate chips

METHOD

Step one: [6] ________________ the oven.
Step two: [7] ________________ egg whites from yolks.
Step three: [8] ________________ egg whites, coconut oil, yogurt and sugar.
Step four: Add cocoa powder and wholemeal flour to wet [9] ________________.
Step five: [10] ________________ mixture until incorporated.
Step six: Add chocolate chips.
Step seven: Spread the [11] ________________ in a pan.
Step eight: Put the pan in the oven for [12] ________________ minutes at 260 degrees Fahrenheit.

C Where does Harry think he went wrong with the recipe?

SPEAKING SKILL

A Work in pairs. Complete the example in the video. Why does Sam use a question tag here?

Sam: Now you did separate the egg whites from the yolks, ________________?

B Read the information in the box. Which strategy (a–c) has been used in the sentences from the video (1–5)?

Repairing misunderstandings

When we don't understand another person or another person doesn't understand us there are a number of things we can do to repair the misunderstanding.

a Tag questions to check that we have understood correctly or that the other person has understood correctly.

b Clarifying instructions to signal that we are going to go over instructions again.

c Restating to clarify what we mean. We can also say what we don't mean.

1 OK … maybe let's go over them again. ___

2 Not whisk … mix. ___

3 Remember to add chips … not chunks … chips of dark chocolate. ___

4 Hold on, Fahrenheit? You mean Celsius, don't you? ___

5 OK, let's go through it one more time. ___

C Work in pairs. Take turns reading aloud the sentences (1–5) in Exercise B. Try to copy the intonation of Sam and Harry in the video.

SPEAKING HUB

A PLAN You are going to give instructions on a process you know well. Choose one of the ideas below or use your own idea.

- recipe
- how to repair something
- sport or exercise tips
- professional or academic process

B PREPARE Write notes on how you are going to explain the process to your partner.

C PRESENT Work in pairs. Explain your process to your partner. Ask your partner to retell you the process. Clarify any misunderstandings. Change roles.

Well, no … that's not exactly right. You should make sure you stretch first.

Explain and give instructions about a process

➤ Turn to page 163 to learn how to write a summary of a text about stress.

Unit 8 Review

VOCABULARY

A Choose the correct word to complete the sentences.

1. I went to see the doctor when I had a *rash* / *sprain* on my chest.
2. I'm really stressed right now, so my blood *pressure* / *rate* is a little high.
3. I'm on crutches because I've *fractured* / *pulled* a bone in my foot.
4. Do you have any eye drops? I've been looking at a screen all day and my eyes are really *inflamed* / *sore*.
5. I *pulled* / *sprained* my wrist when the ball hit my hand.
6. I think I *fractured* / *pulled* a muscle at the gym, so I'd better put some ice on it.
7. Do you ever track your heart *rate* / *pressure* while you're exercising?

B Match the questions (1–12) with the answers (a–l).

1. Do you ever get cold feet before speaking in public?
2. Do you always give it your best shot when you play sports?
3. Do you always keep an eye out for good places to eat?
4. Which sports are not your cup of tea?
5. Have you heard something that you've had to take with a pinch of salt?
6. Did you feel like throwing in the towel when it got tough?
7. When was the last time you felt out of your league?
8. Who is a sports player who is head and shoulders above his peers?
9. Do you offer to help out when you see someone making a meal of something?
10. What was the last thing you read that gave you food for thought?
11. Are your gut feelings usually right?
12. Has anyone ever moved the goal posts while you were working on something?

a. Yes, because I'm incredibly competitive.
b. Messi is clearly one the best players in history.
c. At times in the race I wanted to give up, but you have to keep going.
d. No, I don't usually get nervous.
e. A teacher once changed the title of an essay.
f. I'm not a big fan of football or baseball.
g. There was a great article in the paper about innovation the other day.
h. Yes, a friend told me a story. But he always exaggerates.
i. Not usually, I find it a little embarrassing.
j. Not really. I search for things online.
k. I once took an exam that was much too difficult for me.
l. Rarely. I'm not good at predicting things.

C Choose the correct word to complete the sentences.

1. I don't like soft cookies. They need to be *crunchy* / *tangy* / *soggy*.
2. I don't often eat seaweed. It's a little too *crisp* / *murky* / *slimy* for me.
3. Pasta can often be too *bland* / *pungent* / *sour*, so I always add a lot of parmesan cheese.
4. I tend to order a *mild* / *gritty* / *sticky* curry when I have Indian food.
5. I like lemon dressing on my salad to give it a *creamy* / *soggy* / *tangy* flavor.
6. I never buy *mild* / *pungent* / *fizzy* drinks in case they've been shaken up.
7. I love eating *cheesy* / *gritty* / *sticky* things like toffee apples and cotton candy.

GRAMMAR

A Correct the mistakes in the sentences.

1. My smartwatch has a feature that you can share your exercise data with friends.
2. There's an app which in you can record your fitness data.
3. This is the device that being used to monitor people's blood sugar levels.
4. The inventor is someone which people like to read about.
5. I don't know who's smartwatch this is.
6. This is the diet tracking service which I subscribe.

B Complete the text with the words or phrases in the box.

a large number of	both	either
most people	one	others	some people

The raw food diet

These days, there are [1] ____________ diets that claim to be the best way to stay healthy. [2] ____________ is the raw food diet. According to this diet, [3] ____________ cooked and processed foods are unhealthy, so people should not eat [4] ____________. [5] ____________ follow a raw vegan diet, whereas [6] ____________ eat animal products, too. The diet includes fruits, vegetables, nuts, seeds and, for the non-vegans, meat. [7] ____________ who follow the diet, whether vegan or not, also eat fermented foods, such as sauerkraut and kimchi.

9 BEHAVIOR

Behavior is the mirror in which everyone shows their image.

Johann Wolfgang von Goethe

Caught red … and blue … and green handed.

OBJECTIVES

- talk about group behavior
- discuss factors that affect behavior
- discuss animal behavior
- talk about behavioral experiments
- give and justify your opinion on social engagement
- write a conclusion to an academic report

Work with a partner. Discuss the questions.

1 Look at the picture. How do children learn to behave? What influences our behavior as we grow?

2 Read the quote. What aspects of our image/character might we deliberately try to show through our behavior? What might we reveal accidentally?

3 What would a stranger guess about your character from your behavior? What might they assume incorrectly?

9.1 Language and behavior

- Talk about group behavior
- Discuss factors that affect behavior

G noun phrases V slang P pronouncing vague expressions S understanding rapid colloquial speech

VOCABULARY
Slang

A SPEAK Read the dictionary definition. Work in groups and discuss the questions.

1 Can you think of any examples of slang (in English or your language)?
2 What problems can slang cause for language learners?

> **slang** – definition and synonyms
> NOUN Pronunciation /slæŋ/
> Words or expressions that are very informal and are not considered suitable for more formal situations. Some slang is used only by a particular group of people.

9.1 **B** Read and listen to some examples of informal English. In pairs, try to work out the meaning of the underlined slang expressions.

1 I could do with some new wheels but they'd set me back at least ten grand … and I'm completely broke.

____

2 Hey, can you lend me ten bucks? Ah, sweet. That's awesome, dude.

____

3 I don't mean to gripe, but the office bash last night was a hot mess. I was so bummed!

____

4 This guy offered me a brand new TV for fifty bucks, so I'm like 'Sounds shady to me – it's probably hot or something.'

____

5 I wanted to hang out with my buddies tonight but I'm totally beat, so I guess I'll just chill out and crash instead.

____

6 I'm so stoked cuz I got myself a new crib. It's so cool.

____

9.2 **C** Now listen to a more neutral version of the same sentences to check your ideas.

D DISCUSS Work in small groups. Discuss the questions. Use words in Exercise B.

1 When was the last time you griped about something?
3 What events have you been to that were a hot mess? What happened?
4 When was the last time you felt stoked or bummed? Why?

LISTENING

A SPEAK Work in pairs. Do you speak or behave differently depending on who you are with?

3 **B LISTEN FOR GIST** Listen to a group of people taking part in a psychology experiment. Then answer the questions.

1 How many participants are in the group?

____

2 Where are the experimenters?

____

3 What's the purpose of the experiment?

____

4 What five tasks does the experiment include?

____

3 **C LISTEN FOR DETAIL** Listen again. Are the statements true (T) or false (F)? Correct the false sentences.

1 Lisa volunteered to take part for free. T / F
2 Lisa's group was due to start at 11:30. T / F
3 All four members of the group agree to eat the doughnuts. T / F
4 Lisa knew for certain that her answer about the lines was wrong. T / F
5 Sometimes PTU affects everyone in a group. T / F
6 The participants think 'yummy' is a cool word. T / F
7 Groupthink is mainly associated with teenagers. T / F
8 The experimenters were surprised by Lisa's behavior. T / F

4 **D LISTEN TO RAPID SPEECH** Listen to some extracts from the conversation. Cross out the words and sounds that the speakers leave out. Put brackets [ ] around the phrases they link together. The first two have been done for you. Use the information in the box to help you.

Understanding rapid colloquial speech

Rapid colloquial English is especially difficult to understand because:

- speakers use a lot of slang and idioms.
- sounds, syllables or even whole words are often left out.
- common phrases like *what do you* and *going to* are linked together.

1 ~~Good~~ morning. How ~~are~~ [you doing?]
2 [Don~~'t~~ know] what they're testing.
3 Are we supposed to wait?
4 We have to go and teach.
5 Should we get going?
6 It's obvious.
7 Do you think they're for us?
8 What about you, Jake?
9 Can we have some more?
10 What are you going on about?

E SPEAK Work in groups and discuss the questions.

1 Do you think you would respond to the tasks in the same way as Lisa?
2 Have you ever experienced PTU? Think about your experiences as a language learner.
3 Have you ever encountered groupthink or something similar? What happened?

PRONUNCIATION

Pronouncing vague expressions

A Underline the vague expressions in the extracts from the conversation. Use the information in the box to help you.

Pronouncing vague expressions

Vague expressions are a way of showing that we're not being too precise. They are especially common in informal English.

Vague expressions are usually pronounced very quickly, with no stressed syllables. The word *of* is often reduced to *a* (e.g. *kinda*, *sorta*). The word *and* becomes *n*.

1 Something about perception skills and stuff like that.
2 There were two guys here earlier, psychology professors or whatever.
3 How groups influence our behavior, and so on.
4 I thought my eyes were playing tricks on me in some way!
5 Sometimes it's easier to follow the crowd, in a sense, than to trust your own eyes!
6 Everyone else is nodding their heads, or something like that.
7 I felt kind of stupid.
8 You must think I'm some kind of sheep!

9.5 **B** Listen to check your answers. Then practice saying the sentences.

SPEAKING

DISCUSS Work in small groups and discuss the question. Use the vague expressions in the list and slang from this lesson in your discussions.

How can we avoid the problems of group behavior? Think of at least five practical steps.

- and so on
- and stuff like that
- in a/some sense/way
- kind/sort of (+ adjective/verb)
- more or less
- or something (like that)
- or whatever
- some kind/sort of (+ noun)

READING

A SPEAK Work in pairs. Do you think the language you speak could affect any of the areas below? Why/Why not?

- how rich you are
- how you play
- your health

B SKIM Read *Does your language affect your behavior?* Were any of your ideas from Exercise A mentioned?

C READ FOR MAIN IDEA Read the article again. Answer the questions.

1. How did Chen try to show that language (not other factors) affects our behavior?
2. Why does our language affect our behavior, according to Chen?
3. How could Chen's ideas make the world a better place?
4. What other behaviors are connected with our language, according to Chen?
5. What other factor (apart from grammatical structures) might affect how speakers of certain languages behave?
6. What claim is the main focus of the article?
7. What's the problem with the classification of English?
8. Which language feature did Chen use to categorize languages?

D SPEAK Work in groups and discuss the questions.

1. Do you agree with Chen's claims?
2. How else could we explain his correlations?
3. Do you often make long-term plans for the future (e.g. saving for retirement)?
4. Do you consider yourself an impulsive person or someone who likes to plan?

DOES YOUR LANGUAGE AFFECT YOUR BEHAVIOR?

In 2013, Keith Chen, a behavioral economist at Yale University, made headlines around the world with the extraordinary claim that the language we speak can have a significant impact on [1]our propensity to save, plan and prepare for the future.

Chen divided the languages of the world into two categories: strong FTR (future tense reference) languages, which need markers like 'will' to signal the future, and weak FTR languages, which don't. In English (a strong FTR language), you can't say 'it snows tomorrow'; you usually have to add 'will' or 'going to'. In weak FTR languages like Mandarin, it's normal to say, 'it snows now' and 'it snows tomorrow', using the same verb form in [2]both these cases.

Chen's remarkable finding was that speakers of weak FTR languages save 25% more money for the future than speakers of strong FTR languages. Chen's interpretation of this correlation is that for speakers of weak FTR languages, the future feels like part of the present, while speakers of strong FTR languages save much less because the future feels more remote to them.

Remarkably, Chen's correlations held not only for savings rates, but also for overeating, smoking, drinking, debt and lack of physical exercise. In each case, speakers of weak FTR languages were significantly healthier and took fewer risks, presumably because they felt [3]a strong connection with their future selves.

While Chen's study provoked considerable interest and enthusiasm from the general public, the backlash from linguists and other academics has been just as striking. One criticism involves the possible confusion of correlation with causation. The link between languages and behavior may in fact be due to other factors, such as age, education or income levels. Chen took great care to control for all these factors, by comparing families where the only difference was [4]the language spoken at home. However, many academics still feel deeply uncomfortable with the idea of a causal relationship behind the apparent correlation.

One alternative possibility is that it's the connotations of a language that affect our behavior, rather than any grammatical properties of the language itself. For example, languages such as English might encourage a live-for-today attitude as a result of people's associations of that attitude with English-speaking countries.

In a 2010 study, Dirk Akkermans and colleagues set out to find out more by asking bilingual speakers of English and Dutch to play a game. [5]Those who had lived in English-speaking countries were found to be considerably more competitive when playing in English rather than Dutch. However, those who had experienced only limited exposure to the culture of English-speaking countries were found to be no more competitive when playing in English or Dutch, strongly suggesting that it's the culture of English-speaking countries, not the language itself, that is making the difference.

A second major concern with Chen's study is that his division of the world's languages into two categories, strong and weak FTR, seems overly simplistic. For example, while English does require a future tense marker in predictions like 'it'll rain tomorrow', future markers are optional in other future constructions (e.g. 'I'm leaving tomorrow') and virtually outlawed in conditional clauses (e.g. 'If it rains …'). The future in English is complex, as [6]pretty much every learner can attest, so its classification as strong FTR feels debatable at best. Similar objections could be raised for many other languages.

Overall, despite [7]the many legitimate concerns, Chen's analysis of the correlation can't be dismissed out of hand. Further research is needed, ideally with a more sophisticated classification of languages. However, if [8]Chen's conclusions that grammar influences behavior prove correct, the implications will be profound. Wouldn't it be great if we could solve [9]all our financial and health problems simply by outlawing words like 'will'!

"Chen, M Keith. 2013. "*The Effect of Language on Economic Behavior: Evidence from Savings Rates, Health Behaviors, and Retirement Assets.*" American Economic Review, 103 (2): 690-731."

Glossary

backlash (n) a strong, negative and often angry reaction to something that has happened, especially a political or social change
legitimate (adj) fair and reasonable
outlaw (v) to make something illegal
propensity (n) a natural tendency to behave in a particular way
provoke (v) to cause a reaction, especially an angry one
simplistic (adj) treating something in a way that makes it seem much simpler than it really is

GRAMMAR
Noun phrases

A Complete the rules with the examples (1–9) from the text.

Noun phrases

Long noun phrases (NPs) are especially useful in formal and academic writing because they can contain as much information as a full sentence.

Most NPs start with a number, a quantifier (e.g. *some*, *all*) and/or another determiner (e.g. *the*, *my*, *these*).

a *all* and *both* can be used before a determiner without *of*: ___ / ___

b *many*, *few*, *little* and numbers can be used after a determiner: ___

c Some quantifiers can be modified with phrases like *almost* or *not exactly*: ___

Common structures at the end of an NP include:

d adjective clauses: ___

e reduced adjective clauses: ___

f preposition phrases: ___

g *that*-clauses: ___

h infinitive: ___

B Go to the **Grammar Hub** on **page 138**.

C **SPEAK** Work in small groups. Build 'monster noun phrases' around the nouns in the box, as in the example.

behavior   experiments   language

A: My friends' behavior is strange.
B: A lot of my best friends' behavior is strange.
C: A lot of my best friends' behavior when they're tired is strange.

SPEAKING HUB

A **DISCUSS** Work in small groups. Go to the **Communication Hub** on **page 152**.

B **PLAN** Choose one of the ideas in Exercise A. Create a list of at least five pieces of evidence to support or challenge the idea.

C **PREPARE** Work in pairs. Explain your pieces of evidence to your partner. Listen to your partner's evidence. Give feedback and ask questions.

D **PRACTICE** Practice presenting your evidence. Use your partner's feedback to improve your presentation.

E **PRESENT** Report your evidence to the class. Be prepared to answer questions.

F **REFLECT** Decide which evidence you found most convincing and why.

Talk about group behavior
Discuss factors that affect behavior

- Discuss animal behavior
- Talk about behavioral experiments

G participle clauses and verbless clauses
P intrusive stops
V verb + object + base form; gestures and body language
S identifying outcomes of scientific research

READING

A SPEAK Work in pairs and discuss the questions.

chimpanzees dolphins crows and jays dogs

1 Which of the animals listed in the box are intelligent?
2 How do we know?
3 How could we find out?

B SKIM Read *Understanding animal behavior* quickly. What does the writer say about the questions in Exercise A?

Understanding animal behavior

By Peter Aldhous

We gaze into the eyes of a chimp and see a reflection of ourselves. We glance at a crow and see an alien being. Such biases skew our understanding of what non-human intelligence looks like.

The best known experiment designed to probe animal minds is the 'mirror test'. Having been given time to interact with a mirror, chimps are marked with a dye and anesthetized. After coming around, they look into the mirror while touching the marked area. From this behavior, researchers have concluded that the chimps know they are looking at themselves – one of the hallmarks of an advanced mind. Other animals that have passed the test include manta rays and dolphins.

My issue with the mirror test isn't the meaning of success, but rather how to interpret failure. Do most animals fail because they lack a concept of self, or is the test irrelevant to species that don't use vision for social communication? How would you design a similar test using smells for a dog or ultrasound for a dolphin? When a dolphin **hears its own echoes coming** back in altered form, it might well be thinking: 'Yes, that's me' – but how would we know?

In New Caledonian forests, Gavin Hunt of Massey University **watched crows fashion** twigs into hooks to capture insects from holes. Seeming to understand cause and effect, crows are capable of astounding feats of meta-tool use: using one tool to manipulate another in order to achieve an ultimate goal.

In fact, they seem better than chimps at translating their skill in solving one problem to another conceptually similar one. In the trap-tube test, an animal must use a stick to obtain food from a tube. Pushing it in one direction **helps them get** the reward; pushing it in the other **makes the food fall** into a trap. Crows that have already solved this problem can apply their skills when presented with the trap-table test, which looks different but has the same rule: Don't **let the food drop** down the hole. For chimps, prior experience with the trap tube gives no advantage on the trap table.

Understanding the wider scope of corvid cognition meant entering the birds' world to devise experiments to probe their mental processes. Nicky Clayton did this while at the University of California in the late 1990s. After being told confidently by a psychologist colleague that animals lack 'episodic' memory – an ability to remember the 'what, where and when' of past events – Clayton decided to check for herself. While studying western scrub jays, she realized that the birds' habit of burying food provided a prime opportunity to test their memories.

Clayton first **had the jays bury** insect larvae and peanuts in sand-filled trays. Having learned that the larvae tasted bad after a few days, if just four hours had elapsed, the jays sought out the places where they had hidden them. But if several days had passed, they went for the hidden peanuts. This was an impressive demonstration of 'episodic-like' memory. Clayton has also found that jays will selectively bury certain types of food when aware that it is likely to be scarce in future. So now we apparently have jays planning ahead, in addition to acting on specific memories of the past.

When I visited Clayton and her scrub jays, it was a while before I **saw one of the birds bury** an item of food – apparently my presence had interrupted them. 'They're checking you out,' Clayton told me. I stared back, struck by the gulf between us. Despite having read the scientific papers and knowing how cognitively sophisticated scrub jays are, I experienced no emotional connection.

Glossary

elapse (v) if time elapses, it passes
feat (n) something impressive and often dangerous that someone does
gulf (n) a large and important difference between people or groups
hallmark (n) typical feature

C READ FOR OUTCOMES Complete the notes about the research. Use the information in the box to help you.

Identifying outcomes of scientific research

When you read about scientific research, it's important to distinguish between:

- results (what happened?)
- conclusions (what did we learn?).

You can then decide if you agree with the conclusions.

Mirror test

1 **Results:** Chimps look in mirror and ________________.

2 **Conclusions:** Chimps know ________________.

Trap-tube/-table test

3 **Results:** Crows ________________ from one test to another; for chimps ________________.

4 **Conclusions:** ________________ at translating skills to conceptually similar problems

Insect larvae vs peanuts

5 **Results:** Jays went to larvae locations after ________________, but to peanut locations after ________________.

6 **Conclusions:** Jays possess ________________.

D SPEAK Work in pairs and discuss the question. How might research like this change the way we treat animals?

VOCABULARY

Verb + object + base form

A Look again at the examples in bold in *Understanding animal behavior*. Then complete the rules with verbs from the text.

Verb + object + base form

A very small number of verbs are followed by an object or a base form.

1 Sense verbs: ________________, ________________, ________________ and *feel* are followed by a base form to describe a complete event, or an *-ing* form to describe a process or series of events.

2 Causative verbs: ________________, ________________ and ________________. After *help*, both a base form or an infinitive are possible.

B Go to the **Vocabulary Hub** on **page 147**.

GRAMMAR

Participle clauses and verbless clauses

A Complete the sentences from the article with one word.

1 ________________ been given time to interact with a mirror, chimps are marked with a dye.

2 After coming around, they look into the mirror while ________________ the marked area.

3 Nicky Clayton did this ________________ at the University of California in the late 1990s.

4 After ________________ told confidently by a psychologist colleague that animals lack 'episodic' memory … Clayton decided to check for herself.

5 Having ________________ that the larvae tasted bad after a few days … the jays sought out the places where they had hidden them.

6 Clayton has also found that jays will selectively bury certain types of food when ________________ that it is likely to be scarce in the future.

7 I stared back, ________________ by the gulf between us.

B Match the sentences (1–7) in Exercise A with the rules (a–c).

Participle clauses and verbless clauses

Participle clauses use participles (e.g. *doing, done, being done, having done, having been done*) instead of a subject + verb.

a When a clause starts with a participle, the meaning is often *when/after* ___, ___ or *because* ___.

b Many participle clauses start with prepositions (e.g. *before, after, despite*) ___.

c After some conjunctions (*if, when, while, although*), we can leave out the subject and *be*. Usually this leaves a participle ___.

When *be* was the only verb, we are left with a 'verbless clause' ___, ___.

C Go to the **Grammar Hub** on **page 138**.

SPEAKING

SPEAK Work in groups. Discuss your experiences and opinions of animal intelligence. Then use participle clauses to report back to the class.

LISTENING

A SPEAK Work in groups. Discuss the questions.

1 Do you have any lucky charms that you use before exams or other stressful situations? Do you know anybody who uses these lucky charms?

2 Do you have any lucky rituals or routines that you follow, e.g. before watching your favorite sports team? Do you know anybody who follows these lucky rituals?

9.6 **B LISTEN FOR MAIN IDEA** Listen to a radio show about behavioral psychology and answer the questions.

1 How did the pigeons get food?

____

2 What's the connection between the experiment with pigeons and the one with people?

____

3 How do the three people at the end try to influence events?

____

9.6 **C LISTEN FOR DETAIL** Listen again. Choose the correct endings.

1 In the famous pigeon experiment, the mechanism always delivered food …

a after the same amount of time had passed.
b at random times.
c when the pigeons performed a particular action.

2 As the food continued to be delivered, the pigeons …

a changed their actions.
b became more sure they could affect the delivery.
c became more desperate.

3 The experiment with people …

a showed humans weren't so easily convinced.
b showed very similar results.
c used food as well to trick the participants.

4 The person who seems most convinced of their power to control events is …

a the soccer fan.
b the exam-taker.
c the lottery player.

D SPEAK Work in groups and discuss the questions.

1 Do the behaviors and rituals described in the radio show prove that pigeons and people are stupid/irrational? Or is there a benefit in believing we can influence things beyond our control?

2 What other examples can you think of, where people (or animals) try to control things that are beyond their control?

3 What are some dangers of this type of behavior?

PRONUNCIATION

Intrusive stops

9.7 **A** Listen carefully to some extracts from the radio show. Which sound (/p/, /t/ or /k/) can you hear in each of the underlined words?

1 A kind of bizarre pigeon <u>dance</u>. /p/ /t/ /k/

2 Such actions can <u>influence</u> <u>something</u> beyond our control. /p/ /t/ /k/

3 After completely random <u>lengths</u> of time. /p/ /t/ /k/

4 I was young, and my aunt gave me a lucky <u>hamster</u> toy. /p/ /t/ /k/

B Work in pairs. Practice saying the sentences in Exercise A.

9.8 **C** Which six words in the box can have intrusive stops? Listen to check. What's different about the other three words?

becomes	influence	intense	once
prince	strength	things	warmth	wins

D Work in pairs. Write a sentence using at least three of the words in Exercise C. Then give it to another pair for them to attempt to say correctly.

The more influence the prince has, the more intense he becomes.

VOCABULARY

Gestures and body language

A Match the gestures (1–7) with the body parts (a–g). Choose each body part once. When would you use each gesture?

1	blink / wink	a	your finger(s)
2	shrug	b	your eyebrows
3	point / bend / wiggle	c	your head
4	nod / shake	d	your legs
5	fold / cross	e	your eyes
6	cross / bend	f	your shoulders
7	raise	g	your arm(s)

B Complete the sentences with the correct form of a verb in the box. Which body part does each verb involve?

beckon fidget gaze glare grin lean smirk stare

1 Stop ________________ at those people's clothes! It's really rude! They're looking back now!

2 You look so happy in that photo! You're ________________ from ear to ear!

3 I love ________________ out to sea and dreaming of what's on the other side.

4 Stop ________________ with your keys and pay attention!

5 During the test, the teacher ________________ for me to come to the front of the class.

6 Don't ________________ against that cupboard! It's not very stable.

7 When he beat me at tennis, Harry just ________________ and said, 'I guess I'm better than you.'

8 I could tell you were angry by the way you ________________ at me.

C Go to the **Vocabulary Hub** on **page 147**.

D SPEAK Work in groups and discuss the questions.

1 Which gestures can you use to show that you're happy/ interested/bored?

2 How might you show that you don't like someone?

3 How could you communicate with a stranger who doesn't speak your language?

E Work in groups to play a game. One of you is the facilitator; the others are players. Facilitator – go to the **Communication Hub** on **page 153**. Players – go to the **Communication Hub** on **page 150**.

SPEAKING HUB

A PREPARE Work in groups. You are going to design and conduct a behavioral experiment to test an assumption. You can use one of the ideas below or your own ideas.

Assumption 1: Our body language communicates more information than the words we use.

Assumption 2: We can't help nodding or shaking our heads when we say *yes* or *no*, or shrugging our shoulders when we say *I don't know*, even if the movements are extremely tiny.

Assumption 3: We can't help mirroring other people's gestures and body language. We copy them subconsciously.

B PLAN Work out how you could test the assumption on other members of the class.

- How will you set up the experiment?
- What will you tell the participant(s)?
- What will you be looking out for?
- How might your observations confirm or undermine the initial assumption?

C CONDUCT Take turns to conduct your experiments with other members of the class.

If you're participating in another group's experiment, try to act naturally. Don't try to guess what the experimenters are testing – and don't try to influence their results.

If you're an observer, watch both the experimenters and the participants carefully. Try to work out what the experiment is testing.

D DISCUSS Report back to the class on what you learned from your experiment. Ask other observers for their conclusions. How could you refine your experiment to learn more?

Discuss animal behavior

Talk about behavioral experiments

All together now

A Work in pairs. Look at the picture and discuss the questions.

1 What is happening in the picture?

2 Which other animals behave in this way? Why?

B 00.00–01.51 Work in pairs. Watch the first part of a video. Check your answers to Exercise A.

Glossary

evacuation (n) the process of removing people from a building or an area that is not safe

scenario (n) a situation that could possibly happen

simulate (v) to produce the features of something in a way that seems real but is not

swarm (v) to go somewhere as part of a large crowd

C 00.00–01.51 Watch the first part of the video again. Complete the sentences with the best option (a, b or c).

1 Doctor Ed Codling is a …

a mathematician.

b biologist.

c mathematical biologist.

2 The experiment replicates how people on their own react in …

a a fire.

b an earthquake.

c a plane accident.

3 Doctor Codling wants to observe participants that …

a look confident and assume they can find the exit.

b remain calm and find the exit.

c panic and follow another person.

4 When Doctor Codling blows his whistle he wants them to leave out of …

a the north exit.

b the south exit.

c either the north or south exit.

D Work in pairs. Discuss the questions.

1 What do you think the result of the experiment will be?

2 How many people do you think will go the right or the wrong way?

3 Why did people behave in the way they did?

E 01.51–02.35 Watch the second part of the video. Check your answers to Exercise D.

AUTHENTIC ENGLISH

A Work in pairs. Read the sentence from the video. Choose the correct options in the box.

I mean, I've done it before, you just ***end up*** *following someone who looks the most confident in the room.*

end up

We use *end up* to describe being in a particular place or state after doing something or because of doing it. It is used when the subject ***did / didn't*** intend or expect this.

B Work in pairs. Respond to the sentences using *ended up*.

1 You missed your plane.

I ended up sleeping at the airport.

2 The movie you wanted to see was sold out.

3 After traveling around the world for years, Marta unexpectedly settled down in Ireland.

4 I thought I'd passed the exam but I failed.

5 Alan kept on arriving late for work.

6 We had booked a vacation but had to cancel it because my boyfriend was sick.

C Compare your answers with another pair.

Follow the herd

SAM MALCOLM AMANDA HARRY EMILY

A Work in pairs. What do you think the phrase *follow the herd* means?

B Watch the video. Answer the following questions.

1 What is Amanda writing an article about?
2 What motivated people to use the Social Stairs?
3 What doesn't Harry understand?
4 Why does Sam want Amanda to tell him what she finds out?

SPEAKING SKILL

A Work in pairs. Complete the examples from the video.

1 Oh, ______________________ like that piano staircase in Stockholm?
2 ______________________, the piano staircase had an escalator next to it.
3 You ______________________ about that other example – the Social Stairs or something like that?
4 Oh, yeah. The Social Stairs. ______________________.
5 Or ______________________, they liked hanging out together.

B Watch the video again to check your answers to Exercise A.

C Choose the correct options to complete the information.

Backtracking and reformulating

When we correct something that has been previously said we [1]*backtrack / reformulate*. When we say something previously said in a different way we [2]*backtrack / reformulate*.

D Work in pairs. Decide which of the examples in Exercise A are backtracking (b) and which are reformulating (r).

1 ___ 2 ___ 3 ___ 4 ___ 5 ___

SPEAKING HUB

A PREPARE You are going to discuss the following question.

Do you think a sense of community is declining in modern society? Why/Why not?

Write notes on what you are going to say and how to justify your opinion. Be prepared to reformulate your arguments.

B DISCUSS Work in small groups. Present your opinion to the rest of the group. Respond to what the other members in your group say.

We've ended up being very isolated ... or to put it another way ... lonely.

C REFLECT Give feedback to the other members of your group. Consider the following points.

- reformulation
- fluency
- pronunciation
- interaction

Give and justify your opinion on social engagement

➤ Turn to page 164 to learn how to write a conclusion to an academic report.

Unit 9 Review

VOCABULARY

A Complete the conversation with the words in the box.

awesome	bucks	bummed	chill out		
dude	guy	mess	shady	stoked	was like

A: Hey, [1] ______________. You look happy. What's up?

B: I'm so [2] ______________! I just got ten [3] ______________ for taking part in an experiment.

A: [4] ______________! What did you do?

B: I had to use sticks to push food out of a tube, but it kept dropping into a hole. It was a hot [5] ______________! I was so [6] ______________, but the [7] ______________ who was in charge [8] ______________, '[9] ______________, man! Don't worry!'

A: Sounds a little [10] ______________ to me. What were they testing?

B: Whether people are smarter than crows! Crazy, huh!

B Find and correct the mistake in three of the sentences.

1 The researchers watched one chimp hide the food.

____

2 We weren't let to watch the experiment.

____

3 I'll have my assistant to contact you next week.

____

4 I felt a mosquito bite me last night.

____

5 I can't help you pass the exam, but I can help you avoid mistakes.

____

6 A crow was seen use one tool to make another.

____

C Choose the correct words to complete the blog post.

How to listen – and show you care

- [1]*Lean* / *Glare* / *Raise* toward the other person slightly.
- Don't [2]*fold* / *gaze* / *wink* your arms or [3]*fidget* / *shake* / *wiggle* with pens, keys, etc.
- Keep neutral facial expressions – a smile might look like a [4]*gaze* / *raise* / *smirk*.
- Don't speak. Instead, [5]*bend* / *nod* / *wink* your head slowly to show understanding, [6]*cross* / *point* / *raise* your eyebrows to show interest, or [7]*bend* / *shrug* / *wiggle* your shoulders to show you don't know.
- Keep eye contact but don't [8]*cross* / *grin* / *stare*. You're allowed to [9]*beckon* / *blink* / *glare*!

GRAMMAR

A Reorder the sentences to make noun phrases.

1 You usually have to use / forms / available / future / the / two / that / of / one / are /

______________________________.

2 The research focused on / for / are making / the / that / worrying / of / preparation / the future / lack / extremely / most people /

______________________________.

3 all / behavior / Practically / into / research / my / animal / shows they're smarter than we think

______________________________.

4 The accident occurred because of / the event / for / failure by / such / the organizers / almost / to plan / the / large crowds / complete / to attend /

______________________________.

5 problem / the / ways / these / approaching / Both / of / are flawed

______________________________.

6 We are aware of / that / be expressed / the / only / animal intelligence / of / many / a / can / few / ways /

______________________________.

B Complete the sentences with participle clauses. Use the verbs in parentheses.

1 ______________________ a big breakfast earlier, I skipped lunch. (*eat*)

2 The octopus uses a coconut shell as a shelter if ______________________. (*attack*)

3 ______________________ to understand the rules, the pigeon solved the puzzle quickly. (*seem*)

4 ______________________ to be at the airport at 4 am, we weren't happy about the 10-hour delay. (*tell*)

5 When ______________________ your bags, remember to leave space for souvenirs. (*pack*)

6 Despite not ______________________ at college, she has produced some excellent research. (*study*)

10 SOCIETY

Society exists only as a mental concept; in the real world there are only individuals.

Oscar Wilde

A castle village in Burj Al Babas, Bolu, Turkey

OBJECTIVES

- discuss issues related to tourism
- present solutions to urban problems
- talk about political activism
- discuss how to make a difference
- debate for and against a motion
- write a persuasive essay

Work with a partner. Discuss the questions.

1 Look at the picture. What type of person might live in a place like this?

2 Read the quote. What do you think Wilde means? Do you agree?

3 What would be the advantages and disadvantages of living in an unusual place like the one in the picture?

10.1 Urban problems

- Discuss issues related to tourism
- Present solutions to urban problems

G discourse markers
P introducing new information
V culture and heritage; nouns with *to*
S integrating information from different texts

READING

A SPEAK Work in pairs. What are some advantages and disadvantages of increased tourism for a city?

B SCAN Read the three newspaper articles. What problem of tourism are they discussing?

Has tourism reached its limit?

Being **designated** as a UNESCO World **Heritage** site helps **preserve** a site and **refurbish** its facilities – as well as boosting tourism. Yet, it can end up **endangering** the site. A famous example is Machu Picchu, the **ruins** of an Inca **settlement** in Peru, which is being destabilized owing to tourists littering, climbing on the ruins or even taking pieces of it home.

In response to similar problems, Venice has capped the number of tourists allowed to enter its most famous areas. Niagara Falls requires visitors to buy tickets which say when they can enter the site, whereas the Taj Mahal has increased entrance fees for tourists to actually try to put people off visiting.

Glossary

booming (adj) if an activity is booming, it is becoming very popular

destabilize (v) to cause problems for a country, government, or person in authority so that they become less effective

elitist (adj) supporting or based on a system in which a small group of people have a lot of advantages and keep the most power and influence

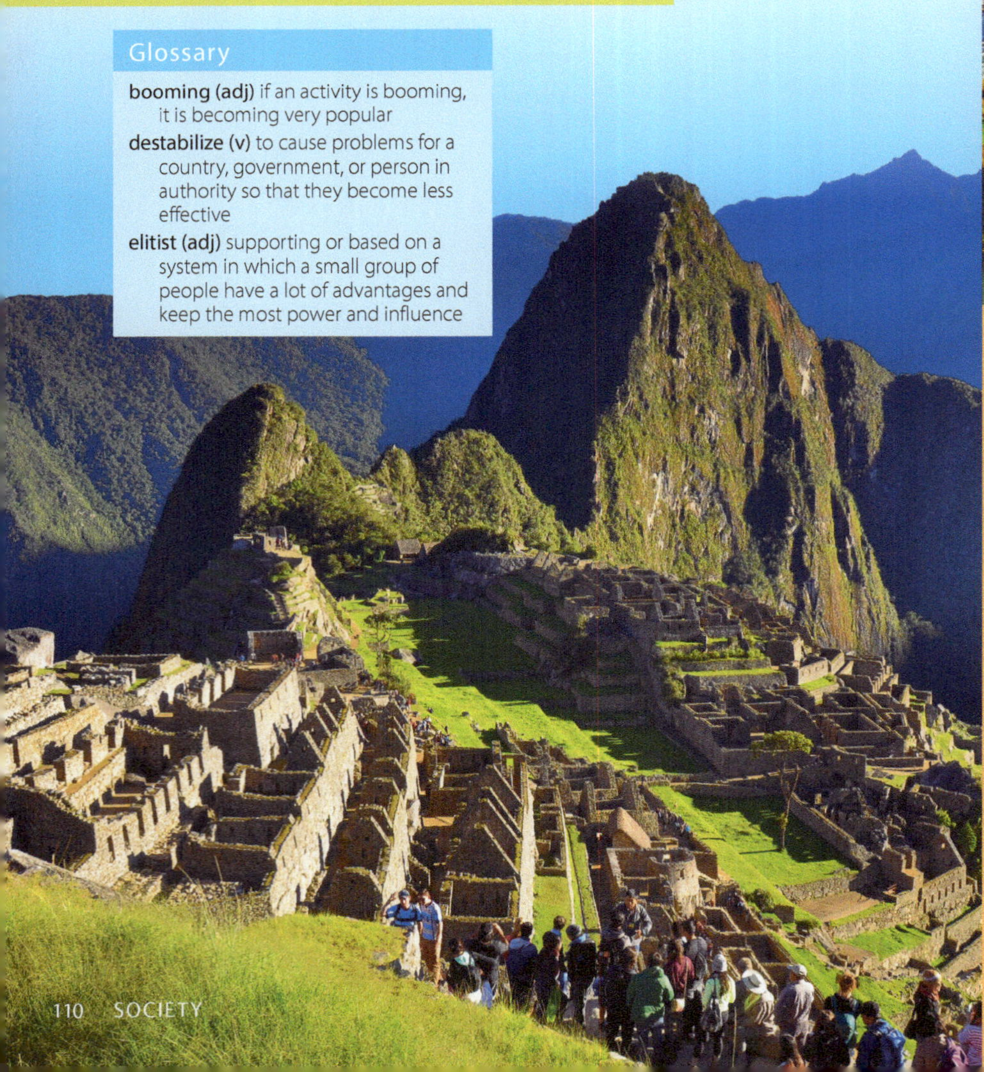

C SYNTHESIZE INFORMATION Imagine that you are writing an essay about tackling the problem you identified in Exercise B. Complete the notes using information from all three articles. Use the information in the box to help you.

Integrating information from different texts

Sometimes you need to get information from multiple sources to understand a topic.

- Be clear about your purpose for reading. What questions are you trying to answer?
- Underline the main ideas in the texts and look for arguments connected to your topic.
- Use headings to organize the information you are looking for. Write notes under these headings as you read more texts.

Notes

Issues caused by the problem

Ideas for dealing with the problem

Criticism of these ideas

D DISCUSS Work in pairs. Look at your notes in Exercise C and discuss the best methods for solving the problem.

Is tourism tax fair?

The New Zealand government recently announced that it will start charging tourists a tax of approximately NZ$35 (£18). The government claims this **fund** will be spent on infrastructure and the natural **habitat** of New Zealand's wildlife.

Is this reasonable? Tourists already contribute to the economy by paying for hotels, food and souvenirs. It's not as elitist as charging higher entrance fees to attractions, but it is still enough to put some tourists off.

Some might question if the fee is masking a failure to manage tourism properly. Should governments be responsible for not only attracting tourists, but better ensuring they are able to handle the influx of visitors?

VOCABULARY

Culture and heritage

A Match the words in bold in the articles with the meanings (1–10).

1 ________________ = the type of place where an animal lives or a plant grows
2 ________________ = the parts of a building that remain after it has been damaged
3 ________________ = a large amount of money
4 ________________ = to take care of something and prevent it being damaged
5 ________________ = a place where people live
6 ________________ = relating to the style or design of a building
7 ________________ = to formally choose someone or something for a role or special status
8 ________________ = objects, traditions and beliefs important to a society's history or culture
9 ________________ = to put something at risk of being destroyed or becoming extinct
10 ________________ = to repair or improve a building

B Go to the **Vocabulary Hub** on **page 148**.

C SPEAK Work in pairs and discuss the questions.

1 Are there any habitats where endangered species live in your country?
2 Should your country's government provide a larger fund to preserve cultural sites?
3 How important is architectural style to your country's heritage?

Tackling tourism with tech

Tourism in Amsterdam is booming, with over 14 million visitors a year to enjoy the canals and the mix of **architectural** styles. The Amsterdam tourism board felt limiting tourist numbers was too extreme, so they turned to technology to deal with potential overcrowding.

Many tourists visit the Van Gogh Museum in the morning and take a cruise on the canal in the afternoon. So the tourism board has launched an app providing information on how busy the attractions are and suggesting alternative destinations.

GRAMMAR

Discourse markers

A Choose the correct discourse markers to complete the sentences.

1 A top tourist attraction is the Grand Bazaar in Istanbul ***owing to*** / ***despite*** its spectacular architecture and wide range of stores.
2 The Zócalo in Mexico, another very popular attraction, hosts a large number of events throughout the year. ***Yet*** / ***Moreover***, it is home to the Metropolitan Cathedral and the National Palace.
3 Some of the most popular tourist attractions are in the US – ***as a matter of fact*** / ***namely*** Times Square, Central Park and Union Station.
4 Theme parks are also among the most popular tourist destinations. Walt Disney World in Florida, ***in any case*** / ***for instance***, is a very popular destination.
5 ***Conversely*** / ***Whereas*** several of the world's most popular tourist attractions are in the US, one of the most popular destinations in Europe is Paris.

B Complete the rules with words and phrases in Exercise A.

Discourse markers

1 Use *despite*, ________________ and ________________ to join two clauses. They can come at the beginning of the sentence (followed by a comma) or in between the two clauses.
2 Use *as a matter of fact*, *conversely*, *in any case*, ________________ and ________________ to connect ideas in two sentences.

C Go to the **Grammar Hub** on **page 140**.

D Work in pairs. Make sentences using the prompts below plus a discourse marker.

1 there are some great tourist sites in my city
2 people who live near tourist sites often get angry with tourists
3 tourists have a reputation for bad behavior
4 many cities around the world are eager to attract tourists

SPEAKING

A SPEAK Work in pairs and discuss the questions.

1 How important is tourism to your country?
2 Do you believe tourism is mainly good or bad for a city? Why?

B DISCUSS Work in groups. Try to gain a consensus on question 2 in Exercise A. Use the steps below to help you.

- Get everyone's view.
- Allow speakers time to justify their views.
- Establish agreement: think about ways of doing this fairly.

C PRESENT Present and justify your position to the class.

LISTENING

A SPEAK **Work in pairs and discuss the questions.**

1. What kind of place do you like to work or study in? Why do you like this place?
2. What are your favorite buildings in your city? Why do you like them?

10.1 **B LISTEN FOR GIST** **Listen to the first part of a radio report about building design. Generally speaking, how can the design of a building affect people?**

10.2 **C LISTEN FOR DETAIL** **Listen to the next part of the radio report and note down how these specific features can affect people.**

1. Light: ______
2. Shapes and lines: ______
3. Colors: ______
4. Store facades: ______
5. Spaces between buildings: ______

D SPEAK **Work in pairs and discuss the questions.**

1. What do you think of the different ideas? Do you think they make a difference?
2. Why do you think many buildings don't follow the recommendations discussed in the program?

VOCABULARY

Nouns with *to*

A **Circle the nouns followed by *to* in the extracts from the radio program. Use the information in the box to help you.**

> **Nouns with *to***
>
> Several nouns are often followed by an infinitive. You can remember which ones they are by thinking about the adjective or verb forms of these words – because they are also normally followed by an infinitive, e.g. *Architects normally start with the wish to design innovative buildings.*

1. And if people feel better about their environment, they have a higher inclination to interact positively with the people around them.
2. People have a tendency to be less productive if their desk is more than 7.5 meters away from a window.
3. … whereas plain, monotonous facades make people anxious and give them the urge to hurry past.
4. The project's failings were a reminder for architects to think not just about the look of buildings, but also about how people would interact within the spaces they create.

B **Match the underlined nouns (1–10) with their meanings (a–j).**

1. Most architects have a desire to create beautiful rather than functional buildings. ___
2. Most people in big cities show a reluctance to talk to strangers. ___
3. Governments have an obligation to limit the population of their cities. ___
4. Cities need to be doing a lot more in readiness to deal with swelling populations. ___
5. The refusal of many cities to provide seating in public places is a mistake. ___
6. A failure to learn from environmental psychology will lead to higher crime rates. ___
7. People need frequent reminders to behave considerately in cities. ___
8. Companies have a responsibility to make sure building design has a positive effect on their staff. ___
9. People in cities have a tendency to feel isolated because they are too busy to socialize. ___
10. There should be a greater urge to limit noise and sound pollution in cities. ___

a something that helps you remember something
b an unwillingness
c preparation
d not doing something that you were expected to do
e a wish
f saying that you will not do something
g a strong feeling of wanting or needing to do something
h responsibility
i a habit of behaving in a particular way
j a duty

C **Work in pairs. Do you agree with the sentences in Exercise B?**

D **Work in pairs. Complete the sentences with your own ideas.**

1. Architects have a tendency to …
2. In my city, most people show a reluctance to …
3. Most people have no desire to …
4. Local planners have a responsibility to …

Google Global HQ

PRONUNCIATION
Introducing new information

0.3 **A** **Listen to the extracts from the radio program. Does the pitch of the speaker's voice go up or down on the underlined words?**

1 As the city evolves, its population has swelled to over 21 million, making Beijing one of the most populated cities in the world. <u>And</u> the more people there are, the more challenging it becomes to provide comfortable environments for people to live and work in.

2 They found that people strongly preferred daylight to electric light – and, <u>as a matter of fact</u>, other research has shown that people have a tendency to be less productive if their desk is more than 7.5 meters away from a window.

3 Apparently, people feel more comfortable in places with round shapes and curved lines. <u>On the other hand,</u> straight lines and sharp edges have been shown to create feelings of fear.

4 One interesting study showed that people are more relaxed when they see lively and interesting store facades, <u>whereas</u> plain, monotonous facades make people anxious and give them the urge to hurry past.

B **Work in pairs. Practice saying the sentences. Listen carefully. Did your partner use a higher pitch on the correct word?**

1 Although most people think that living in a city is exciting, it's actually fairly boring for many people.

2 Rather than developing urban areas, we should be developing rural areas.

3 Companies are now embracing ideas from environmental psychology rather than ignoring them.

4 The offices of large companies are being designed to encourage positive feelings in staff. People's homes, however, are much less likely to receive the same attention.

SPEAKING HUB

A **PLAN** Work in small groups. Imagine that your city is holding an election for a new mayor. Make a list of some of the biggest problems about living in your city and brainstorm some solutions to these problems.

B **PREPARE** You support a candidate in the election. Prepare a short speech to try to persuade people to vote for your candidate. You should:

- decide which three problems your candidate will solve
- be ready to explain the problems
- be ready to explain how your candidate will fix them
- make sure that each member of your group has something to say.

C **PRESENT** Give your speeches and listen to the other groups' speeches.

D **DISCUSS** As a class, decide which candidate you want to be mayor.

For me, the best speaker by far was ...
While I liked all the candidates, the one that really stood out was ...

Discuss issues related to tourism
Present solutions to urban problems

10.2 How to change the world

- Talk about political activism
- Discuss how to make a difference

G – ellipsis and substitution V – word building P – managing conversations S – recognizing shifts in register

READING

A SPEAK Work in pairs and discuss the questions.

1 If you were concerned about a local issue, would you contact your local politician about it?

2 Do you think that political activism (e.g. demonstrations or petitions) can make a difference?

B READ FOR MAIN IDEA Read the article *Political activism* and choose the best summary.

1 The younger generation is becoming very active in politics and many are choosing to become politicians so they can make the world a better place.

2 The younger generation is more interested in campaigning for specific causes than getting behind a particular political party.

3 The younger generation is completely uninterested in politics and prefer to focus on their friendships, hobbies and interests.

C READ FOR DETAIL Read the article again and answer the questions.

1 Is the writer part of the younger or older generation?

2 Why is the younger generation disillusioned with the political system?

3 What three issues has the Harry Potter Alliance taken an interest in?

4 What does the writer mean when he says that 'we're moving from a vision of civics that is party-based and partisan to one that's personal and pointillist'?

D SPEAK Work in pairs. Discuss the question. Some people label the kind of political activism described in the article as 'slacktivism'. Do you think this is a fair criticism?

Political activism is as strong as ever, but now it's digital – and passionate

The new generation of digital natives are not apathetic about politics, but they see online campaigns as more effective than lobbying a politician or joining a party.

Like most Americans of my generation – born in 1973 – I learned about civics from television. On Saturday mornings, our childhood diet of cartoons was regularly interrupted for *Schoolhouse Rock*, three-minute animated musical lessons on science, grammar and the workings of government. Today, it's hard to teach civics in three-minute snippets because the way we participate in civic life is changing shape – and changing very quickly. The vision of participatory citizenship that I grew up with – read a newspaper, vote in elections and if you're really incensed, write to your congressional representative – is utterly unpersuasive and unappealing to the students I teach. Digital natives, born and raised in an atmosphere of interactivity, are acutely aware of how insensitive most governments are to participation and how little meaningful interaction they can expect from their elected representatives and other government officials.

This distaste for participation in dysfunctional political systems is easily misread as apathy, leading legislators and educators to declare 'a crisis in civics' as young people participate in elections at a much lower rate than their parents. But that misses a key shift: Digital natives are participating in civic life in ways where they feel they can have an impact and these points of impact are often outside government.

Take the Harry Potter Alliance, a group of teen and twenty-something fans of J.K. Rowling's books and movies, who are organizing online and searching for ways to live out the values of Harry Potter and Dumbledore's Army here in the Muggle world. Their past campaigns have purchased thousands of books for underfunded public libraries and sent planeloads of health supplies for Haitian crisis response. Now they're working to persuade Warner Bros. to buy fair-trade chocolate for the candies sold as tie-ins to the movies, bombarding the company with 'howlers', open, digital letters that demand it consider the ethical concerns of Harry Potter's fans.

VOCABULARY

Word building

A Complete the Example column with words from the article. Use the information in the box to help you.

Word building

We use suffixes to change the form of words. For example, we can add *-ness* to the end of an adjective to turn it into a noun (*ready* becomes *readiness*). Being aware of different suffixes can help you to understand what kind of word is being used.

Suffix	Add to …	to make…	Example
-al	a noun	an adjective	ethical
-ate	a noun	an adjective	
-ic	a noun	an adjective	
-ical	a noun	an adjective	
-ive	a verb	an adjective	
-hood	a noun	a noun	
-ity	an adjective	a noun	
-ship	a noun	a noun	

B Go to the **Vocabulary Hub** on **page 148**.

SPEAKING

DISCUSS Work in small groups. Discuss the questions.

1 What do you think are some of the biggest problems in the world today? Make a list and rank the problems.

2 What could people do to raise awareness of the top three issues on your list? How could people try to get companies, individuals or governments to change their behavior?

3 If a friend of yours wanted to become involved in political activism, would you encourage him or her or dissuade him or her from doing so? Why?

Not every digital native is an engaged, active citizen (and not every young person is a digital native) and not every online campaign has an impact. But it's too easy to dismiss digitally-rooted activism as naive 'slacktivism'. Online activism is having an impact, but it frequently focuses on areas outside formal political participation. Civic participation of the young uses a broad suite of tools to affect a wide range of targets.

Coders write open-source security software in the hope of frustrating NSA surveillance, while community organizers fund neighborhood gardens through Kickstarter. This emergent civics targets governments, corporations, communities and the media. It harnesses social media, crowdfunding, social entrepreneurship and open-source software as well as law and politics, to bring about change.

No wonder it's hard to get our heads around it. We're moving from a vision of civics that's party-based and partisan to one that's personal and pointillist. Parties offer a way to have an opinion (often an ill-informed one) on every issue, while participatory civics centers on issues that people are passionate about. While my generation tends to see the world in terms of issues important to Republicans or Democrats, my students often see the world in terms of the issues their friends care about, a political identity built on the passions of people important to them. This isn't civics in crisis – it's civics in flux, civics that's changing with the people who practice it.

Glossary

dysfunctional (adj) not working normally
howler (n) a silly and embarrassing mistake
incensed (adj) extremely angry
lobby (v) try to influence politicians or people in authority on a particular subject
snippet (n) a small piece of something, especially information or news

LISTENING

A SPEAK Work in pairs. Discuss the questions.

1 What job did you want to do when you were younger?

2 Do you still want to do that job? Why/Why not?

B LISTEN FOR MAIN IDEA Listen to a conversation about finding a job after college. Answer the questions below.

10.4

1 What kind of job was Robin interested in before?

2 What kinds of jobs is Robin thinking about doing now?

C LISTEN FOR DETAIL Listen again and answer the questions.

10.4

1 What made Robin think about pursuing a different career?

2 What does Joanna think about the jobs Robin is thinking of applying for?

3 What advice does Mr. Evans give Robin about finding the job he wants to do?

4 How did the philosophy graduate decide to help people?

5 Does Joanna agree with Mr. Evans' advice?

D LISTEN TO REGISTER Listen to extracts from the conversation. For each, decide if Robin is using formal or informal register. Use the information in the box to help you.

10.5

Recognizing shifts in register

People speak differently in formal and informal/casual situations.

In formal situations, speakers:

- use longer, more complete sentences
- use careful pronunciation
- are less direct
- use formal words and phrases.

In informal/casual situations, speakers use:

- short sentences, contracted forms and often omit words
- less careful pronunciation
- more informal words and phrases (phrasal verbs, vague language and slang).

1 *informal / formal*

2 *informal / formal*

3 *informal / formal*

4 *informal / formal*

5 *informal / formal*

6 *informal / formal*

E SPEAK Work in pairs and discuss the questions.

1 What kind of job do you think Robin should pursue? Why?

2 What do you think about the idea of working in finance to help charities?

3 If you want to donate to charity, what's the best way to choose the charity?

GRAMMAR
Ellipsis and substitution

A Look at the extracts from the conversation. The speakers omitted some words. Complete the sentences with the omitted words.

1 I've just been trying to look over my résumé and ______________ looking for some interesting stuff to apply to.

2 ______________ any idea what you're going to do?

3 You could train to be a teacher or ______________ just volunteer in your spare time.

B Look at the underlined words in the sentences. What words do they replace?

1 **A:** So … you going to work at your dad's company then?
B: Hmm … hope not.

2 If you haven't read it, you should do.

3 **A:** I was thinking about some kind of volunteer work.
B: You should definitely do it.

C Complete the rules using examples in Exercises A and B.

Ellipsis and substitution

Ellipsis means omitting unnecessary words. We can omit:
1 the subject + modal: ______________
2 the subject + auxiliary verb: ______________
3 a verb phrase
4 an adjective: ______________.

In spoken English, it's also common to leave out words if our meaning is obvious from the context. We can omit:
5 the subject
6 the subject + auxiliary verb.

Substitution means avoiding repeating something by using words like:
7 *do*: ______________
8 *not*: ______________
9 *do so / do it / do that*: ______________.

D Go to the Grammar Hub on page 140.

E SPEAK Work in pairs. Cross out the words that can be omitted in these sentences. Then discuss whether you agree or disagree with them.

1 Charity workers should not receive high salaries and they should not get bonuses.

2 Some charity workers are very persistent and I wish they weren't so persistent.

3 Animal charities often receive the most money, but they shouldn't receive the most money.

F Work in pairs. Replace parts of the questions with *do so*, *not* or *so*. Then ask your partner the questions.

1 Would you ever go overseas to do volunteer work? If you went overseas to do volunteer work, where would you go?

2 Do you think having volunteer work on your résumé makes a big difference to recruiters or does it not make a big difference to recruiters?

3 If your company or college allowed you to take a week off to do volunteer work, would you take a week off to do volunteer work?

PRONUNCIATION
Managing conversations

10.6 **A** Listen to extracts from the conversation. For each extract, decide if the intonation on the second speaker's words rises (↗) falls (↘) or rises then falls (↗↘).

1 ___ 2 ___ 3 ___ 4 ___ 5 ___

B SPEAK Work in pairs. Think of an anecdote for one of these topics. Listen to your partner and use appropriate reactions to keep the conversation going.

- some good advice a teacher gave me
- a time I made a difference

SPEAKING HUB

A PREPARE Work in two groups. You are going to role-play an event where charities look for funding. Group A – you are fundraisers for a charity. Decide what type of charity you work for. Group B – you are funding organizations. Decide what types of charities you want to give money to and why.

B PLAN Group A – plan how you will persuade people to support your charity. Group B – think of questions you will ask charities that want your funding.

C PRESENT Talk to students from the other group. Try to persuade them to support your charity or ask them questions about their work.

D REFLECT Who was able to convince the most people to support their charity? Why were they successful?

- Talk about political activism
- Discuss how to make a difference

Café Hub

10.3 Changing cities

A – describing a scene in real-time   S – using vague language

Mexicable

A Work in pairs. Look at the pictures and discuss the questions.

1 What are some of the different uses of cable cars?

2 Are there cable cars in your city or country? How are they used?

B Watch the video. Check (✓) which of the following you see.

1 A man admiring spectacular views from a cable car. ☐

2 A man in a wheelchair going up a ramp. ☐

3 A man in a wheelchair entering a cable car. ☐

4 Tourists taking photos from a cable car. ☐

5 Mechanics repairing an engine. ☐

6 A man wheeling himself along a sidewalk. ☐

C Watch the video again. Complete the sentences with between one and three words.

1 Ade likes the cable car station because there's a wheelchair entrance and ______________.

2 From the cable car, Ade points out a mural of ______________.

3 The cable cars from Stations 1 to 4 are moved by ______________.

4 *Mexicable* connects some of the poorest and ______________ areas of the city.

Glossary

feat (n) something difficult needing a lot of skill, strength, bravery, etc to achieve it

haphazard (adj) done in a way that does not seem to be carefully planned or organized

loop (n) a round shape or curve made by a line curling back toward itself

mural (n) a large painting on the wall of a room or building

D Work in pairs. Try to remember what you heard. What do these numbers and dates refer to? One number isn't mentioned.

1 22 million ______ 5 30,000 ______

2 2016 ______ 6 4 ______

3 6 ______ 7 7 ______

4 26 ______ 8 3 ______

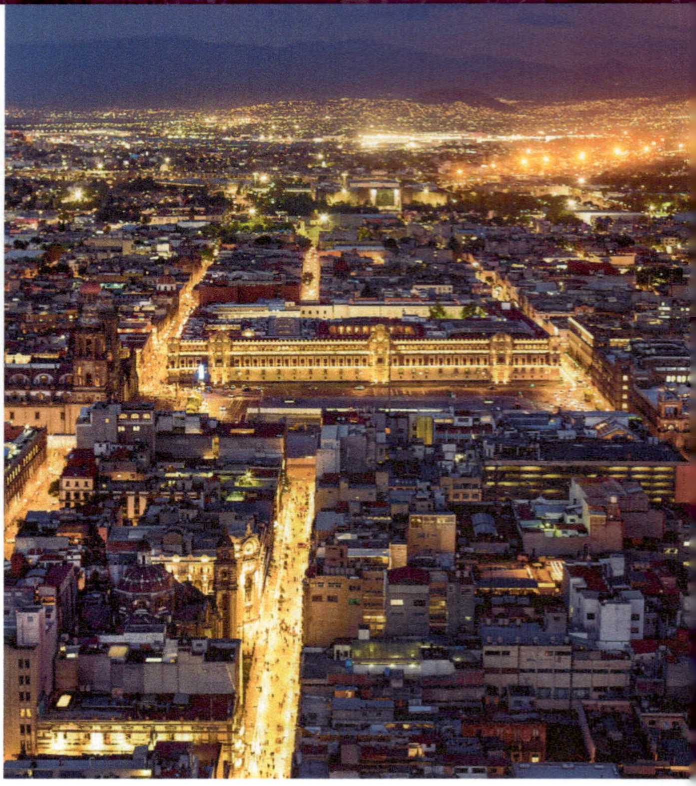

AUTHENTIC ENGLISH

A Work in pairs. Read the sentence from the video and the information in the box. Underline the descriptive words. What do they mean?

The views from the Mexicable – you've got this sprawling city and these murals and the amazing colors on the houses, it's just breathtaking!

Describing a scene in real-time

When we describe a scene in real-time we often use visually descriptive language to bring the scene to life and paint a mental picture in the listener's mind.

B Read the sentences. What is being described in each sentence?

1 There's this sea of golden shifting sand, spectacular dunes and a fierce, burning sun.

2 Just look at the gorgeous lush green meadows and peaceful grazing sheep.

3 I've never seen such deep valleys and magnificent snow-capped peaks.

4 Everywhere you look there are towering skyscrapers, bustling streets and stunning street art.

5 You have these picturesque narrow streets, an enchanting medieval square and beautiful, cozy cottages.

C Work in pairs. Describe a scene to each other using descriptive language. Student A – go to the Communication Hub on page 152. Student B – go to the Communication Hub on page 155.

Everything's changing

SAM MALCOLM AMANDA HARRY EMILY

A Work in pairs. Discuss the questions.

1 What developments are happening where you live?
2 Are the developments positive or negative? Why?

B Watch the video. Does everybody have a similar opinion about the new cable car?

C Watch the video again. Answer the following questions.

1 Why is parking and traffic worse according to Emily?
2 What is being built over the river?
3 What does Malcolm say will happen to the area soon?
4 How much would it cost Emily to rent a bigger office?
5 Why is Harry looking forward to the cable car?
6 What improvements have there been to the area according to Amanda?
7 How was Sam able to set up his café according to Harry?

SPEAKING SKILL

A Work in pairs. Look at the extracts from the video. Why have the speakers used the underlined phrases?

Amanda: Also, the area was quite run down with high unemployment and <u>all the rest of it</u>.
Malcolm: I had to park all the way over on <u>whatsitsname</u> and walk here.

B Read the information in the box. Underline the vague language in the sentences from the video.

Using vague language

We often use vague words when we can't find the exact expression we need.

a List completers – when someone is unable to complete everything on a list.
b Placeholders – a speaker cannot remember something.
c Evasion – not wanting to say something exactly.
d Quantities – when we're not sure of the exact figure.

1 It doesn't help either that they're building that thingy over the river.
2 I hardly recognize the neighborhood any more with all the new shops, the road system and stuff like that.
3 It was two thousand odd pounds for the month.
4 Well, yeah, sort of … it is convenient … but if I can't afford to stay in the area they won't be much good to me.
5 It will also encourage tourism and who knows what else.
6 Crime in the area is down about 20% in the past four years.

C Work in pairs. Match the examples (1–6) from the video with the functions (a–d) in the box.

SPEAKING HUB

A PREPARE You are going to debate the following motion. Decide who in the class will be *for* and *against* the motion.

All vehicles should be banned from city centers.

B PLAN In your groups, write notes for your side of the argument. Think about:

- environment
- public transportation
- convenience
- cost

C PRESENT Join together with the other group and hold a debate.

Without cars you could have more public spaces, street cafés and all the rest of it.

D REFLECT Hold a vote on whether you agree or disagree with the motion.

Debate for and against a motion

➤ Turn to page 165 to learn how to write a persuasive essay about living in the city or country.

Unit 10 Review

VOCABULARY

A Complete the article with the words in the box.

architectural designated endangered fund habitat heritage preserve refurbish ruins settlement

UNESCO

World Heritage Sites

The goal of the World [1]______ list is to help countries [2]______ sites of 'outstanding universal value'. To be [3]______ as a World Heritage site, a place must meet one of ten criteria, such as being an [4]______ masterpiece, a human [5]______ or the [6]______ of one representative of a particular culture, a place of exceptional natural beauty, or a place that is the natural [7]______ of an [8]______ species.

Once a site is selected for the list, the World Heritage [9]______ can provide money to protect or [10]______ the site – and being on the list usually provides a significant boost to the number of tourists visiting the site.

B Choose the correct words to complete the sentences.

1. Architects have ***an urge*** / ***a responsibility*** to provide people with enough daylight.
2. People have a ***reluctance*** / ***tendency*** to be less productive if there is background noise.
3. The government needs frequent ***desires*** / ***reminders*** to tackle the problem of air pollution.
4. The government's ***readiness*** / ***refusal*** to invest in rural areas has led to overcrowding in cities.
5. Architects have ***a failure*** / ***an obligation*** to talk to the people who will use a building before they design it.

C Choose the correct words to complete the sentences.

1. Young people don't like politics because it is too ***formal*** / ***formality***.
2. People often vote for the person with the strongest ***personal*** / ***personality*** rather than the best plans.
3. The ***public*** / ***publicity*** should have a vote on major political decisions.
4. Social media enables much easier ***interactive*** / ***interactivity*** with politicians.
5. Politicians' ***personal*** / ***personality*** lives should remain private.
6. People who don't vote have let down their ***communal*** / ***community***.

GRAMMAR

A Complete the article with the words or phrases in the box. There are five you do not need to use.

as a matter of fact conversely despite for instance in any case moreover namely owing to whereas yet

Tourism

Cycle Model

Tourist sites go through similar stages as they grow. First of all, adventurous tourists start coming to a place. [1]______ this interest, local people set up businesses to cater for tourists. They open hotels and restaurants, [2]______. After that, larger companies start to invest in the area – [3]______, by building large hotels and catering to large groups. The tourism industry begins to dominate the area, while, [4]______, other industries begin to shrink. As the number of visitors increases, the area becomes less attractive and visitors begin to go elsewhere. [5]______, the facilities begin to become dated and damaged. If there is no further investment, the area will go into decline.

B Match numbers (1–6) to letters (a–f) to form full sentences.

1. It's better to give money to a charity than
2. You should donate clothes or
3. Some charities are really wasteful with their donations
4. If a friend asks you to donate to a charity,
5. Some people are really good at volunteer work,
6. It's a good idea to choose one or two charities to support

a volunteer your time rather than give money.
b and when you do, you can give bigger donations.
c you should do so.
d to an individual.
e and I wish they weren't.
f but I'm not.

Irregular Verbs

Base form	Simple past	Past participle
be	was/were	been
become	became	become
begin	began	begun
break	broke	broken
bring	brought	brought
build	built	built
buy	bought	bought
can	could	(been able to)
catch	caught	caught
choose	chose	chosen
come	came	come
cost	cost	cost
cut	cut	cut
do	did	done
drink	drank	drunk
eat	ate	eaten
fall	fell	fallen
feel	felt	felt
find	found	found
forget	forgot	forgotten
get	got	got
give	gave	given
go	went	gone/been
grow	grew	grown
have	had	had
hear	heard	heard
hit	hit	hit
hold	held	held
hurt	hurt	hurt
keep	kept	kept
know	knew	known
leave	left	left
lend	lent	lent

Base form	Simple past	Past participle
let	let	let
lose	lost	lost
make	made	made
mean	meant	meant
meet	met	met
must	had to	(had to)
pay	paid	paid
put	put	put
read	read	read
ride	rode	ridden
run	ran	run
say	said	said
see	saw	seen
sell	sold	sold
set	set	set
shut	shut	shut
sing	sang	sung
sit	sat	sat
sleep	slept	slept
speak	spoke	spoken
spell	spelled	spelled
spend	spent	spent
stand	stood	stood
steal	stole	stolen
take	took	taken
teach	taught	taught
tell	told	told
think	thought	thought
throw	threw	thrown
understand	understood	understood
wear	wore	worn
win	won	won
write	wrote	written

PHONETIC SYMBOLS											
Single vowels			Diphthongs			Consonants					
/ɪ/	f**i**sh	/fɪʃ/	/uw/	n**ew**	/nuw/	/p/	**p**en	/pen/	/s/	**s**nake	/sneɪk/
/iː/	b**ea**n	/biːn/	/eɪ/	f**a**ce	/feɪs/	/b/	**b**ag	/bæg/	/z/	**z**oo	/zuː/
/ʊ/	f**oo**t	/fʊt/	/ɔɪ/	b**oy**	/bɔɪ/	/t/	**t**ea	/tiː/	/ʃ/	**sh**op	/ʃɒp/
/uː/	sh**oe**	/ʃuː/	/oʊ/	n**o**se	/noʊz/	/d/	**d**og	/dɒg/	/ʒ/	televi**si**on	/ˈtelɪvɪʒən/
/e/	**e**gg	/eg/	/ju/	**u**se	/juz/	/ʧ/	**ch**ip	/ʧɪp/	/m/	**m**ap	/mæp/
/ə/	moth**er**	/ˈmʌðər/	/aɪ/	**eye**	/aɪ/	/ʤ/	**j**azz	/ʤæz/	/n/	**n**ame	/neɪm/
/ɜː/	w**o**rd	/wɜːrd/	/aʊ/	m**ou**th	/maʊθ/	/k/	**c**ake	/keɪk/	/ŋ/	ri**ng**	/rɪŋ/
/ɔː/	t**al**k	/tɔːk/				/g/	**g**irl	/gɜːrl/	/h/	**h**ouse	/haʊs/
/æ/	b**ack**	/bæk/				/f/	**f**ilm	/fɪlm/	/l/	**l**eg	/leg/
/ʌ/	b**u**s	/bʌs/				/v/	**v**erb	/vɜːrb/	/r/	**r**oad	/roʊd/
/ɑː/	**ar**m	/ɑːrm/				/θ/	**th**ing	/θɪŋ/	/w/	**w**ant	/wɔnt/
/ɒ/	t**o**p	/tɒp/				/ð/	**th**ese	/ðiːz/	/j/	**y**es	/jes/

Grammar Hub

1.1 Nominal clauses

- Nominal clauses function like nouns. They can be used as the subject or object of a sentence, after a preposition, an adjective or the verb *to be*.
- Nominal *-ing* clause (also known as a 'participle clause'):

  Wearing a uniform *can help people feel part of the team. (as subject)*

  I don't enjoy ***wearing formal clothes****. (as object)*

  I'm excited about ***buying some new outfits****. (after a preposition)*
- Nominal *that* clause:

  That she won again this year *is not surprising. (as subject: this use is rare)*

  I explained ***that she would have to buy a new outfit****. (as object)*

  I'm worried ***that I won't fit in****. (after an adjective)*
- Nominal question clause:

  What you wear *is entirely up to you. (as subject)*

  My appearance certainly affects ***how I feel****. (as object)*

  Fiona felt embarrassed because of ***how she looked****. (after a preposition)*
- Nominal infinitive:

  To spend so much money on clothes *is totally unnecessary. (as subject: this use is rare)*

  It's a good idea ***to wear dress clothes for an interview****. (as object)*

  I was surprised ***to learn about the dress code****. (after an adjective)*
- We frequently use phrases like *The fact/idea that …* or *The experience/problem of …* to introduce a nominal clause.

  The fact that you got a high grade shows how hard you worked.

  The experience of traveling on the Orient Express was one she would never forget.

Be careful!

- Because *that* clauses and infinitive clauses can sometimes sound unnatural as subjects, we usually use *it* as an empty subject.

  It doesn't surprise me that you hate shopping.

  NOT ~~That you hate shopping doesn't surprise me.~~

1.2 Comparatives and superlatives

- We only use *than* after comparative adjectives and adverbs when it is followed by the thing we are comparing it with.

  CDs are ***more expensive than*** *they used to be.*

Be careful!

CDs are only fractionally more expensive today. NOT ~~CDs are only fractionally more expensive than today.~~

- We don't put *the* before a superlative when we use a determiner.

  Here's our ***cheapest*** *smartphone.*

  NOT ~~Here's our the cheapest smartphone.~~
- To compare things that are the same, we can use *as* + adjective/adverb + *as* …

  Dance music is ***as popular as*** *it ever was.*
- We leave out the second + *as* when the adjective/adverb isn't followed by the thing we're comparing it with.

  None of our audiences have been as large!

  NOT ~~None of our audiences have been as large as!~~
- We can use *the … the* with comparatives to show that two changes are closely connected. As one thing changes, it makes the other thing change.

  The *cheaper* ***the*** *technology, the worse quality it is.*

  The *bigger,* ***the*** *better!*
- We can use the structure *more than* with a small number of verbs (*compensate for, double, fulfill, make up for, meet*)

  His enthusiasm and intelligence more than compensated for his lack of experience.
- To show that there is a big difference between two things we can use one of these modifiers before the comparative adjective: *a good/great deal, a lot, considerably, dramatically, far, significantly, much.*

  The new building is ***considerably*** *bigger than the old one.*
- To show that there is a small difference, we use these words and phrases before the comparative adjective: *a little, a fraction, fractionally, marginally, rather, slightly, somewhat.*

  The first movie was ***fractionally*** *longer than the sequel.*
- We can modify superlative adjectives using: *by far, far and away, easily, the very.*

  Tom is ***by far*** *the smartest boy in the class.*

  Tom is the smartest boy ***by far****.*
- We can also make a superlative stronger by inserting *possible* after the superlative and before the noun.

  The shopping mall was built in the best ***possible*** *location.*
- We can also use modifiers before the structure *as … as*: *almost, at least, easily, every bit, half, just, twice.*

  My old phone was every bit ***as good as*** *this new one.*

1.1 Nominal clauses

A Correct the mistakes in each sentence.

1 It's an unwritten rule what employees must stick to the dress code.
2 The fact of you wear a uniform sends a certain message about your status.
3 You'll regret not to wear nicer clothes to yesterday's interview.
4 David insisted on that he pay for all the designer clothes I'd chosen!
5 The reason for Sarah's absence that she never received her invitation.
6 That I had forgotten was that the restaurant only lets in nicely dressed customers.
7 The clothing company more than double its annual profits.
8 Sandra always wants to buy clothes at the possible lowest price.

B Choose the correct options to complete the conversation.

Joey: I'm really eager [1]***to start / about starting*** my new job next week.
Phoebe: I'm sure [2]***you to / that you will*** fit in really well.
Joey: They explained [3]***that they have / having*** a dress code there. So … [4]***that I buy / buying*** a business suit is my first priority! Will you come and help me choose one?
Phoebe: Of course. I think you should be prepared [5]***to spend / that you spend*** a lot of money.
Joey: What do you mean?
Phoebe: You must know [6]***that / the fact*** an expensive suit will last longer than a cheap one?
Joey: Oh, I see [7]***what / that*** you mean. OK. But [8]***I'm needing to know / what I really need to know*** is what color to choose!

C Complete the second sentence so that it has a similar meaning to the first sentence, using the word given. Write between two and five words.

1 That designer clothes are hugely expensive is well-known.
FACT
_______________ designer clothes are hugely expensive is well-known.
2 It's none of my business what he does in his free time.
SPENDS
_______________ his free time is none of my business.
3 The purchase of expensive school uniforms is a problem which many parents face.
OF
Many parents face _______________ _______________ expensive school uniforms.

➤ Go back to page 3.

1.2 Comparatives and superlatives

A Choose the correct options to complete the sentences.

1 Thank goodness I have tech-savvy friends like you – you're _______________.
a the best b the best friend
2 I think we need to replace our company logo with something _______________.
a funkier than b funkier
3 Winning the Young Tech Designer of the Year was _______________ _______________ moment!
a the my proudest b my proudest
4 Your handwriting is _______________ Carol. Well done!
a the neatest handwriting b the neatest
5 We've redesigned our website so that it's _______________.
a more user-friendly b user-friendlier
6 CDs weren't around for very long, and CD burners disappeared almost _______________.
a as quickly b as quickly as

B Write one word in each blank to complete the sentences.

1 My sister is a great _______ more concerned about appearances than I am.
2 A tailored jacket is _______ and away the most important item of clothing in your closet.
3 I dress _______ fraction more informally on Fridays, but I don't feel comfortable in casual clothes.
4 In my opinion, having the right image is every _______ as important as saying the right thing.
5 Chelsea only ever buys the _______ best in terms of clothing and accessories.

C Complete the sentences using a word from the box and your own ideas.

considerably	half	marginally	twice

1 The green dress costs $25. The blue dress costs $27.
The blue dress costs _______________ _______________.
2 My sister is a fashion vlogger and earns ten times more than I do!
My sister earns _______________ _______________.
3 We were expecting 100 people at the fashion show, but only 50 came.
Only _______________ we expected came to the fashion show.
4 I believe that you have to do double the work of others to be sure of success.
I believe that you have to work _______________.

➤ Go back to page 7.

Grammar Hub

2.1 Narrative tenses

	Active Voice	Passive Voice
Simple past	**I realized** it was a great idea.	**We were given** a month to finish the job.
Past progressive	**We were hoping** for a better result.	**The plans were being drawn up** at the time.
Past perfect	**They had already bought** the site.	**The architects had been chosen.**
Past perfect progressive	**We had been walking** for hours.	

- We use the simple past in a story or narrative to explain the main events.

  *We **met** on Saturday, outside Victoria train station.*
- We use the past progressive to describe the background to a story, actions in progress at a particular point or together with the simple past, to describe actions or situations that were interrupted by shorter events.

  *The sun was shining when Amy **left** the house.*
- We use the past perfect to show that one event happened before the other.

  *He **had waited** for over an hour by the time she finally arrived.*
- We usually use the past perfect progressive together with the simple past, for actions that were in progress before another action in the past.

  *I **had been working** all day so I **decided** not to go out that night.*
- We can use the simple past with *did* + base form for emphasis.

  *He **did** look very anxious when he left.*

Be careful!

- We don't usually use the passive voice form of past perfect progressive.

  Someone had been watching us. NOT ~~We had been being watched.~~

2.2 Future in the past

	Future in the past
Past progressive	We **were traveling** to Australia the next day.
was/were going to	Sam **was going to start** looking for another job.
would + base form	I thought it **would be** nice to take a gift.
was/were + infinitive	Jody **was to contact** me as soon as her plane landed.
was/were + perfect infinitive	Jody **was to have contacted** me as soon as her plane landed.
was/were about to + base form	We **were about to leave** the house when the phone rang.

- When we are talking about the past, we sometimes need to talk about things that had not yet happened. We can use the past progressive or *was/were going to* for this.

  *When I saw her, she **was leaving** the next day.*

  *Jim **was going to** meet Mary that evening.*
- We can use the past form of *will* (*would*).

  *That discovery **would turn** out to be important later on.*
- We can also use past forms of the verb *be* with the infinitive or the perfect infinitive. The infinitive can be used for events that came true or didn't come true.

  *He **was to deliver** the report on Tuesday. (And he did.)*

  *He **was to deliver** the report on Tuesday. (But he failed.)*

  The perfect infinitive is usually only used for events that didn't come true.

  *He **was to have delivered** the report on Tuesday. (But he failed.)*
- We can also use past forms of *be* + *supposed to* + base form or perfect infinitive. These are often, but not always, used for events that didn't come true.

  *He **was supposed to have delivered** the report on Tuesday. (But he failed.)*

  *He **wasn't supposed to look** at the files. (But he did anyway.)*
- To describe something that was going to happen soon, we use the past form of the verb *be* with the word *about*. Sometimes we add the word *just*.

  *She had her coat on because she **was (just) about to take** the dog for a walk.*

Be careful!

- You may need to make other changes to pronouns, times, places, etc, in the same way as you do in reported speech.

  Anna was leaving for Canada the following day. NOT ~~Anna was leaving for Canada tomorrow.~~

2.1 Narrative tenses

A Choose the option in each sentence that is NOT correct.

1 I ___ what he meant.
 a had finally been understanding
 b finally understood
 c had finally understood
2 ___ to wait in the reception area.
 a They told me
 b I was telling
 c I was told
3 Jim had been swimming earlier and his hair ___ wet.
 a was
 b had got
 c was getting
4 Angie was shocked by what she ___ at the film festival.
 a had seen
 b saw
 c has seen
5 He had gotten the job but he ___ the starting date.
 a hadn't been being told
 b wasn't told
 c hadn't been told
6 It was a terrible day and it ___ heavily.
 a was raining
 b had been raining
 c had been rained

B Correct the underlined mistakes. Sometimes more than one answer is possible.

1 I realized I left my money at home.
2 When I looked out of the window, I saw that it rained.
3 I did to realize that I had forgotten my keys before I left.
4 Janine changed her mind about the theater but it was too late as I already bought the tickets.
5 We arrived a little early and we told to wait until the manager was free.
6 Greg went to see the doctor because he wasn't being feeling well.
7 As soon as we had finished the discussion, we had left.

C Complete each sentence with the correct form of the verb in parentheses, active voice or passive voice. Sometimes more than one answer is possible.

1 I was angry because ______________ (*I / keep*) waiting for an hour.
2 The sun was shining and the birds ______________ (*sing*) in the trees.
3 The reason I was tired was that I ______________ (*have to / walk*) all the way home.
4 We ______________ (*only / work*) on the project for a week when it was canceled.
5 Pete ______________ (*not / tell*) about the change of plans so he knew nothing.
6 We couldn't use the living room because it ______________ (*decorate*).

➤ Go back to page 17.

2.2 Future in the past

A Choose the correct options to complete the sentences.

1 I couldn't go to the party because I ***would take*** / ***was taking*** a test the next day.
2 When we were at school together, he was ***becoming*** / ***going to become*** a doctor.
3 They thought it ***will*** / ***would*** be fun to play a trick on us.
4 Our new TV was to have been ***delivered*** / ***delivering*** yesterday but it didn't come.
5 I was ***about*** / ***about to*** ask him where he got the money when he made an excuse and left.
6 When the movie was released, few people thought it ***would be*** / ***was being*** a success.
7 The fingerprints found at the scene of the crime ***were being*** / ***were to be*** vital in solving it.
8 Thinking there was no way he ***was going*** / ***would*** to get into college, he didn't even apply.

B Write one word in each blank to complete the sentences.

1 Sonja ______________ about to get on the train when she realized she'd left her ticket at home.
2 Philippe couldn't believe he was actually ______________ to graduate in three weeks' time.
3 We all knew it ______________ be fun to enter the competition.
4 Both girls truly believed they ______________ going to be famous one day.
5 At that point it dawned on me that London ______________ to be my new home.
6 Marie was ______________ about to give in her report when she spotted the mistake.

➤ Go back to page 21.

Grammar Hub

3.1 Future structures

- We can use a variety of grammatical forms to express the future, such as future forms with *will*, the simple present, the present progressive and *be going to*.

  They'll plant some more trees over the next few weeks.
  When does the presentation begin?
  I'm going to install solar panels on my roof.

- We use the future progressive (*will be* + *-ing*) to describe a situation that will be in progress at a particular point in the future.

  Scientists will be making an important announcement at 3 pm.

- We use the future perfect (*will have* + past participle) to describe changes that will be completed before a particular point in the future.

  He will have fixed the air-conditioning by the end of the day.

- We can use the future perfect with adverbs in the middle position after *will*.

  *Pollution in our city will **surely** have impacted quality of life by the end of the next decade.*

- We use the future perfect progressive (*will have been* + *-ing*) to focus on the future results of an earlier future process, and/or to measure the length of time of that process.

  The crew will have been tearing down the old factory for twelve weeks by the end of June.

Be careful!

- We usually don't use *will* after words which signal conditional sentences such as *if, unless, when, while.* So we use present progressive instead of future progressive, and present perfect instead of future perfect.

  She'll be hanging up flyers while I'm meeting with the council. NOT ~~*She'll be hanging up flyers while I'll be meeting with the council.*~~

- We can use a modal verb such as *may*, *might* or *could* instead of *will* in these future structures to express possibility.

  They'll be switching to renewable energy soon. (= definitely)
  They could be switching to renewable energy soon. (= it's possible)

- We also use phrases such as *be on the verge of* + *-ing*, *be on the brink of* + *-ing*, *be due to* + base form, *be set to* + base form, and *be about to* + base form to refer to the future.

  *Danielle **was on the verge of achieving** her goal.*

3.2 Negative inversion

- We use negative inversion when we want to emphasize a negative element of a sentence. We place the negative element at the beginning and we invert (= swap over) the subject and auxiliary verb.

  *I have never seen such waste in my life. = **Never have I seen** such waste in my life.*
  *I'm not saying we need to leave now. = **By no means am I saying** we need to leave now.*
  ***No way could I ever drive** a gas-powered car again.*

- We add *do*, *does* or *did* in inverted clauses when there is no auxiliary verb.

  *She never received an apology. = Never **did** she receive an apology.*

- We use *than* after the phrase *no sooner*.

  *No sooner had she written the document **than** her computer crashed.*

- Inversion is often used with the structure *not only … but also*.

  Not only did I meet the mayor, but I also met the governor.

- Some words and phrases change in inversions, and negative verbs become positive.

  ***Nobody** told me about that once. → Not once did **anybody** tell me about that.*
  *You **must not** say that under **any** circumstances. → Under **no** circumstances **must** you say that.*
  ***That's not** the only solution by **any** means. → By **no** means **is that** the only solution.*

- There are also some inversions which do not contain negative words and phrases. These include sentences which start with *only* for time expressions, such as *Only after*, *Only when*, *Only once*, *Only if*, *Only by*, *Only rarely*, and *Rarely*, *Hardly* and *Barely*.

  Only by reading the instructions three times did I understand what to do.

Be careful!

- With some inversions, such as *No sooner … than*, *Not only*, *Hardly*, etc, it's the first verb and the subject which inverts.

  *Not only **was he late**, he was also unprepared.*
  *Hardly **had we sat down** when the fire alarm went off.*

- With other inversions, such as *Only after*, *Not until*, etc, it's the verb in the main clause which inverts.

  *Only after I'd arrived **did I realize** I'd gotten the day wrong.*
  *Not until he'd spent hours online **did he find** a suitable photo.*

- We don't use inversion when the negative word or phrase is the subject.

  None of my colleagues take public transportation. NOT ~~*None of my colleagues do take public transportation.*~~

- The verb and subject invert after *neither* and *nor*.

  *None of their staff knew the answer, and **neither did we**.*
  *I haven't told anyone, and **nor has Jake**.*

3.1 Future structures

A Match the statements (1–7) with their purposes (a–g).

1 We're going to build a zero-emissions home. ___
2 I'll call the manager, if you like. ___
3 I think you'll be famous someday! ___
4 When are they going to close down that factory? ___
5 The talk begins at 10 am. ___
6 I think I'll just take the bus instead. ___
7 With all these clouds, it's going to rain very soon! ___

a making a prediction from strong evidence
b explaining plans
c talking about a fixed scheduled event
d making a prediction based on opinion more than evidence
e making an offer
f asking about plans
g making a decision while speaking

B Choose the correct options to complete the sentences.

1 We'll *be testing* / *have tested* the new equipment for a few hours tomorrow.
2 They'll have *been laying* / *laid* the foundation by the end of next week.
3 I'll *be meeting* / *have met* Jim later today, if you'd like to join us.
4 Will you have *be working* / *been working* with the company for very long when you retire?
5 The company will have *built* / *been building* two new hotels by the end of the year.
6 They won't *have taken* / *be taking* questions from the audience after the talk.
7 By the time she finishes the marathon, Kayla will have *jogged* / *been jogging* for six hours.
8 He'll probably still be working unless he *decides* / *will decide* to leave it for next week.

C Complete the second sentence so that it has a similar meaning to the first sentence. Use between two and five words, including the word in bold.

1 Thirty minutes from now, the meeting will conclude. **DUE**
The meeting ______________________ conclude in half an hour.
2 The scientists will make the discovery any day now. **VERGE**
The scientists are ______________________ the discovery.
3 In less than a minute, the rocket will launch. **ABOUT**
The rocket ______________________ launched.
4 The two companies are close to sealing the deal. **BRINK**
The two companies ______________________ sealing the deal.
5 By the end of the year, the agreement will have expired. **SET**
The agreement is ______________________ by year's end.
6 I'll be collecting samples and she'll be recording them. **WHILE**
She'll be recording samples ______________________ them.

➤ Go back to page 26.

3.2 Negative inversion

A Rewrite the sentences (1–6) using inversion and the words given.

1 Nobody asked me if I passed my driving test.
Not once ____.
2 I'd just arrived home when they called me back to the office.
No sooner ____.
3 We seldom see players with such natural ability.
Rarely ____.
4 He is really smart and incredibly funny.
Not only ____.
5 Tina realized her purse had been stolen when she went to pay her bill.
Only when ____.
6 You must not open that door.
Under no circumstances ____.

B Write one word in each blank.

Anna was in charge of organizing her company's annual conference. She had met the manager a week before to make the plans, and no [1] ______________ had they sat down to talk than the manager was called away. She waited forty-five minutes, and [2] ______________ until she got up to leave did the manager re-appear. On the day of the conference, [3] ______________ no means did everything go according to plan. Not [4] ______________ was the turnout low, but she [5] ______________ had trouble with the conference venue. [6] ______________ in a million years would she have thought things could go so wrong.

➤ Go back to page 31.

Grammar Hub

4.1 Conditionals without *if*

We can use inversions to replace the word *if* in some conditional sentences.

- In first conditional sentences, we can use *should* to replace *if*.

  __Should__ you have any questions, please don't hesitate to call. (= If you have … OR If you should have …)
- In second conditional sentences, we can use *were* to replace *if*.

  __Were__ it banned, there would be an outcry. (= If it were banned…)

  __Were__ I to do the quiz, I'm sure I would win! (= If I were to do …)
- In third conditional sentences, we can use *had* to replace *if*. This use of inversion is more common in formal language.

  Had he used a brain training game, he would have remembered more. (= If he had used …)
- We can also sometimes use verbs, *-ing*, past participles and the imperative in place of *if*.

Imagine / Suppose (that)	**Suppose** (that) I had a chip in my brain, would I be smarter?
Assuming / Supposing / Presuming / Providing (that)	**Assuming** (that) you complete the experiment, will you have all the data? **Providing** (that) we didn't make any mistakes, the results should be correct.
Provided (that)	**Provided** (that) you believe in yourself, you will definitely succeed.
Imperative … , and	**Read** more books, **and** you will improve your memory.

Be careful!

- With the imperative and *Imagine/Suppose (that)*, you cannot swap the clauses around.

  Imagine you were offered a brain implant, would you want it?

  NOT ~~Would you want a brain implant imagine you were offered it?~~

4.2 Wishes and regrets

wish / if only + simple past/progressive	to wish that the present was different	**I wish / If only I didn't blush** so easily.
wish / if only + could/would		**I wish / If only I could stop** stammering. **I wish / If only you would speak** more clearly.
wish / if only + past perfect simple/progressive	to wish that the past was different	**I wish / If only I had participated** in the study.
wish / if only + could have + past participle		**I wish / If only I could have participated** in the study.
ought (not) to / should (not) have + past participle *ought (not) to / should (not) have been + -ing*		**I shouldn't have gazed** at the floor all the time!

- *If only* often sounds more dramatic or emphatic than *wish*. It can be used about other people, but usually suggests the speaker's opinion.

  __If only__ David had known the answer! (= I wish David had known the answer!)
- To be more formal, we use *were* instead of *was* after *I/he/she/it*.

  If only I __were__ more confident.

  He wishes he __were__ more confident.
- When you want to talk about your own wishes, use *could* instead of *would*.

  I wish I __could__ speak Chinese. NOT ~~I wish I would speak Chinese.~~
- We can also use *ought to have* + past participle to talk about things that were ideal or desired in the past.

  They __ought to have managed__ the meeting better.
- We can use *would love to have* + past participle to talk about regrets.

  I __would love to have had__ enough time to explain my views. (= I didn't have enough time and that's a shame.)
- We can also use *if* + past perfect simple + modal verbs (subordinate clause) and modal verb + *have* + past participle to talk about imagined situations in the past with regret.

  I __could have learned__ more, __if I had prepared__ for the classes.

4.1 Conditionals without *if*

A Complete each second sentence so it means the same as the one before it.

1 If I had dropped my coffee on her carpet, I would have felt embarrassed!
Had ______________________________, I would have felt embarrassed!

2 If brain implants were available to everyone, I would definitely get one!
Should ______________________________, I would definitely get one!

3 If you practiced Sudoku puzzles more, you would get better at them.
Were ______________________________, you would get better at them.

4 If you become dizzy after taking the medication, please contact your doctor.
Should ______________________________, please contact your doctor.

B Choose the correct options to complete the sentences.

1 *Imagine / Imagining* that you met Elon Musk, what would you say to him?

2 *Suppose / Providing* that we didn't make any errors during the experiment, the data should be correct.

3 *Look / Suppose we look* at the problem from a different angle, we might be able to find a solution.

4 *Imagine / Assuming* that she told us the truth, I think we can conclude that she's innocent.

5 *Supposing / Provided* all the participants had been men, would that have made a difference to the results?

6 *Conducting / Conduct* more research, and you will have a clearer picture.

C Complete the sentences with the correct form of the verbs in parentheses.

1 ________________ (*act*) confidently, and you will never again feel embarrassed.

2 Suppose you ________________ (*arrive*) late for an exam, what would you do?

3 Provided that you think before you speak, you ________________ (*not say*) anything silly.

4 Were I ________________ (*say*) the wrong thing, I would apologize.

5 Assuming you ________________ (*prove*) he was cheating, would you tell the examiner?

6 Should AI become a reality, we ________________ (*need*) to improve human intelligence.

7 ________________ (*I know*) that the research was unethical, I would never have taken part in it.

8 Unless the government ________________ (*increase*) funding for the program, the researchers will never be able to complete their study.

➤ Go back to page 41.

4.2 Wishes and regrets

A Choose the correct options to complete the sentences.

1 I wish I had made a better first impression. = I ***made / didn't make*** a good impression.

2 I wish I could understand what the lecturer was saying. = I ***understand / don't understand***.

3 You shouldn't have been so clumsy! = You ***were / weren't*** clumsy.

4 Helena wishes her new boss was more friendly. = Her new boss ***is / isn't*** friendly.

5 I would love to have taken part in the experiment. = I ***took / didn't take*** part.

6 You ought not to have worn that eccentric outfit. = You ***wore / didn't wear*** an eccentric outfit.

7 If only I didn't feel so socially awkward. = I ***feel / don't feel*** socially awkward.

8 If only he could express himself more clearly. = He ***is / isn't*** able to express himself clearly.

B Complete the sentences with the correct form of the verbs in parentheses.

1 I wish I ________________ (*prepare*) more thoroughly for my interview yesterday.

2 If only I ________________ (*know*) whether or not I got the job!

3 I wish I ________________ (*can / get*) her autograph but I wasn't brave enough.

4 If only I ________________ (*not / say*) that I'm disorganized!

5 I wish I ________________ (*can / think*) clearly under pressure but I get so stressed.

6 I wish I ________________ (*not / have to*) go through job interviews!

C Correct the mistakes in each sentence.

1 You shouldn't have copy your essay from the internet.

2 The girls wish they was on vacation.

3 You could had told me the truth – I would have believed you!

4 I would love to had taken part in the research.

5 The scientists ought to have make their findings public.

6 Gemma doesn't wish she was so shy.

7 If only I hadn't get embarrassed with new people.

8 I could have done better, if I haven't been so nervous.

➤ Go back to page 43.

Grammar Hub

5.1 The passive voice

	Passive voice
make sb do sth	We **were made to wait** for over an hour.
Passive voice with *-ing*	I hate **being kept** waiting.
Passive voice with infinitive	He would like **to be given** the chance to retake the test.
get passive voice (informal)	They **got thrown** off the course.
Causative *have* and *get*	I need to **have** my phone **serviced.**

- Remember that we use the passive voice when we don't say who or what causes the action (usually because the person or thing is not known, not important or not obvious).

  *We **were made to take** the exam again. NOT ~~We were made by the examination board to take the exam again.~~*
- We use *by* when we know who does/did an action and we want to mention it.

  *I don't mind being told **by my boss** to work late but I don't like it when I have to cover for other people.*
- We can use an infinitive or *-ing* passive voice form, depending on the verb or construction that comes before it. Some verbs can be followed by an infinitive or *-ing* with no or little change in meaning. Prepositions are always followed by *-ing*.

  *We arranged **to be** paid in cash.*
  *I appreciated **being** told about the delay.*
  *The child loved **to be / being** thrown up in the air.*
  *Johnny never talks about **being** thrown out of college.*
- We use the causative (in any tense) when someone does something for us, or when we are victims of a crime or accident. The causative with *have* is more formal than the causative with *get*.

  *I **got** my hair cut. OR I **had** my wallet stolen on the train.*
- We can use *get* + object + past participle when we talk about causing something to happen or be done by somebody else.

  She is popular because she gets things done.
  They are angry because they are not getting their packages delivered on time.
- We can also use *get* + object + *-ing* to talk about causing someone or something to do something.

  The book on game theory got Susan thinking.

Be careful!

- In both the *get* passive voice and the causative, *get* is usually less formal than *have*. Don't use it in formal situations.

  The letter asked us when we had had the house built. NOT ~~The letter asked us when we had got the house built.~~

5.2 Passive voice reporting structures

- Some verbs, such as *allege, assume, believe, expect, know, say, report, rumor, suppose, understand*, are often used in the passive voice as reporting verbs. The verb *rumor* can only be used in this way.
- We frequently use the impersonal *it* with these verbs.

  ***It** is rumored that the President will announce her resignation today. (= There is a rumor that …)*
- With an impersonal *it* passive voice, we can follow the reporting verb with either an infinitive or *that*.

  *It is understood **to be** a complicated situation.*
  *It is understood **that** the situation is complicated.*
- With a personal reporting structure, beginning with *I/you/he/she/it/we/they*, we use the past participle of the reporting verb, followed by infinitive.

infinitive	He **is known to be** a thief.
progressive infinitive	She **is thought to be planning** a comeback.
perfect infinitive	They **are rumored to have started** a secret mission.
perfect progressive infinitive	They **are believed to have been watching** us.

- We can sometimes use modal verbs before the reporting verb.

  *It **can** be assumed that the business is still profitable.*
- In both personal and impersonal constructions, we can use the reporting verb in the past if we are referring to something people *expected/knew/thought*, etc. However, if the action was done in the past, and we are reporting it now, the verbs must reflect this.

  *He **was** known to be hiding.*
  *It **was** thought that they **had** failed.*
  *He **is** understood to **have made** contact.*
  *It **is** believed that he **discovered** America.*

Be careful!

- Do not use *that* in a personal passive voice (one that begins with *I/You/He/She*, etc).

  He is rumored to be planning to make cuts. NOT ~~He is rumored that he is planning to make cuts.~~

5.1 The passive voice

A Find the mistakes and correct them. Some sentences are correct.

1 I was made to fill in pages of details on the form.
2 I dislike to be spoken to as if I don't understand anything.
3 He looks forward to be spoiled when he visits his family.
4 In my school, we used to get told off for the slightest things.
5 You look different – have you had your hair done?
6 Do you know what we were made do in the intelligence test?

B Complete the sentences with the correct *-ing* or infinitive passive voice form of the verb in parentheses.

1 I miss ________________ spend summer vacation days on the beach. (*be able to*)
2 Justine begged ________________ for the things she'd said in anger. (*forgive*)
3 The taller kids tended ________________ for basketball, regardless of their ability. (*choose*)
4 The manager wouldn't tolerate ________________ with. (*disagree*)
5 Paul didn't mention ________________ by the police – do you think he's hiding something? (*stop*)
6 He couldn't remember ________________ onto an elephant, although he had the photo to prove it had happened. (*lift*)

C Complete the sentences in the passive voice or causative form.

1 Active: They made him sign the document.
Passive: He ________________.
2 Active: If you're not careful, they'll throw you out.
Passive: If you're not careful, you'll ________________.
3 Active: I'd like to know how much it costs for you to clean my car professionally.
Causative: I'd like to know how much it costs to ________________.
4 Active: How on earth are we going to find someone to repair that window on a Sunday?
Causative: How on earth are we going to get ________________?
5 Active: I'm sure they didn't tell me to be here half an hour early.
Passive: I don't remember ________________.
6 Active: Someone will steal your car if you leave it there.
Causative: You'll get ________________.

➤ Go back to page 51.

5.2 Passive reporting structures

A Choose the correct options to complete the sentences.

1 We are supposed *to be* / *to be being* there at nine o'clock.
2 It is rumored *to be* / *that* the company is having difficulty.
3 Two members of staff are alleged to *transfer* / *have transferred* money into private accounts.
4 It *is* / *was* originally thought that they were related.
5 They are believed to *plan* / *be planning* a trip overseas.
6 The police are known to *be* / *have been* following him recently.
7 It was thought that there *was* / *to be* a secret tunnel, but nothing has been found.
8 On her first day, *it* / *she* was expected to write three reports.

B Complete the text with a suitable form of the verbs in the box.

announce discuss focus look make plan

Director disputes

Home Articles About us Contact

Following tomorrow's meeting, Collins is expected [1] ________ his resignation. The company is thought [2] ________ to specialize in the near future. They are expected [3] ________ on only one product, and Collins is known [4] ________ his objections to this very clear on several occasions in the past. Although Collins is understood [5] ________ the situation with top management for several weeks, the company is now rumored [6] ________ for a way to force him out.

C Rewrite the sentences using both personal and impersonal passive voice structures. Use the reporting verb in bold.

1 People **believe** he is very rich.
He ________________.
It ________________.
2 Some people **report** that he was awarded over one million dollars.
He ________________.
It ________________.
3 They **say** she knows her subject inside out.
She ________________.
It ________________.
4 Critics **claim** that the game's story is too complex.
The game ________________.
It ________________.
5 Many **think** that it is a complex problem.
The problem ________________.
It ________________.
6 People **assume** she is shy but she's just quiet.
She is ________________.
It is ________________.

➤ Go back to page 55.

Grammar Hub

6.1 Past modals of speculation and deduction

- We use *must* + *have* + past participle for things we believe logically happened.

  *It's a huge book, so it **must have taken** her a long time to research and write.*
- We use *could/might/may well* + *have* + past participle for things we believe likely happened.

  *They're still not sure what caused the fire but it **may well have been started** deliberately.*
- We use *could/might/may* + *have* + past participle for things we think possibly happened.

  *The plane **might have crashed** in the mountains but they never found the wreckage.*
- We use *can't/couldn't* + *have* + past participle to say something was not logically possible.

  *They **couldn't have built** this massive fort in just a week.*

Be careful!

- Although *could/might/may have* + past participle all mean the same thing, *might/may not have* expresses possibility, whereas *couldn't have* expresses certainty.

  It's possible that Aled didn't see the email. = Aled may/might not have seen the email. NOT ~~*Aled couldn't have seen the email.*~~

- We can use phrases that start with *There is* + *a/an/the* + adjective + noun + (*that*) to speculate, with adjectives such as *distinct*, *fair*, *high*, *remote*, *slim* and *slight*, and nouns such as *chance*, *likelihood* and *possibility*.

  ***There is a distinct possibility that** he picked up the illness while in the jungle.*
- We can also use phrases that start with *It is* + adverb + adjective + (*that*) to speculate, with adverbs such as *extremely*, *highly*, *reasonably and somewhat* and adjectives such as *likely* and *possible*.

  ***It's extremely possible that** rival explorers sabotaged their plans.*

6.2 *-ing* and infinitive forms

- We use *-ing* after a preposition.

  *She praised the journalist **for exposing** the injustice.*

  *They're not interested **in finding** out the truth.*
- We also use *-ing* after expressions such as *It's no good…*, *It's not worth…*, *There's no point (in)…* and *…have a good time/difficulty/fun/problems…* .

  *It's **not worth publishing** the article if it will get you fired.*

  *There's **no point (in) helping** people who are ungrateful.*

  *You'll **have difficulty justifying** that answer.*
- We use an infinitive after adjectives, nouns, quantifiers and the word *time*.

  *She's **eager to get** started on her work.*

  *They urged **people to take** shelter in the new facility.*

  *The report is lengthy, and there's **too much to read** in one night.*

  *Let's pick a good **time to review** the materials.*

Be careful!

- We use an infinitive after the word *time*, but after the phrase *have a good/great time…*, we use *-ing*.

  It's time to make a decision. NOT ~~*It's time making a decision.*~~

  We had a great time painting the wall. NOT ~~*We had a great time to paint the wall.*~~

- Some verbs can be followed by *-ing* (e.g. *appreciate*, *suggest*) and some can be followed by infinitive (e.g. *attempt*, *manage*). Some can be followed by *either*, *usually* with a change of meaning (e.g. *remember*, *stop*, *try*).

  *Why don't you **try doing** some research online?*
  (= experiment)

  *I **tried to get** in touch with Jan but couldn't find her anywhere.*
  (= attempt)
- We can use *-ing* or base form after the object of sense verbs like hear, see, etc. The base form emphasizes a complete action that is seen or heard, while the *-ing* emphasizes an ongoing activity.

  *I **saw her drinking** the coffee.*
  (= The action was in progress. I didn't see her finish the coffee.)

  *I **saw her drink** the coffee.*
  (= The action was completed. I saw her finish the coffee.)

6.1 Past modals of speculation and deduction

A Find and correct mistakes in some of the sentences.

1 You may have been exhausted after such a long trip.
2 She must be lying. She might not have traveled all that distance in one day. It's impossible!
3 They could have taken a wrong turning, but it's hard to tell at this stage.
4 He must well have taken his bike with him as he loves biking.
5 Janessa couldn't possibly have climbed Mt. Kilimanjaro with a broken ankle.
6 She can't have been a globetrotter in her youth because she has souvenirs from all around the world.
7 Jonathan must not have gotten our message. I suppose we'll only find out when we hear from him.
8 They must have already left because their room is empty and their bags are gone.

B Choose the correct options to complete the sentences.

1 There is *a distinct possibility* / *extremely possible* that they checked in under a false name.
2 It is *a slim chance* / *somewhat likely* that the courier company had the wrong address.
3 There's *highly possible* / *a remote chance* that the Sphinx was carved more than 10,000 years ago.
4 There isn't *the slightest possibility* / *highly unlikely* that anyone survived that plane crash.
5 It's not *a distinct likelihood* / *completely impossible* that she made her way out of the cave alive.
6 There's *somewhat possible* / *a reasonable chance* that Geoff kept copies of all the correspondence.

C Complete the text with the words in the box.

couldn't it might must there well

Cabeza de Vaca may [1] ________________ have been one of the luckiest and unluckiest explorers ever. Of the 600 men on his 1527 expedition to the Americas, he was one of only four to survive. While they probably imagined a difficult journey, they [2] ________________ have known the misfortune that awaited them. They risked it because [3] ________________ was a possibility of finding gold. Before they even set foot on land, 100 men deserted. They [4] ________________ have been too exhausted to continue.

Shortly before reaching the coast, a hurricane killed 60 more. On land, the Apalachee people they encountered weren't very hospitable. [5] ________________ is likely they sensed the explorers' ill intentions. The Spanish tried to escape, and they [6] ________________ have been successful except for another hurricane! More men died, the natives in Texas enslaved them, and it was ten years before Cabeza de Vaca and his last three men were finally free.

➤ Go back to page 63.

6.2 *-ing* and infinitive forms

A Choose the correct options to complete the sentences.

1 It's no good ___ him for information. He doesn't give anything away.
  a to ask b asking
2 It's time ___ our invention to the test!
  a putting b to put
3 Despite putting his heart and soul into the project, he had a hard time ___ it.
  a to finish b finishing
4 Even though the city has money, they have little ___ to those in need.
  a to give b giving
5 It's correct ___ that her life was a true rags-to-riches story.
  a saying b to say
6 I'm not very interested in ___ a meeting on a Saturday.
  a to arrange b arranging
7 The police didn't have enough evidence ___ the crime.
  a to solve b solving
8 Jason found it harder ___ with his colleagues after the disagreement.
  a to work b working

B Write the correct form of the verb in parentheses.

1 Justin was disciplined for not ________________ (*finish*) his assignment.
2 She brought food for the picnic, but there wasn't enough ________________ (*go*) around.
3 It's not worth ________________ (*do*) such hard work for so little money.
4 I'm sorry, but this is a bad time ________________ (*discuss*) this topic.
5 Is she having difficulty ________________ (*adjust*) to her new life?
6 They advised him on ________________ (*invest*) in new business ventures.
7 There are many ideas here ________________ (*help*) you get started on the project.
8 Your plan failed miserably. Have fun ________________ (*explain*) that to the boss!
9 I saw them ________________ (*steal*) the bike. I witnessed the whole thing from start to finish.

➤ Go back to page 67.

Grammar Hub

7.1 *it* clefting

- We can use the structure *It* + *is/was* + 'focus' + defining adjective clause to focus on a particular piece of information in a sentence. This focus could be:

a person/people	It was **Tenzing Norgay and Edmund Hillary** who first reached the summit of Mount Everest.
a time	It was **1953** when Sir John Hunt successfully led the expedition to reach the summit of Mount Everest.
a place	It is **Mount Everest** which has always captured people's imaginations.
a thing or idea	It was **the challenge of the climb** which inspired generations of climbers.
a clause with *because*	It was **because he had almost reached the summit one year previously** that Tenzing Norgay was hired for the expedition.
a clause with infinitive	It was **to show his respect for the people of Nepal** that Sir Hunt asked Tenzing to make the final climb to the summit.
a clause with *until*	It wasn't **until years later that Tenzing revealed** which climber had first stepped onto the summit of Mount Everest.

Be careful!

- In sentences like this, we usually leave out the second defining adjective clause to avoid repeating the same information.

  It wasn't John Hunt who first climbed Everest – it was Edmund Hillary.
  NOT ~~It wasn't John Hunt who first climbed Everest – it was Edmund Hillary who first climbed Everest.~~

7.2 *what* clefting and *all* clefting

- We can use a *what* clause + *be* + second clause in order to emphasize the information in the second clause.

  With this structure, the information in the *what* clause is usually known or understood whereas the information in the second clause is usually new and therefore the main focus of the sentence.

  What Prianka wants is to escape the rat race.
  What they needed, after their walk in the snow, was a hot bath.
  What he decided to do was to change careers.
- To emphasize a verb in the second clause, we can use the structure: *what* clause with *do* + *be* + second clause. We can use the infinitive or the base form after the verb *be*.

  What he does is (to) climb cellular phone towers.
- We can use *All* instead of *What* at the beginning of the first clause. This emphasizes the idea of there being 'only one thing'.

  All you need to do in the interview is (to) act naturally. (= the only thing you need to do)
- It is also possible to use *Why*, *Where*, *How*, *When* to begin this kind of cleft sentence.

  Why he enjoys extreme sports is a mystery to me.

Be careful!

- The structure *what* clause + *be* + second clause is reversible.

  What he enjoys about his job is living in the wilderness. OR Living in the wilderness is what he enjoys about his job.
- The structure *what* clause with *do* + *be* + second clause is not reversible.

  What they did was move to the country. NOT ~~Move to the countryside was what they did.~~

7.1 *it* clefting

A Write one word in each blank to complete the responses.

1 Did you know that Jack was going to come with us?
No, it ________ a surprise that he decided to come.

2 What time did Antonio arrive home?
It was seven o'clock ________ I heard his key in the lock.

3 Was he worried about the cost of fixing his laptop?
No, it was losing all his work ________ he was more worried about.

4 You've met my sister, haven't you?
No, it was your brother ________ I met.

5 Did you recognize Stella right away?
No, it wasn't ________ somebody introduced us that I realized it was her!

B Read the questions. Use *it* clefting and the information in parentheses to complete the answers.

1 What first got you interested in rock climbing?
(*my friend Seb*)
________________ first got me interested in the sport.

2 What do you think attracts people to Yosemite?
(*the idea of being in the wilderness*)
I think ________________ attracts so many people to go there.

3 When did you set out to climb the Half Dome?
(*early in the morning*)
________________ we set out.

4 When did you realize how high the Half Dome is?
(*only when I reached the top*)
________________ I realized how high up it is!

C Complete the second sentence so that it has a similar meaning to the first sentence, using the word given. Write between two and five words.

1 Susan wasn't hysterical, Jane was.
WAS
It ________________ hysterical, not Susan.

2 Not until after we were rescued did I realize the danger we had been in.
UNTIL
It ________________ were rescued that I realized the danger we had been in.

3 We took part in the charity walk because we wanted to raise money.
IT
________________ money that we took part in the charity walk.

4 What caused her to fail the interview was her over-confidence.
WAS
It ________________ caused her to fail the interview.

5 I believe yoga will help you to relax.
THAT
It ________________ yoga will help you to relax.

6 Somebody else upset Mzia, not you.
YOU
It ________________ upset Mzia.

➤ Go back to page 74 .

7.2 *what* clefting and *all* clefting

A Reorder the words to make sentences.

1 about the winter / dislike / is / What / the long nights / I
________________.

2 I / want / a normal life / All / is
________________.

3 we're / a solution to our problems / to find / is / here / What
________________.

4 the last train / we missed / happened / that / What / was
________________.

5 I / to ask you / did / All / a simple question / was
________________.

6 I / remember / All / is / really difficult / the questions / were / that
________________.

B Rewrite these sentences using *what* clefting or *all* clefting.

1 I've found that working underwater isn't as bad as it sounds.
What ________________.

2 I'm only saying that you should think twice before moving to Antarctica.
All ________________.

3 I'm going to look for a job as a window cleaner.
What ________________.

4 I only asked for your opinion.
All ________________.

5 I bought a ladder and a bucket.
What ________________.

➤ Go back to page 79.

Grammar Hub

8.1 Adjective clauses with complex relative pronouns

- We use *whose* to add information about someone's possessions.

  I was happy to meet Georgia, ***whose*** *sister had helped me find a place to stay.*

- We use *whereby* to add information about a method (formal).

  They introduced a new system in the company ***whereby*** *everybody has a full induction on their first day.*

- We use *whom* to add information about a person where they are the object of the clause (formal).

  The people ***whom*** *I asked were all in favor of the plan.*

- In very formal English, we place the preposition (generally only with *whom*, *whose* and *which*) before the relative pronoun.

  The President, ***in whose*** *honor the event was being held, welcomed all the guests.*

  The person ***on whom*** *I depend the most …*

  The place ***to which*** *I often return …*

- In less formal English, we put the preposition at the end of the clause.

  Martin, ***whose house I was staying in,*** *was a very neat person.*

  *The person (****who****) I depend* ***on*** *the most …*

  *The place (****which****) I often return* ***to*** *…*

- Formal constructions can use a variety of prepositions depending on meaning.

  The person ***in whom*** *I have the most confidence …*

  The person ***to whom*** *I sent the letter …*

  The person ***for whom*** *the money was being raised …*

Be careful!

- The relative pronoun *whom* is very formal. We don't usually use it with a preposition at the end of the clause.

  The person to whom you gave the money …

  NOT ~~The person whom you gave the money to …~~

8.2 Pronouns and determiners

- We use determiners before nouns to identify a number, an amount or a group.

  We have ***a few*** *tomatoes.*

  I had ***a couple of*** *cups of coffee while I was waiting.*

  You need to get ***some*** *fresh air.*

- Some common determiners include: *a/an, the, this/that/these/those, all, some (of), none, (a) little, (a) few (of), my/your/their/its*/etc, *any, much, more, both (of), enough, a lot of, other, each/every, one/two/three*/etc, *either (of).*

- We can use some common determiners like *millions of, loads of, tons of* when we want to exaggerate a point, especially in informal English.

  I feel so guilty because I ate a lot of chocolate last night.

- Pronouns can be the same words as determiners but they are not followed by a noun. They replace the noun, often to avoid repeating it.

  You look like you need water – I'll get you some.

  NOT ~~You look like you need water – I'll get you some water.~~

- Some common pronouns include: *I/he/they*/etc, *me/you/him/her*/etc, *this/that/these/those, there, some, mine/yours/his*/etc, *both, several, anyone/something*/etc, *others, none, either.*

- We can also use *one* or *one's* as pronouns to refer to people in general. These are especially used to make generalizations in formal English. *One's* indicates possession.

  Diets make ***one*** *realize how much food can impact* ***one's*** *life.*

Be careful!

- Some pronouns cannot be used as determiners.

  That glass is mine. NOT ~~That is mine glass.~~

- Some determiners cannot be used as pronouns.

  That is my glass. NOT ~~That glass is my.~~

8.1 Adjective clauses with complex relative pronouns

A Choose the correct options to complete the sentences.

1 Do you know the name of the person to *who* / *whom* the letter must be addressed?
2 That's Melanie, *whose* / *who* mother is the manager of our company.
3 This is the cell phone *which* / *whereby* I am most interested in.
4 His father, *to whom* / *whom* he would often go for financial help, had refused to give him more money.
5 We need to find a solution *whereby* / *which* everyone will be happy.
6 The new grocery store will benefit the villagers, *among whom* / *for whom* there are a number of families without cars.

B Complete each sentence with a word or phrase from the box.

for whom · into which · into whose · whereby · whose · with which

1 A pedometer is a mechanical or digital device ________________ we count steps taken while walking.
2 The owner, ________________ pocket the pedometer can be slipped, can then use it to calculate their distance traveled.
3 More recently, cell phones have started featuring fitness apps, ________________ pedometers or 'step counters' have been incorporated.
4 Some experts claim that people ________________ daily number of steps is lower than 10,000 should be concerned about their health and fitness.
5 Most fitness experts agree that any method ________________ our steps can be counted is a useful one.
6 Pedometers make people ________________ exercise is not a priority aware of their daily activity and motivate them to do more.

C Match the sentence beginnings (1–6) with the endings (a–f) to make sentences.

1 We reached an agreement ___
2 He was uncomfortable because it was a situation in ___
3 Paula is a person whose ___
4 This will be popular with the team, among ___
5 The explorer contracted an illness from ___
6 We still hadn't met Mr. Dawson, in whose ___

a mood never changes.
b which he never recovered.
c house we were all staying.
d whereby everyone was satisfied.
e whom any extra support is appreciated.
f which he had never been before.

➤ Go back to page 88.

8.2 Pronouns and determiners

A Underline the determiners in each sentence. Some sentences have more than one determiner.

1 I could do with a little help starting this fitness program.
2 The doctor said I should leave the car at home and do more walking.
3 Both of the recreational centers in my area are too far to walk to.
4 There was little point in talking to him since he wouldn't listen.
5 One of the techniques is bound to suit you.
6 The cafeteria had two healthier options but I didn't want either of them.

B Change one determiner into a pronoun in each sentence by crossing out some words.

1 Some people have a gluten-free diet because they genuinely can't eat it without getting sick, but many people believe that avoiding gluten is just healthier.
2 I try to drink a couple of liters of water every day, but I'm pretty sure that I don't drink enough water.
3 A lot of people I know are cutting back on sugar and caffeine, but I don't want to cut back on either sugar or caffeine.
4 I've started following a vegan diet so I like to try vegan restaurants, but there are only a few vegan restaurants in my area.
5 I prefer fruits and vegetables that have been grown organically to those fruits and vegetables that haven't.
6 The government should make companies that produce food with a lot of sugar use less sugar to help people have better diets.

C Complete each sentence with the correct pronoun. More than one answer is sometimes possible.

1 Jack couldn't decide which of the two sandwiches to get so he just bought ________________.
2 Some people enjoy running, while ________________ find it really boring.
3 Now I can't tell which shoes are ________________ – they look the same as yours.
4 'Which of the two games do you want to watch on TV?' '________________ – I really don't mind.'
5 I know we said we'd buy oranges but ________________ don't look very nice.
6 We don't have any soccer shoes in stock but we'll be getting some new ________________ in next week.

➤ Go back to page 93.

Grammar Hub

9.1 Noun phrases

- We can use possessive adjectives, quantifiers, numbers and modified quantifiers before nouns to make noun phrases.

Article/determiner	**Those** researchers are highly qualified.
Possessive adjective	**Their** study is well funded.
Quantifier	**Many** eager participants started immediately
Number	**Two of the five** speakers disagreed.
Modified quantifier	**Almost every single** student showed up early.

- We can use adjective clauses, prepositional phrases, *that* clauses and an infinitive after nouns to make noun phrases.

Adjective clause	**The clinic where she works** just closed.
Reduced adjective clause	**The woman sitting down** is my colleague.
Prepositional phrase	They shared **a wealth of knowledge**.
that clause	I question **the idea that humans are still evolving**.
infinitive	They looked for **a cheap place to eat and sleep**.

- We can use phrases such as *the fact that*, *the idea that* and *the belief that* to turn a sentence into a noun phrase.

A language dies every two weeks. That is regrettable. (= The fact that a language dies every two weeks is regrettable.)

People believe language strengthens social ties. This is supported by research. (= The belief that language strengthens social ties is supported by research.)

9.2 Participle clauses and verbless clauses

- We use present and past participles as well as combinations of both to form participle clauses.

__Feeling__ unsure of the results, Mary tested the configuration once more.

__Left__ to their own devices, children can solve complex problems.

__Having__ just finished his research, Travis went for a walk to relax.

- We can use prepositions such as *before*, *after* and *despite* before participle clauses with present participles (but not past participles).

__Before arriving__ at the office, Susan texted her boss.
NOT ~~Before arrived at the office, Susan texted her boss.~~

- We can use conjunctions such as *if*, *when* and *while* before participle clauses with both present and past participles.

__While waiting__ for the bus, Paula had a marvelous idea.
__When pressed__ to answer questions, Jonathan became very nervous.

Be careful!

- Participle clauses appear near the nouns they refer to. When that noun is missing, or the clause appears closer to another noun which it doesn't refer to, it becomes a 'dangling participle' and is grammatically incorrect.

While doing research, Frank noticed the room getting cold. NOT ~~While doing research, the room got cold.~~ (Incorrect: the room wasn't doing research)

- When the participle clause involves using the verb *be*, we can omit the verb altogether and the clause becomes 'verbless'.

Too impatient to wait, Paul barged in and demanded the results. (= Being too impatient to wait, ...)

- We can start a clause with just a participle, with words such as *when*, *after* or *because* being implied.

Hearing the news, Alex leaped for joy! (= After hearing the news, Alex leaped for joy!)

9.1 Noun phrases

A Choose the option which is closest in meaning to the sentence.

1 Lisa questioned many of her professors, and only one gave a clear answer.
 a Many of the professors Lisa questioned only gave one clear answer.
 b Only one of the many professors Lisa questioned gave a clear answer.
2 I have two younger brothers, and they are language experts.
 a Both of my younger brothers are language experts.
 b Two of my younger brothers are language experts.
3 Very few of the participants enjoyed the study.
 a Almost all of the participants disliked the study.
 b Quite a few of the participants enjoyed the study.
4 Jake is standing at the workstation, and he's running reports.
 a The man standing at the workstation is running reports.
 b The man standing at the workstation and running reports is Jake.
5 They're looking for a safe location so they can try out their experiment.
 a They're searching for a safe location to try out their experiment.
 b They're looking to try out their experiment at a safe location.
6 Many people applied for the trial, but few were qualified to join.
 a Many of the few people applying for the trial were qualified to join.
 b Few of the many people applying for the trial were qualified to join.

B Rewrite these sentences using noun phrases. Use the words in bold to help you.

1 I speak **three** languages and **two** of **them** are Latin-based.
 ________________ languages I speak are Latin-based.
2 I have **little** money, but I save **it all** ... well, **almost**.
 I save ________________ money I have.
3 I've read **very few** pieces of research, but this is **one of them**.
 This is ________________ pieces of research I've read.
4 **The writer** draws **two** conclusions and they **both** seem dubious to me.
 ________________ conclusions seem dubious to me.
5 **The researchers** interviewed **many** people. **Quite a few** had no savings at all.
 ________________ interviewees had no savings at all.
6 They **can't conduct the experiment** in peace. That is annoying.
 ________________ is annoying.
7 That **man** is in charge of the experiment. He's wearing a **white lab coat**.
 The ________________ is in charge of the experiment.
8 Many linguists **believe language is alive**, and this is factored into their theories.
 ________________ factored into linguists' theories.

➤ Go back to page 101.

9.2 Participle clauses and verbless clauses

A Choose the correct options to complete the sentences.

1 *Sensing* / *Sensed* danger, Henry shut down the machine immediately.
2 *Having already left* / *Leaving the building*, Danielle didn't feel like returning to get her phone.
3 Before *notifying* / *notified* her supervisor, Anna wanted to make sure the experiment was a success.
4 When *asking* / *asked* about the research, Kyle refused to reply.
5 *Too* / *Too being* cautious to take risks, Martin decided to stay on at his job.
6 Despite *handed* / *handing* in her notice, Sarah put in great effort during her last days at work.
7 *Having been told* / *Being told* to speed up the study, David cut corners to make his deadlines.
8 If *successful* / *being successful*, we can publish the results in a science journal.

B Rewrite these sentences using participle clauses or verbless clauses and the word in bold.

1 I understand animal behavior better now that I've read the article. **having**
 ________________________________.
2 The octopus hid in the coconut shell because it felt threatened. **feeling**
 ________________________________.
3 These experiments can teach us a lot if you do them properly. **done**
 ________________________________.
4 I guessed the answer because I didn't know. **knowing**
 ________________________________.
5 The crow had never seen the tool before but used it perfectly. **despite**
 ________________________________.
6 She wasn't fast enough to win the race, but she came in a close second. **too**
 ________________________________.

➤ Go back to page 103.

Grammar Hub

10.1 Discourse markers

- We use discourse markers to connect ideas, or to give further information regarding our attitude to what we're saying or writing.
- We use some discourse markers to join two clauses within a sentence. They can be positioned either at the beginning of a sentence (followed by a comma) or in between the two clauses. They may be used to express cause and consequence, or to describe a contrast.

despite	**Despite** having a degree in Business Studies, Karla didn't get the job. Karla didn't get the job **despite** having a degree in Business Studies.
owing to	**Owing to** his lack of certifications, Omar was unable to find a job in the field. Omar was unable to find a job in the field **owing to** his lack of certifications.
whereas	**Whereas** Kim is determined to succeed, her sister lacks ambition. Her sister lacks ambition, **whereas** Kim is determined to succeed.

- We use some discourse markers to connect ideas in two separate sentences. These discourse markers can be positioned at the beginning of the second sentence, in which case they should be followed by a comma. Some can also be placed after the subject of the second sentence, and should in this case be followed by a comma, or at the end of the second sentence.

as a matter of fact	He's doing research into Arctic animals. **As a matter of fact**, he's leaving for Greenland next week. / He's leaving for Greenland next week, **as a matter of fact**.
conversely	The novel was a huge bestseller. **Conversely**, the movie version was never as successful. / The movie version, **conversely**, was never as successful.
for instance	Mediterranean resorts are making a comeback. **For instance**, Mykonos is now seen as a vacation hotspot for Europe's young celebrities. / Mykonos, **for instance**, is now seen as a vacation hotspot for Europe's young celebrities. / Mykonos is now seen as a vacation hotspot for Europe's young celebrities, **for instance**.
in any case	It seems that no crime had taken place. **In any case**, it wasn't a matter for the police. / It wasn't a matter for the police, **in any case**.
moreover	Tax income increased because of tourism. **Moreover**, it has created hundreds of new jobs. / It has, **moreover**, created hundreds of new jobs.

10.2 Ellipsis and substitution

- Ellipsis involves leaving out words and phrases to avoid repeating them.
- In written English, there are a number of grammatical items that are often left out.

repeated subject	**He**'s into politics and (**he**) is passionate about activism.
repeated subject + modal	**They should** organize a campaign and (**they should**) create some positive publicity.
repeated subject + auxiliary verb	**We're going to** start a petition and (**we're going to**) organize a protest meeting.
repeated verb phrase	'I thought you were **going on the march**.' 'Yes, I am (**going on the march**).'
repeated adjective	So many students are **apathetic**, but Kiera isn't (**apathetic**).

- In spoken English, we can also leave out some grammatical items for the sake of brevity, when it's clear who/what we're talking about.

  subject: *Can't believe we managed to save the forest from developers! (= I can't believe …)*

  auxiliary verb: *You planning to join the group? (= Are you planning …)*

  auxiliary verb + subject + verb: *Any preference as to which route we take? (= Do you have any preference …)*

- We often substitute the following words and phrases to avoid repeating words.

  do: *Are you going into town? Will you post my letter if you **do**?*
  (to avoid repeating 'go into town')

  not: *I may have to organize the campaign, but I hope **not**.*
  (to avoid repeating 'that I don't have to organize the campaign')

  do so: *Deactivate the security alarm. In order to **do so**, you'll need to key in this code number.*
  (to avoid repeating 'deactivate the security alarm')

  do it: *I often read English-language newspapers. I **do it** to improve my vocabulary.*
  (to avoid repeating 'read English-language newspapers')

  do that: *I specifically asked you not to read my emails. Why did you **do that**?*
  (to avoid repeating 'read my emails')

10.1 Discourse markers

A What is the function of the discourse markers in bold? Read the sentences and choose the correct options.

1 Large hotel complexes consume huge amounts of water, **whereas** smaller family-run hotels tend to use less.
 a contrasting two different ideas
 b comparing two related ideas
2 Walking vacations, **for instance**, are an environmentally-friendly choice.
 a suggesting a possibility
 b giving an example
3 Huge building projects tend to attract investors. **Conversely**, small businesses sometimes struggle to raise money.
 a repeating and reinforcing an idea
 b contrasting two different ideas
4 The room wasn't expensive at all. **As a matter of fact**, it was one of the cheapest places we stayed.
 a adding more information
 b giving an example
5 Farmers are warning that crops may fail **owing to** the lack of rain.
 a offering an explanation
 b trying to persuade someone
6 **Despite** placing advertisements on various websites, Aisha didn't manage to sell her products.
 a describing a situation
 b contrasting two different ideas

B Choose the correct options to complete the sentences.

1 We haven't visited all the monuments yet. ***Owing to / In any case***, Farid isn't that interested in sightseeing.
2 We managed to visit all the most important museums in the city ***whereas / despite*** our limited budget.
3 Because the cost of living in Venice is so high, many people are leaving. ***Moreover / For instance***, many inhabitants are worried about the danger of flooding.
4 Many of the streets in Venice are very narrow. The 'Calleta Varisco', ***conversely / for instance***, is just 53 centimeters wide!
5 ***Owing to / Despite*** rising water levels, Venice city authorities are building flood barriers to protect the city.
6 Riding on a gondola is a bucket list experience for many visiting Venice. Some say it is one of the most iconic tourist experiences, ***as a matter of fact / moreover***!

➤ Go back to page 111.

10.2 Ellipsis and substitution

A Cross out the words that can be omitted in the conversation.

Dom: Do you know who I saw the other day?
Ali: No, who did you see?
Dom: Klaus.
Ali: Do you mean your old roommate from college?
Dom: Yeah! I can't believe it – I saw him again after all these years.
Ali: What happened when you saw him?
Dom: He gave me his phone number and he gave me his email address.
Ali: Are you planning to meet up soon?
Dom: He's going to be visiting the area again next month, so he'll give me a ring when he does visit the area again.

B Replace the phrases in bold with the words and phrases in the box.

do do it do so doing that don't

1 'Do you have time to help out at the animal shelter?'
 'No, I'm afraid I **don't have time to help out at the animal shelter.**'
2 'I'd like to volunteer with you on the weekend.'
 'That's great. You'll have to fill out this form in order to **volunteer with us on the weekend**.'
3 'I volunteer at an animal shelter every weekend.'
 'I really admire you for **volunteering at the animal shelter**.'
4 'Are you enjoying your volunteer work?'
 'Yes. I didn't know how fulfilling it would be, but now I **know how fulfilling it is**.'
5 'I've always wanted to volunteer at the Cats' Home.'
 'So why don't you **volunteer at the Cats' Home**?'

➤ Go back to page 117.

Vocabulary Hub

1.1 Clothes and fashion

A Choose the correct word to complete the sentences.

1 There is a ***dress code / uniform*** at my work – for example, we aren't allowed to wear torn jeans or shorts.

2 Many people try to copy Audrey Hepburn's style – she was a real trend ***setter / follower***.

3 The theme of the party is *Superheroes* – everybody has to wear a(n) ***outfit / costume***.

4 You need a new pair of pants – those are so old and ***scruffy / casual***.

5 People who work in fashion usually dress boldly to ***fit in with / stand out from*** the crowd.

6 I like ***baggy / oversized*** clothes in the summer because they keep you cool.

B Work in pairs. Look again at both options in Exercise A. What is the difference between each option? What do they have common?

➤ Go back to page 2.

1.2 Experimenting with prefixes and suffixes

Add the correct prefix or suffix from the box to the words in bold to complete the sentences.

friendly ish prone proof re resistant savvy super

1 It doesn't matter if he dropped the camera in the pool – it's **water**________________ and **shock**________________.

2 She's really up-to-date with new recording and video equipment. She's very **tech**________________.

3 The sound quality is awful and it looks like it was made at home. It's just too **amateur**________________ to be taken seriously.

4 She has a lot of experience making vlogs. She has every reason to feel ________________**confident** about her abilities.

5 He's always breaking the stuff on the set. I guess he's just **accident**________________.

6 The themes on the show are too adult. I couldn't show my children that – it's not **family**________________.

7 You've made a mess of that video. You'll have to ________________**start** it.

➤ Go back to page 8.

2.1 Describing art

Choose the correct words to complete the sentences. Then discuss the sentences with your partner. Do you agree?

1 Some people enjoy looking around galleries, but I find it very ***tedious / unconventional***.

2 Some modern theater is incredibly ***pretentious / groundbreaking*** – it's more about making the writer feel smart than actually saying anything important.

3 Art needs to be ***hilarious / thought-provoking***. Without a deeper meaning, it's just a pretty picture.

4 Some of the most ***iconic / sensational*** photographs can be disappointing when you see them up close.

5 When a writer uses the same idea in his or her work too many times, it feels really ***repetitive / overrated***.

➤ Go back to page 14.

2.2 Compound adjectives

Make compound adjectives with the words in the box to complete the sentences. Use each word only once.

highly late open part self thick well world

1 I work for a company now, but, in the future, I'd like to be ________________**-employed**.

2 Traveling can introduce you to new ways of seeing the world and make you more ________________**-minded**.

3 Sandra's looking for a ________________**-time** job so she can study and work at the same time.

4 Sometimes as a writer you need to be ________________**-skinned** – you can't take criticism personally.

5 Rob is a ________________**-motivated** person who loves his job and wants to excel at it.

6 It's important that my job is ________________**-paid**, so I have some disposable income after I pay all my bills.

7 He is definitely a celebrity in his own country, but he isn't ________________**-famous** yet.

8 There is a ________________**-night** convenience store below our apartment that will be open.

➤ Go back to page 20.

3.1 Sustainability

Complete the text with the words in the box.

biodegradable consume emission exploitation neutral offsetting renewable

Home Articles About Contact

How to be green

[1]______ energy from sun, wind, rain and waves is one possible solution to the environmental problems we face today. It helps us to address the over-[2]______ of natural resources that are finite like minerals, oil, natural gas and coal. Some businesses and organizations aim to be carbon-[3]______ by [4]______ the amount of carbon they release. There are even some zero-[5]______ buildings which actually create as much energy as they [6]______. Also using [7]______ materials, for example, in food packaging, is another important step because these materials break down naturally and cause less waste.

➤ Go back to page 26.

3.2 Verb–noun collocations

Cross out the incorrect word or phrase in each group.

1 We managed to *achieve* / *attain* / *deliver* / *perform* / *meet* our goals.
2 We have made *a concerted effort* / *limited progress* / *reasonable headway* / *advances in the right direction* / *room for improvement*.
3 They performed *impressively* / *particularly* / *reasonably* / *relatively* / *surprisingly* poorly.
4 The statistics *demonstrated* / *hindered* / *displayed* / *showed* a marked imbalance.
5 We should set *significant progress* / *realistic goals* / *clear objectives* / *measurable targets*.
6 We have seen *little movement* / *a deadline* / *a new record* / *regression* / *incremental progress*.

➤ Go back to page 33.

4.2 Science and research

Choose the correct word to complete the sentences.

1 What are some examples of social *findings* / *norms* in your social group?
2 Can you *conduct* / *speculate* how most people would react if they were publicly told they had a low score on a test?
3 Do you think the study above proved the theory that the researchers *demonstrated* / *hypothesized*?
4 What did this study *conduct* / *demonstrate*?
5 Can you think of another idea for *an experiment* / *some findings* to prove the hypothesis?
6 Is it important to read the *findings* / *participants* of a study to understand the conclusions?
7 Have you ever *conducted* /*speculated* an experiment at school or college?
8 What have you *concluded* / *conducted* about embarrassment by reading the texts?

➤ Go back to page 43.

Vocabulary Hub

4.2 Thinking

Choose the correct options to complete the sentences.

1 While she is very smart, she just isn't very practical. She doesn't have much ***common sense*** / ***wishful thinking***.

2 I was lying on the beach when I had an amazing idea for my business – it was a ***eccentric*** / ***eureka*** moment.

3 He is very ***eccentric*** / ***absent-minded*** – he really stands out from the crowd and doesn't mind doing things in his own unique way.

4 I'd say I'm a little ***curious*** / ***absent-minded*** – for example, I left my key card at home this morning and couldn't get into my office.

5 If you make a resolution but put no effort into planning how to achieve it, then your idea is just ***wishful thinking*** / ***common sense***.

6 We need someone who can analyze and solve serious problems – in other words, ***troubleshooting*** / ***overthinking*** skills are essential for this job.

7 Lara always ***troubleshoots*** /***overthinks*** things; sometimes she should just follow her instincts.

8 Tim describes himself as ***curious*** / ***eccentric***, but I would describe him as nosy.

➤ Go back to page 44.

5.1 Competition and cooperation

A Read the definition of *outmaneuver*. What does the prefix *out-* mean?

outmaneuver – definition and synonyms
VERB Pronunciation /ˌaʊtməˈnuːvə(r)/
to defeat or gain an advantage over someone by being more smart or skillful than they are

B Complete the sentences with the correct form of the verbs in the box.

outdo outnumber outplay outrun outsmart outweigh

1 You'll need to be fast to ________ your rivals and win the race.
2 When we played tennis, she completely ________ me, and I lost every game.
3 It's not perfect, but on balance, the advantages ________ the disadvantages.
4 When I bought a new car, my neighbor didn't want to be ________, so he bought one too!
5 I managed to ________ my opponent by solving the clues faster.
6 In my class, women ________ men by three to one.

➤ Go back to page 53.

5.2 Reporting verbs

Complete the second sentences with a reporting verb from the box and reported speech.

alleged boasted clarified doubted speculated

1 'The new bridge is supposed to reduce traffic congestion, but I don't think it will.'
Daniel ________ whether the new bridge ________ traffic congestion.

2 'Sorry – I think you misunderstood me. I didn't offer to do all the work for you.'
Tania ________ that ________ for me.

3 'Who knows? If you'd studied harder, you might have gotten a better grade.'
Max ________ that I ________ harder.

4 'I was awesome at the Take or Share game! I made over $200!'
Victoria ________ that ________ Take or Share game.

5 'I can't prove it, but I know that Andy lied on his résumé to get the job.'
Michael ________ that ________ to get the job.

➤ Go back to page 55.

5.2 Motivation and manipulation

Complete the text with the correct form of the phrases in the box.

act coax go nuts inclined spur steer tap into

A day in the life of... a salesman

I wouldn't say my job involved [1] __________ people into buying things that they don't actually want. I would never convince someone to buy a faulty product or [2] __________ against their best interests. But I totally believe in the quality of our products – they have been well-designed and [3] __________ what the market really wants. My job is just to [4] __________ people toward the most appropriate products in our range to meet their needs. To be honest it's not difficult. The products sell themselves. Customers are [5] __________ for them. It is the quality of the product that [6] __________ me on to do my job as well as I can. If the product is no good, you're not [7] __________ to make the same effort to sell it.

➤ Go back to page 56.

6.1 Journeys and adventures

A Complete the sentences with a word or phrase. Use the definitions in parentheses to help you.

1 Can you think of a time that you went __________ (*away from frequently visited places*)?
2 How do/would you pass the time on a __________ (*long distance*) flight?
3 Do you prepare in advance before you __________ (*leave*) on a trip? What do you do?
4 Is there any __________ (*places not covered by maps*) left in the world? Where?
5 Imagine you had to camp in the __________ (*middle*) of a rainforest. What __________ (*supplies of food, drink, equipment*) would you take with you?
6 Would you like a job that required you to be a __________ (*frequent traveler*)? Why/Why not?

B Work in pairs. Discuss the questions in Exercise A.

➤ Go back to page 63.

6.2 Binomial expressions

Work in pairs. Complete the sentences with a binomial expression from the box.

by and large far and wide heart and soul life or death safe and sound side by side slowly but surely time after time

1 Marco Polo traveled __________ in Asia.
2 Brothers Louis and Auguste Lumière worked __________ to create motion pictures.
3 Edmund Hillary and Tenzing Norgay were the first to climb Mount Everest and return __________.
4 The American conservationist Dian Fossey won the trust of the gorillas __________.
5 The German physicist Albert Einstein is, __________, thought to be the smartest person that ever lived.
6 Passengers on the sinking *Titanic* faced a __________ situation.
7 __________, numerous climbers have tried to reach the summit of the mountain. But all have failed.
8 Van Gogh put his __________ into his art and inventions, working tirelessly on both.

➤ Go back to page 69.

Vocabulary Hub

7.1 Feelings

Choose the correct options to complete the text.

Home Articles About Contact

The psychology of everyday life

Extreme and stressful situations can always be difficult to cope with. But it's actually how we deal with mundane, everyday tasks, that has the biggest impact on our well-being. Here are some tips on how to cope.

- Learn to control your emotions – be the calm and collected person rather than the [1]***hysterical*** / ***courageous*** / ***devastated*** one when the pressure is on.
- Try not to fire back emails when you're [2]***humble*** / ***grumpy*** / ***resilient*** – an angry message may make you feel better immediately. But, you'll be [3]***indifferent*** / ***disgusted*** / ***devastated*** when your boss fires you and you're suddenly jobless.
- If you just aren't getting anywhere with something and are [4]***frustrated*** / ***devastated*** / ***disgusted***, recognize that you may need a break or even to ask for help.
- Sometimes it's important to be [5]***courageous*** / ***humble*** / ***superior*** and take risks rather than play it safe. Bravery is something you can practice and get better at.
- Just because you are busy, don't be [6]***indifferent*** / ***hysterical*** / ***resilient*** to other people's problems – it's important to help out the people around you.
- No matter how well you think you're doing right now, try to stay [7]***humble*** / ***courageous*** / ***resilient*** about your achievements. Nothing annoys people more than a [8]***superior*** / ***disgusted*** / ***hysterical*** attitude.

➤ Go back to page 76.

7.2 Polysemy

Complete the sentences with the correct form of one of the words from page 79. You can use some words more than once.

1 It can be difficult to ________________ a job with the right balance between intellectual challenge and not too much ________________ to succeed.

2 One of the most important ________________ of barometers (which measure atmospheric ________________) is to calculate the height at which a plane is flying.

3 There's too much ________________ between hundreds of people who have sent in their ________________ for the job; there should be a ________________ to find the successful candidate instead!

4 The pilot says he will ________________ the plane shortly as ________________ have improved.

➤ Go back to page 79.

7.2 Intensifiers

Choose the correct intensifiers to complete the advice about job interviews. What other intensifiers are used?

1 It's perfectly normal to exaggerate your achievements *remarkably* / *somewhat*, but you should never tell *noticeably* / *outright* lies.

2 If you're not *altogether* / *immensely* sure what the interviewer is asking, it's completely fine to ask for clarification.

3 *Practically* / *Radically* all interviews are highly stressful, but as long as you're extremely well-prepared, it should be *relatively* / *utterly* painless.

4 Remember that for the interviewers, it's *practically* / *exceptionally* boring to hear the same answers from every single interviewee. If you give *immensely* / *radically* different answers, you'll stand out from the crowd.

➤ Go back to page 81.

8.1 Health problems

Cross out one word in each sentence which does not make a collocation.

1 Tony fractured a(n) ***muscle / arm / bone*** when he went skiing last year.
2 Do you sell anything for a ***twisted / sore*** throat?
3 Some studies have claimed that ***low / slow*** blood pressure may be more common among athletes.
4 When I was running I may have ***pulled / dislocated / sprained*** a muscle.
5 After intense exercise your ***skin rash / blood pressure / heart rate*** is usually higher.
6 You can buy a number of products over the counter to help relieve skin ***fractures / inflammation / rashes***.

➤ Go back to page 86.

8.2 Describing taste

Complete the sentences with words from Exercise A. More than one answer is possible for some sentences.

1 I love ________________ drinks, but I'm trying to be healthy so I usually order sparkling water at restaurants.
2 I know I should eat more citrus fruits to get my daily dose of Vitamin C, but they are just too ________________ for me.
3 Presentation is so important for me – if food doesn't look ________________, I can't eat it.
4 I ate a delicious curry on the weekend, which wasn't too spicy at all – in fact, it was fairly ________________.
5 My dad loves blue cheese, so I get some really ________________ aromas when I open the fridge sometimes.
6 I try to eat salad for lunch occasionally, but it doesn't taste like much. It's really ________________ unless I put some unhealthy dressing on the top.
7 I'm trying to eat healthy snacks, like carrot sticks – they're nice and ________________.

➤ Go back to page 93.

9.2 Verb + object + base form

Complete the sentences with the correct form of the verbs in parentheses.

1 The scientists observed the dolphin ________________ itself in the mirror for hours. (admire)
2 Snakes' heat sensors help them ________________ prey ________________. (detect, approach)
3 Scientists must be seen ________________ procedures very carefully. (follow)
4 Oh! You're here! I didn't notice you ________________! (arrive)
5 I woke up because I could feel a spider ________________ on my arm. (crawl)
6 I was made ________________ for over an hour before they let me ________________ in. (wait, come)
7 The experimenters had the participants ________________ a form before they could start. (sign)

➤ Go back to page 103.

9.2 Gestures and body language

Complete the sentences with the correct form of the words in the box.

beckon fidget glare grin lean wink nod gaze

1 Sally was ________________ across the bay, looking at nothing in particular, when the ship suddenly came into view.
2 Phillip just can't sit still in meetings – he's always ________________.
3 James ________________ at Emma, so she knew he was joking.
4 'Shhh … we have to be quiet … just ________________ if you agree with me.'
5 The bookshelf fell over when I ________________ against it.
6 Steven was so happy when he got the job that he couldn't stop ________________.
7 The teacher ________________ his student over to the board.
8 Elizabeth was so angry that she just ________________ at them without saying a word.

➤ Go back to page 105.

10.1 Culture and heritage

Complete the text with the words in the box.

architectural endangered funding habitat heritage preserve refurbishment settlement

HOMETOWN GLORY

My hometown has a very rich history – it is where a famous treaty was signed and is close to the site of an ancient [1] ________________. In fact some of ruins of the site are still standing today and are of special [2] ________________ interest as they show the precise engineering methods of the Romans.

For these reasons alone, the town is a very important part of my country's national [3] ________________. The nearby forests are the [4] ________________ of a lot of different wildlife, including some rare species which are unfortunately now [5] ________________. As such they have been designated as an area of outstanding natural beauty and are protected.

Unfortunately we don't receive a lot of [6] ________________ from the government to [7] ________________ areas of the old town. Some of the unlisted buildings are in real need of [8] ________________ – so please come and visit us. Tourism is a valuable source of income and helps us to keep our heritage and culture alive!

➤ Go back to page 111.

10.2 Word building

A Write the correct form of the word in parentheses to complete the sentences.

1 A good politician is someone who grew up in the ________________ (commune) that they represent.
2 Most politicians are more interested in ________________ (person) success than helping the public.
3 Becoming ________________ (act) in politics is the best way to make a difference in the world.
4 I feel ________________ (passion) about politics and follow the news closely.
5 Most people's political beliefs are formed during their ________________ (child) by listening to their parents.
6 Many people are ________________ (apathy) about politics, because they don't trust politicians.
7 The best politicians are those who had other careers before entering ________________ (politics) life.
8 Local politics is often more ________________ (effect) at improving people's lives than national politics.

B Work in pairs. Do you agree with the sentences in Exercise A? Why/Why not?

➤ Go back to page 115.

2.2 Students A and B

Read what your answers to the quiz say about you.

ARE YOU CUT OUT FOR FAME?

MOSTLY 1S
You have a very clear vision for your future and nothing will stop you from achieving it. You welcome negative feedback as a way to improve and grow as a person. You want to be well-known, even if this won't necessarily make you rich.

MOSTLY 3S
You feel comfortable among large groups of people and don't need a lot of alone time. That being said, you would not particularly enjoy your private life being discussed online. You are fairly ambitious and would like to be respected in your field. But you also have other interests in your life which are important to you. Fame might not be for you.

MOSTLY 5S
You don't enjoy being the center of attention and value privacy. For you, work is a small part of your life, secondary to spending time with friends and family. The purpose of working is to earn money to do the things you enjoy. Fame isn't for you.

➤ Go back to page 20.

4.1 Students A and B

BRAIN TEASERS

Try these fun brain teasers to keep your mind active and increase your intelligence.

1. If you were running in a marathon and you passed the person in third place, what place would you be in now?
2. An electric train is moving north at 100 kph and a wind is blowing to the west at 10 kph. Which way does the smoke blow?
3. If there are six apples and you take away four, how many do you have?
4. I'm tall when I'm young and I'm short when I'm old. What am I?

Answers: 1 Third 2 An electric train doesn't produce smoke. 3 Four 4 A candle

➤ Go back to page 38.

Communication Hub

9.2 Players

You have three minutes to get ten points, but you have to work out the rules to the game by yourselves. For example, maybe you get a point for nodding your head, for blinking your eyes or for saying a particular word (or possibly all three at the same time). Work as a team to see if you can win ten points in three minutes. Good luck!

➤ Go back to page 105.

4.1 Student A

Using your own words, explain each situation to your partner. Then decide what you would do in pairs.

Situation 1

Imagine that a company begins selling brain implants. They allow you to learn and remember information quickly. For example, some people use them to learn languages or other skills instantly. However, the implants have also caused people to lose some of their memories. Would you buy one?

Situation 2

Imagine that a company begins selling highly advanced robots. These robots will take on any tasks that you need them to do, provide companionship for people who live alone, and protect you and your house. They are also smart enough to learn and use their initiative. Would you get one of these robots?

Situation 3

Imagine that artificial intelligence is used for both medical check-ups and treatment in the future. The AI has a higher rate of accurate diagnoses than human doctors. You have the choice between a human doctor or an artificial intelligence system. Which would you pick?

➤ Go back to page 41.

4.2 Students A and B

Think of a time when you did something you regret. Use the prompts below or your own ideas. Discuss it with your partner.

- You failed a test.
- You forgot something.
- You lost something.
- You missed an appointment.
- You sent an email or message to the wrong person.
- You wore the wrong type of clothes.

➤ Go back to page 43.

5.2 Students

Work in small groups to solve the puzzles.

PUZZLE A: THE TAKE OR SHARE IT GAME

You and a stranger are both offered a choice: **TAKE or SHARE.**

If only one player chooses **TAKE**, they keep $1000.

If both players choose **SHARE**, they get $500 each.

But if both players choose **TAKE**, they get nothing.

You can't communicate with each other.

What's the best strategy if you play once?

What if you play multiple times?

PUZZLE B: THE TALENT SHOW DILEMMA

You're watching a TV talent show. The two candidates with the most votes will go through to the final. Your favorite contestant is so popular she's almost certain to win. Your second favorite contestant also deserves to be in the final. You have only one vote. Who should you vote for?

PUZZLE D: THE ROAD NETWORK

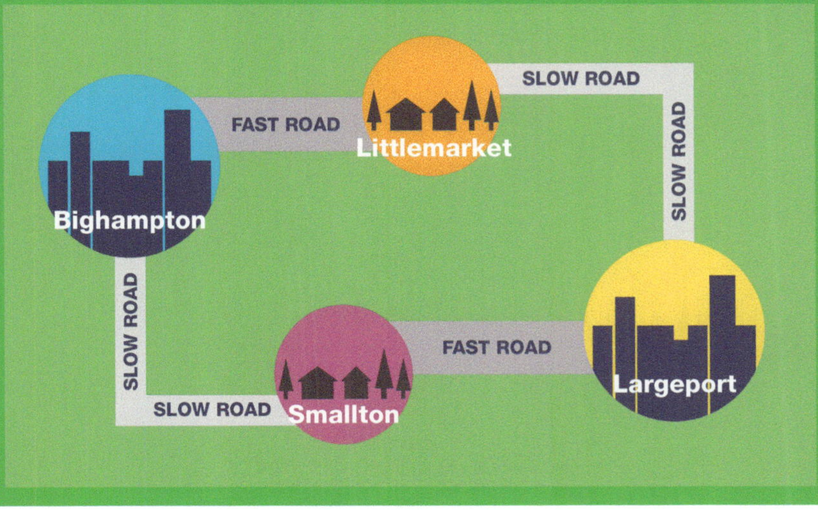

The map shows the road network between four towns. Where (if anywhere) should you build a new road to solve the towns' traffic problems?

➤ Go back to page 54.

Communication Hub

9.1 Students

In your groups, discuss the questions.

- Experiments have shown that speaking English encourages people to be more competitive, thanks to the connotations of English-speaking countries. What effect might your own language have on its speakers?
- Unlike English, many languages have formal and informal words for *you*, so you always have to think about your relationship with the other person before speaking to them. How might that affect your behavior?
- The present perfect in English treats past events as part of the present. How might that affect English speakers' view of the past … and their behavior?

➤ Go back to page 101.

4.1 Student B

Using your own words, explain each situation to your partner. Then decide what you would do in pairs.

Situation 1

Imagine that a company begins selling body upgrades. You can use its technology to make you stronger, faster and more skillful. People can use the upgrades to fix their sight and hearing, or repair injuries. However, the new parts don't look natural, so it will be clear you have had upgrades. Would you use this service?

Situation 2

Imagine that a company begins offering a memory back-up service. You can download the memories from your brain onto its servers and then view the memories whenever you want. You can also share selected memories with others. However, you don't get to choose which memories are downloaded. Everything has to be downloaded together. Would you use this service?

Situation 3

Imagine that a highly advanced robot in the future demanded the same rights as a human. The robot argues that it is as conscious as a human being. Would you support the demands of the robot?

➤ Go back to page 41.

10.3 Student A

SPEAK Describe the following scene to your partner.

➤ Go back to page 118.

4.3 Students

Low frequency sounds, like number 1, are connected to earthy tones like browns and reds.
High frequency sounds like, number 2, are connected to violet tones like blue and purple.

➤ Go back to page 46.

9.2 Facilitator

The 'game' is in fact an experiment to see if you can trick the players into behaving strangely. They think they have to 'win' points, but in fact they simply get a point at regular intervals. When the game starts, count to ten slowly and silently in your head, again and again, saying 'one point' aloud every time you reach ten. Don't let the players work out the real rules – but you can share the secret with them at the end!

➤ Go back to page 105.

6.1 Group A

Work in small groups. Read about a historical mystery. Speculate about what happened.

THE LOST COLONY OF ROANOKE

In 1585, an English settlement was established on a small island off the Eastern coast of the US. In the first year there, they began to run out of food, so the Mayor returned to England to get supplies – but it was three years before he could come back. He left behind his daughter, son-in-law and grandchild among the colonists.

When he returned, the colony and all 117 members of the colony were gone. The only thing left was a fence around the area and a newly built fort on the other side of the island. He never saw or heard from the colonists again.

The Mayor had told the settlers to carve a symbol into a tree if they had been forced to leave the area, but he only found the word CROATOAN. Croatoan was the name of a nearby island, inhabited by a tribe of indigenous people with the same name.

In recent years, some objects of European origin from that period were found at two different locations. Part of a sword was found on Croatoan Island and some pottery was found about 50 miles inland.

Despite modern efforts to solve the mystery, nothing of the actual colonists is known for sure. Several theories exist, but the quest to find out what happened continues.

➤ Go back to page 63.

4.3 Students

Both pictures are brightness illusions known as Munker's illusion. Although the shapes appear to vary in brightness, they are actually the same. It is the colors next to them that make them appear different.

➤ Go back to page 46.

3.2 Student B

Read the situation and prepare what you will say.

You're being interviewed for a radio program about progress. You feel that while there have been a lot of advances, overall life in the modern world is getting worse. You can think about the following points or use your own ideas to prepare:

- the impact of technology
- community
- quality of life
- cost of living
- employment
- the environment

Complain to the interviewer about how life is getting worse in the modern world.

➤ Go back to page 31.

6.3 Students

Underline examples of summarizing, repetition and dynamic words in the transcript.

Hydrogen atoms, carbon atoms, oxygen and sulphur atoms – these basic building blocks react and combine to make everything.

A forest is a complex place – there are oak trees and grass and mosses and ferns, and countless animals and plants all living together in a tangled ecosystem. But there's a simpler level of description – everything is made of atoms. So an oak tree is really just carbon, nitrogen, oxygen and hydrogen and a few other things mixed together. So, when you look at it like that, it's really not that complicated at all.

The atoms that make up this forest have been on an extraordinary journey to get here. Think of a carbon atom in this acorn. It was assembled in the heart of a star billions of years ago out of protons that were built just after the Big Bang. It got thrown out into the universe in a supernova explosion, collapsed as part of a dust cloud to form the sun and then the earth four and a half billion years ago.

It will have spent a lot of time in rocks. It was probably part of some of the first living things on Earth. It would have been breathed out as carbon dioxide by someone that walked through this forest 400 years ago. It will have entered into some ancient oak tree through the action of photosynthesis constructed into this acorn and fallen down to the ground. And there it is. It's got a history that goes back billions of years. In fact, a history in terms of the building blocks of carbon, the protons, that goes back right to the origin of the universe. And in billions of years time when the sun dies and the Earth is vaporized they'll be thrown back out into space and probably condensed into a new world billions of years in the future.

So life is just a temporary home for the immortal elements that build up the universe.

➤ Go back to page 70.

10.3 Student B

SPEAK Describe the following scene to your partner.

➤ Go back to page 118.

6.1 Group B

Work in small groups. Read about a historical mystery. Speculate about what happened.

THE NAZCA LINES

Approximately 2,000 years ago, people living in southern Peru drew pictures of shapes and animals into the dry desert landscape by removing red rocks to reveal the white sand below.

Some of the pictures are as large as the Empire State Building, but when seen from above are very accurate. How did the people draw the pictures without being able to see them from above? And since the pictures are not visible from the ground, who was supposed to see them?

One scientist found that one of the lines pointed directly to the sun during the winter solstice.

Another scientist believes the drawings were used to mark the location of underground rivers and wells.

One image is of a spider, but this species of spider is not found in this area. It comes from the Amazon, over 900 miles away.

➤ Go back to page 63.

Ⓦ making your blog post successful

A Look at the buttons. What do you think *skeuomorphism* means?

B Read *4 things you need to know about skeuomorphism*. Complete the article with the headings (a–d).

- **a** Is skeuomorphism cool?
- **b** Is skeuomorphism useful?
- **c** What are some examples of skeuomorphism in real life?
- **d** What is skeuomorphism?

4 things you need to know about SKEUOMORPHISM

Have you ever wondered why the best websites look fresher and smarter than yours? Do you want to learn the powerful secret of great web design? Then you need to know about skeuomorphism.

1 ___

Here's a simple definition: skeuomorphism involves making digital objects look like things in the real world. The earliest websites just had a lot of text. Instead of a 'click here' button, you simply had the words 'click here'. But web designers soon realized that users prefer life-like buttons and switches.

2 ___

Examples of skeuomorphism are everywhere. Is there a trash can on your phone for 'delete'? A cogwheel for 'settings'? An envelope for 'messages'? The list of examples is endless. Skeuomorphism even brings outdated technologies – like floppy disks and sand-filled hourglasses – back to life.

3 ___

It depends. Early web designers got carried away with skeuomorphism. Every button had a 3D appearance, with shadows and reflections. This led to a backlash in the early 2010s called 'flat design', which gave a cleaner, less fussy appearance. Flat design managed to appear both retro and modern … but also a little boring.

4 ___

Yes and no. Skeuomorphism does make things more user-friendly and intuitive. We all know that a green phone means 'start a call' and a red one means 'end a call', but what if you've never seen an old-fashioned phone? What if you're color-blind? By all means use skeuomorphism in your web design, but don't assume your users can work out what everything means!

Want to learn more about web design trends? Click here to sign up for our online course.

C SPEAK Work in pairs. Discuss the questions in the headings.

D Match the objectives (1–3) with the strategies (a–g).

Making your blog post successful

A successful blog post achieves three objectives:

1. People will find it using search engines. _____, _____, _____, _____
2. They will read it from start to finish. _____, _____
3. They will take some action that helps the writer. _____

- **a** Include a number in your title (i.e. 7, not seven). Search engines prefer them!
- **b** End with a clear call to action (CTA), e.g. 'sign up for our newsletter'.
- **c** Ask questions in your first paragraph, but only answer them later in your blog post.
- **d** Choose one key word or phrase and use it as many times as possible in your blog post.
- **e** Use questions as section headings. Many people use questions to search.
- **f** Speak to readers as 'you' and offer to solve their problems.
- **g** Include a lot of common search terms like 'definition' and 'examples'.

E Find examples of the strategies (a–g) in the blog post.

WRITING

A PREPARE Work in groups. You are going to write a blog post about a trend or trends in general. Think of ideas for topics.

B PLAN Choose your key word or phrase (to be repeated many times in your blog post), your title and a series of questions to use as section headings.

C WRITE Write your blog post. Make sure the first paragraph encourages the reader to keep going to the CTA!

D REVIEW Read some other people's blog posts. Use the box above to evaluate the posts.

Write a review

W – writing concisely

A Read this announcement and answer the questions.

> **Reviews wanted**
>
> Have you recently read a classic book or watched a classic movie? We're starting a series of reviews of classic books and movies and we want your opinions.
> Is the book or movie as good as everyone says it is? Is it still relevant today? Please send us a review for the college paper. Write 220–260 words.

1 What should be reviewed?
2 What questions should be addressed by the review?
3 Who is the target audience?
4 How long should the review be?

B Read the review. Does the writer agree that the book deserves its reputation as a classic? Which parts of the review tell you this?

Alice's Adventures in Wonderland

1 Fantasy children's novel *Alice's Adventures in Wonderland* was published in 1865. The book, adapted for movies and television and translated into over 100 languages, fully deserves its reputation as a classic and is just as fun today as it always was.

2 At the beginning of the story, Alice sees a white rabbit wearing clothes and talking to himself. Following the rabbit, she falls down a hole into a bizarre world of strange and wonderful creatures, including a snooty caterpillar and the mysterious, grinning Cheshire Cat.

3 One of the reasons that *Alice's Adventures in Wonderland* is so popular is that it is a nonsense story. It's not a typical linear story or a story with logic and a moral. It's about the strange situations and unusual characters created by the author, and they surprise and delight readers.

4 Another reason for the book's enduring popularity is Lewis Carroll's playful use of language. The story is full of riddles, puzzles, puns and made-up words. One of the most famous examples is the 'unbirthday party' at the Mad Hatter's tea party.

5 *Alice's Adventures in Wonderland* is without a doubt a classic book that has captured the imaginations of generations of children and adults. Its creative story, characters and playful use of language make it a unique story – and one that everybody should read at least once.

C Look at the review and identify which paragraph contains the following information.

a an overall opinion of the work and a recommendation ___
b key information about the work and a general opinion of it ___
c analysis of a second positive or negative aspect of the work ___
d a plot summary or description of the work ___
e analysis of one positive or negative aspect of the work ___

D Read the review again and answer the questions.

1 Which characters from the book are mentioned?
____
2 How is the story of this book different to most other books?
____
3 What example of playful use of language does the writer give?
____

E Find features of concise description in the text. Use the information in the box to help you.

> **Writing concisely**
>
> If you need to write concisely, you can use some of the following features:
> - noun phrases: *English writer and mathematician Charles Dodgson*
> - reduced adjective clauses: *Charles Dodgson, writer and mathematician, published his first book.*
> - participle clauses: *Educated at home, Dodgson wrote poems and short stories.*

WRITING

A PREPARE Look again at the announcement in Exercise A.

B PLAN Plan your review. Use your answers to question 2 in Exercise A to help you.

C WRITE Write your review. Use your plan to help you.

D REVIEW Exchange your review with a partner. Do you have similar information? Underline any information that you don't think is correct.

E EDIT Read your partner's comments. Rewrite any parts you think should change.

W– persuasive techniques

A SPEAK Read the email. Who is the writer? Who is he writing to? Why?

To: Lakeside residential estate (group)
From: Daniel Hernandez
Subject: Road resurfacing

Dear all

a As you know, the internal roads in our neighborhood are in dreadful condition. Not only does this look ugly, but it also damages our cars. Furthermore, one of our loved ones may be injured by tripping on the uneven surface.

b With that in mind, the housing association has set aside funds to resurface the roads. As I'm sure you remember, the roads were last resurfaced five years ago. One option is simply to use the same cheap materials again (and in five years, the surface will have deteriorated again).

c I would like to propose an alternative: self-repairing concrete. Thanks to cutting-edge technology, self-repairing concrete is infused with billions of tiny limestone-producing bacteria, *Bacillus pseudofirmus*. While sealed in concrete, these bacteria remain inert, but when exposed to air they multiply rapidly. No sooner does a crack appear in the concrete than millions of these bacteria will wake up and plug the crack.

d As you can imagine, although self-repairing concrete is somewhat expensive, it will save us money in the long run (see attached calculations). More importantly, if one serious accident can be prevented over the next five years, I'm sure you'll agree it will have been worth the extra cost.

e I know you are all smart people, so let's make the smart decision. Please support my proposal at our next housing association meeting.

Best regards

Daniel

B Read the email again. Match the questions (1–5) with the paragraphs (a–e). Then discuss the questions in pairs.

1 What is a potential objection and how can it be overcome? ___
2 What is the most likely solution and what's wrong with it? ___
3 What action does the reader need to take? ___
4 What is the problem and why should the reader care? ___
5 What's an alternative solution and why is it better? ___

C Underline examples of each technique in Daniel's email. Use the information in the box to help you.

Persuasive techniques

1 Use words like *we*, *our* and *let's* to build a connection with the readers.
2 Flatter your readers by claiming they're intelligent and knowledgeable.
3 Provide facts and figures to support your claims, in an attachment if appropriate.
4 Use emotive language and imagery to appeal to your readers' fear of loss, damage or injury.
5 Explain technical issues in simple language, but include some impressive technical terms.
6 Use *although* or *while* to link weaknesses with strengths.

D Work in pairs. Use the techniques in Exercise C to make these email extracts more persuasive.

1 Your biggest problem is that you spend too much money on electricity.
2 Please support me so I can solve this problem for you.
3 The road surface is so bad that delivery drivers may refuse to drive into our neighborhood.
4 I admit this solution will be extremely disruptive during the building work.

WRITING

A PREPARE Work in groups. You are going to write a persuasive email about sustainability, smart materials or voluntourism. Generate a list of ideas. Use the following questions to help you:

1 What problem are you trying to solve?
2 Who do you need to persuade?
3 What do you want your reader to do?

B PLAN Plan a five-paragraph email. You can use the five questions from Exercise B to help you.

C WRITE Write your email, using techniques from this lesson.

D REVIEW Exchange your email with a partner. Do you use similar techniques? Comment on how the email could be made more persuasive and underline any mistakes.

E EDIT Read your partner's comments. Rewrite any parts you think should change.

W– hedging

A Study the list of twenty words for one minute. Then try to write them all down.

experiment brilliant eccentric
participant professor memory
argument common sense fashion
metaphor trend brainpower website
conclusion project world-famous
iconic obstacle self-portrait
inspiration

B Work in groups. Compare the words that you remembered. Which words did most people remember?

C Read the report. Which words did the study find were more likely to be recalled? Why were these words more likely to be recalled?

INVESTIGATING SHORT-TERM AND LONG-TERM MEMORY

Introduction

This report describes an experiment to replicate the results of an earlier study. Murdock (1962) investigated the concepts of short-term and long-term memory by getting students to memorize a list of words. He found that students were more likely to recall the words at the beginning and end of the list. [a]He concluded that this **may** be because the words from the beginning of the list were stored in the long-term memory, whereas the words at the end of the list were stored in the short-term memory.

Methods

Thirty participants (16 men and 14 women) were asked to look at a list of 20 words for a minute. They were then asked to try to recall the words.

The words that participants wrote down were analyzed to see which words were recalled the most and if the position of the word in the list affected the students' ability to recall the word.

Results

The results confirmed Murdock's findings and showed that students were more likely to recall words from the beginning and end of the list.

Discussion

Murdock suggested that students studied the words at the beginning of the list more carefully, maybe by saying the words out loud. [b]**He believed that** this meant that the words had been processed enough to enter the long-term memory. [c]The words at the end of the list were the words students had just looked at, so these were **likely** to be stored in the short-term memory. [d]This study replicated Murdock's findings and **suggests** that his theory may be correct.

Conclusion

It can be concluded that when given information as a list, we are more likely to recall items from the beginning and end of the list.

D Look at the report again and match the report headings with the descriptions (1–5).

1 Analysis of the meaning of the findings ________
2 Description of participants and what was done ________
3 The findings ________
4 A summary of the outcome ________
5 An overview and background information ________

E Match the rules with the four sentences (a–d) in the report.

Hedging

In a scientific report unless something is a well-established fact, we should use hedging to make our claims less strong and less open to criticism. Use:

1 auxiliary verbs such as *may*, *might* and *could*: ___
2 adverbs such as *probably*, *possibly* and *likely*: ___
3 verbs that that allow for some doubt, such as *seem*, *appear*, *suggest*, *indicate*: ___
4 introductory phrases to qualify, such as *We believe*, *We understand*, *In our view*: ___

WRITING

A PREPARE Read about a similar experiment. Imagine you have recently replicated this experiment.

B WRITE Write a full report about it.

Glanzer and Cunitz (1966) did a similar experiment to Murdock, but they had two different groups. One group received the test immediately after looking at the words. The other group had a 30-second delay before they did the test and had to count backwards in threes from 99 during the delay. The results showed that although participants could recall the words from the start of the list, they could not recall the words from the end of the list. Glanzer and Cunitz concluded that this was because these words were no longer in participants' short-term memories because of the delay and the distraction.

References

Glanzer, M, & Cunitz, A R (1966) 'Two storage mechanisms in free recall' *Journal of Verbal Learning and Verbal Behavior*, 5(4), 351–360.

W – using depersonalization

A Read the report and answer the questions.

1 Who commissioned the report? Why?

2 What worked well in the two case studies? What went wrong?

3 Which elements does the writer recommend copying? What would the writer change?

Using games to attract tourists to Littlemarket

Background

At a recent meeting of the Littlemarket Tourism Board, [1]it was proposed that an investigation should be conducted into the use of urban gaming and gamification to attract tourists. This report summarizes the research and provides a series of recommendations.

Case study 1: Bighampton

Two years ago, the tourism board in Bighampton launched a series of treasure-hunt worksheets for tourists, which [2]were reported to be enjoyable by 55% of participants. However, they were found to be too easy by 25%. The games were moderately successful in attracting tourists to some lesser known attractions, but the overall impact on tourist numbers was minimal (a 1.5% rise).

Case study 2: Smallton

Last year, the Smallton Tourism Board developed an app to gamify tourists' experience of the town. Badges could be won for visiting particular cafés, museums and other attractions. [3]In spite of widespread frustration with technical problems, the results were impressive, with some cafés and restaurants reporting an 80% increase in sales. [4]It remains to be seen how successful the app has been at boosting overall tourist numbers, but initial indications are positive.

Recommendations

[5]It would be relatively cheap and simple to develop a series of printable treasure hunt maps. Ideally, a range of levels (beginner to expert) would be offered. However, [6]it would be necessary to invest significantly in marketing [7]to raise awareness of the games. [8]It would also make sense to use the gamification techniques from Smallton's experiment to encourage tourists to spend more money. Unlike Smallton, we should involve local businesses in the costs of developing and promoting our games.

The costs of developing an app are currently beyond our budget, so I recommend gaining experience first with a cheaper, low-tech solution and then, if appropriate, upgrading to a sophisticated technical solution in two to three years.

B Complete the examples with the extracts (1–7) from the report.

Using depersonalization

Depersonalization involves removing people from your writing to make it more formal. Depersonalization techniques include:

a *it* + *be* + adjective + infinitive: *we could cheaply and easily* → ___; *we'd need to* → ___

b preposition + noun: *Although many people got frustrated* → ___

c changing verbs into nouns or adjectives: *55% of participants said they had enjoyed* → ___; *to inform people about* → ___

d the passive voice: *somebody proposed that* → ___

e other impersonal phrases: *We still don't know* → ___; *we should also* → ___

WRITING

A PREPARE Work in groups. You have been asked to write a report for a language school about using games to attract new students and improve language skills. Discuss how escape rooms, urban games, game theory or gamification could help your language school.

B PLAN Imagine two or three case studies involving other language schools. Write notes about each case study in your plan.

C WRITE Write your report. Use depersonalization techniques to make it suitably formal.

D REVIEW Exchange your report with a partner. Do you use similar techniques? Comment on how your partner has used depersonalization.

E EDIT Read your partner's comments. Rewrite any parts you think should change.

W– structuring an expository essay

A SPEAK Work in pairs. Read the essay prompt and brainstorm possible answers.

> What are the benefits of deep-sea exploration?

B Read the essay. What benefits does the writer mention? What evidence or examples does the writer give for each benefit?

The benefits of DEEP-SEA EXPLORATION

Did you know that humans have only explored 5% of the world's oceans? This means there is clearly a lot left to be discovered. There are benefits of deep-sea exploration, such as learning more about climate change, addressing the problems of food shortage, and finding cures for diseases.

First, deep-sea exploration is providing vital information about climate change. For example, researchers have been observing how rising temperatures affect the movements of sea creatures. In addition, some studies have found that the sea is able to absorb carbon from the atmosphere.

Second, exploration of the seas will help governments ensure there is enough food for everyone in the future. According to the UN Food and Agriculture Organization, fish stocks are already getting low. However, improvements to fish farming methods will allow countries to support sustainable fishing.

Finally, exploring the seas is leading to advances in medicine to help fight disease. For example, medicines have already been discovered to help with chronic pain, asthma and even cancer. Many scientists believe we are much more likely to discover new medicines in the sea than on land.

In summary, there are many benefits to deep-sea exploration. It can help scientists to understand climate change better as they try to prevent it. It can also help people to ensure the ocean remains a valuable source of food. In addition, discovering new species of plant and animal could lead to the development of new medicines. People have already discovered a lot from just 5% of the ocean. Imagine what they could find in the other 95%.

C Read the essay again and answer the questions. Use the information in the box to help you.

Structuring an expository essay

The typical structure of an expository essay is:

- **Introduction:** Includes a 'hook' to get readers' attention, background information and the thesis statement, which states what the essay will describe or explain
- **Body paragraph one:** Describes or explains the first point
- **Body paragraph two:** Describes or explains the second point
- **Body paragraph three:** Describes or explains the third point
- **Conclusion:** Summarizes the points that were made and leaves the reader with a 'final thought'.

1. Which sentence is the hook? How does the writer get the reader's attention?
2. Which sentence is the thesis statement? What do you notice about the order of the points in the thesis statement?
3. The first sentence of each paragraph is called a topic sentence. What information is included in this sentence?
4. What kind of information is included in each paragraph to support the idea introduced in the topic sentence?
5. The conclusion contains a summary of the points made in the essay. What do you notice about the order of the points in the summary?

WRITING

A PREPARE Work in groups. Read the essay prompt in Exercise A again. Come up with ideas and make a list of possible benefits.

B PLAN Choose the best ideas and organize them into paragraphs.

C WRITE Use your plan to write an expository essay. Write approximately 250 words.

D REVIEW Work in pairs. Edit your partner's essay. Check:

- spelling and punctuation
- use of language
- clarity of the structure

Write a cover letter

W– using power verbs

A Read the job advertisement.

Which skills and abilities:

1 will candidates need to prove from their certifications and experience?

2 will candidates try to show from their life experience and character?

3 are useful but not essential?

Research Technician – Antarctica

The **International Antarctic Research Station (IARS)** is recruiting a research technician. The job involves setting up and maintaining equipment for scientific experiments, collecting data and providing support as part of the IARS team.

No research skills are required but experience with work in glaciology, geology, meteorology or oceanology would be valuable. The main requirements are technical skills (including electrical and mechanical engineering). You will need to cope with extreme conditions (including severe weather, dangerous environments and hazardous materials), work as a reliable member of an international team and follow instructions accurately and intelligently.

Applications to: Dr. Adelia Ross, IARS

B Read the cover letter. Which skills and abilities from Exercise A does Francesca mention? What doesn't she mention?

Dear Dr. Ross,

I am writing to apply for the position of Research Technician at the IARS.

You will see on my résumé (attached) that I have six years' experience as a laboratory technician at an international energy company, where I investigated energy efficiency. During this time, I gained invaluable insights into real-life research, where quick thinking and creativity are just as valuable as patience and precision.

I have explored the Polar regions many times. Last summer, I successfully led an international expedition to a remote part of Greenland, where I demonstrated exceptional organizational skills, resilience in the face of extreme challenges and, above all, the ability to work on a team.

I look forward to the opportunity of an interview.

Best regards,

Francesca Matienzo

C Read the information about using power verbs to apply for a job. Add five power verbs from Francesca's letter to the list of examples.

Using power verbs

In résumé and cover letters, it's more powerful to use verbs to describe your achievements (*I managed the project*) rather than nouns (*I was the manager of ...*) or adjectives (*I was responsible for ...*).

Examples: *achieved, coordinated, designed, implemented, improved, negotiated, organized, persuaded, strengthened, updated,* ________, ________, ________, ________, ________

D Make these extracts more powerful.

1 I was involved in negotiations to buy raw materials.

2 My manager agreed to my idea to switch suppliers.

3 I was in charge of a team of six.

4 Our old records were out of date, so I fixed them.

5 I did general office tasks, like answering the phone and checking emails.

WRITING

A PREPARE You are going to apply for your dream job or one of the jobs below. First, list the skills, abilities, experience and certifications required for the job.

- stunt performer
- safari or mountain guide
- zoo keeper
- astronaut

B PLAN Draft your cover letter, using Francesca's letter as a model.

C WRITE Make your letter more powerful by adding at least five power verbs.

D REVIEW Read some of your classmates' letters. Which letters would persuade you to invite the candidate for an interview? How could you improve the other letters?

Write a summary

paraphrasing

A SPEAK Work in pairs. How does stress affect the body?

B Read *The effects of stress on the body* and circle the specific health problems the article mentions.

The effects of stress on the body

Chronic stress can affect several different parts of the body, including the musculoskeletal system, the cardiovascular system and the gastrointestinal system.

Stress causes muscles to tense and when this happens for an extended period of time, it can cause tension and pain in the back, shoulders and head. For many people, this results in tension headaches and migraines.

It is well known that acute stress causes a temporary increase in heart rate and blood pressure. However, long-term stress means that heart rate and blood pressure remain high, potentially leading to inflammation of the arteries and an increased chance of hypertension, heart attack or stroke.

Stress can have a direct or indirect effect on the gastrointestinal system. Stress often causes people to eat more unhealthy food than they usually would. This can lead to heartburn and acid reflux, which can affect the throat. Stress can upset the stomach too, leading to digestive problems, nausea and even stomach ulcers.

In summary, long-term stress puts extra pressure on the body that can lead to health problems for various parts of the body, such as the muscles, the heart and stomach.

C Look at three draft summaries of the article. What are the problems with each of these summaries?

1 Long-term stress can lead to heart attacks and strokes because of the extra pressure it puts on the cardiovascular system. During periods of stress, our heart rate and blood pressure are raised. This is a natural response to stress, but it becomes harmful if it continues for an extended period of time.

2 It is important to use strategies to help you relax, so that stress does not lead to health problems with your muscles, heart and digestive system. For example, having an increased heart rate and increased blood pressure for an extended period of time can result in heart disease or stroke. Stress can also cause headaches, digestive problems and even panic attacks.

3 Chronic stress can affect different parts of the body, including the musculoskeletal system, the cardiovascular system and the gastrointestinal system. Stress causes muscles to tense, and people to eat more unhealthy food, which can upset the stomach.

D Read the information in the box about writing a summary. Then identify the main points in *The effects of stress on the body*.

Paraphrasing

It's important to focus on the main points of the source text, but not just to copy the text. You need to explain the information in your own words.

1 Identify the main points in the piece of text that you want to summarize. In an academic paper, look at the introduction, the topic sentences at the beginning of each paragraph and at the conclusion. In a newspaper article, look at the opening paragraph and the conclusion.

2 Note down any words you need to re-use from the text (i.e. proper nouns, technical words).

3 Explain the information in your own words. Use different structures and different words to make sure you aren't copying from the text. You can also put the information in a different order.

4 Check your summary. Make sure you have not copied parts of the original, introduced new information or changed the meaning.

WRITING

A WRITE Write a short summary of *The effects of stress on the body*. Do not write more than 60 words.

B REVIEW Exchange your summaries. Give your partner any suggestions for improvements.

C EDIT Use your partner's feedback to improve your summaries.

9 Writing

Write a conclusion to an academic report

W – linking in academic writing

A SPEAK Work in pairs. Say the following sentences aloud five times. Do they make you feel happier/sadder? Why?

1 Two new blue shoes flew to the moon.
2 These green leaves seem free and easy.
3 Our alarm can't harm the calm farmer.

B Read the conclusion to an academic report. Does it agree with your responses to Exercise A?

CONCLUSION

1 Our research set out to test the facial feedback hypothesis that our facial expressions can affect our moods. Strack *et al* (1988) famously asked respondents to evaluate cartoons while holding a pen in their mouths. Some held it between their teeth, forcing them to smile; others held it between their lips, forcing a frown. The 'smilers' found the cartoons significantly funnier than the 'frowners'. Similarly, Zajonc *et al* (1989), demonstrated a causal relationship between vowel sounds and mood: the repetition of 'smile vowels' (/e/, /iː/) and the 'aha vowel' (/ɑː/) put the respondents in a significantly better mood than 'frown vowels' (e.g. /uː/). However, recent research by Wagenmakers *et al* (2016) has cast serious doubt on this hypothesis.

2 Our own research provides limited support for the hypothesis. We found that repeating sentences with 'smile vowels' did indeed provoke a mood improvement compared to 'frown' vowels. However, in neither case were the results conclusive: the majority of respondents reported no change in mood. The one exception was that the 'aha vowel' had a significant positive effect on almost every respondent's mood.

3 Our evidence suggests that facial expressions do indeed affect mood, but it is principally the open-mouthed 'aha smile' rather than the wide-mouthed grin that has the greatest impact. This may explain the failure of Wagenmakers *et al* to repeat the effects of the pen experiment: they were focusing on the wrong type of smile.

4 If refined and confirmed by further research, the facial feedback hypothesis could be used by psychotherapists and carers to improve patients' moods. Additionally, marketers may use vowel sounds in product names to influence customers' connotations. If products such as 'New You' are renamed as 'Calming Spa', it may well be because of the effect of vowel sounds on our mood.

C Match the topics (a–d) with the paragraphs (1–4).

a Analysis: What did you learn? ___
b Implications: What do your findings mean? ___
c Background: What question were you trying to answer? ___
d Key findings: What information did you collect? ___

D Answer the questions. Use the information in the box to help you.

Linking in academic writing

Use linking words (e.g. *however*) to show the relationships between ideas.

Use colons (:) to show that one idea 'explains' another.

Use semi-colons (;) to show that two related ideas are 'equal' in importance.

1 Find a semi-colon in paragraph 1. In what way are the two ideas equal?
2 Which two linking words in paragraph 1 link all the research together?
3 Find three colons in paragraphs 1–3. How does the second idea explain the first in each case?
4 What linking word in paragraphs 2 and 3 relates expectations to reality? What grammar structure is often used with this word?
5 How does the writer link the main ideas in paragraph 4?

WRITING

A PREPARE Choose one of your own ideas or a piece of academic research from this unit.

B PLAN Write notes about the points you will cover in your conclusion.

C WRITE Write a four-paragraph conclusion. Use linking words, colons and semi-colons in your writing.

D REVIEW Exchange your conclusion with a partner. Do you agree with their analysis? Comment on how they use linking words.

E EDIT Read your partner's comments. Rewrite any parts of your conclusion that you think could be improved.

10 Writing

Write a persuasive essay

W using counter-arguments and rebuttals

A SPEAK Work in pairs. Look at the essay title and discuss the questions.

1 What is gentrification?

2 What do you think of gentrification? Is it a good or bad thing?

B Read the example essay and answer the questions.

1 What is the writer's opinion of gentrification?

2 What reasons does the writer give for her opinion?

3 What reason to support the opposite opinion on gentrification does the writer mention?

DOES GENTRIFICATION HAVE A POSITIVE OR NEGATIVE IMPACT ON CITIES?

In cities all over the world, 'gentrification' is changing entire neighborhoods. Some people argue that this improves the areas by making them cleaner and safer. However, on the whole, gentrification actually has a negative impact. It prices people out of the areas where they have lived for years, destroys the unique character of neighborhoods, and it only benefits the rich.

The most obvious negative impact of gentrification is that it forces long-term residents to move away from their homes. As an area becomes trendy, landlords are able to increase the rent and attract wealthier tenants to the area. Meanwhile, lower income families are forced to move away from their friends, schools and jobs to find cheaper places to live.

Gentrification also results in the area losing its individual character. People may have first been attracted to an area by its unique stores and restaurants. However, as this area becomes gentrified, these establishments are unlikely to be able to pay increased rent. Gradually, these stores and restaurants are replaced by clothing chains so the area becomes just like many other neighborhoods in the city.

Some people argue that gentrification has a positive impact because the area becomes cleaner and safer. While it is true that gentrification leads to less crime and better facilities, the local people who deserve to benefit from these changes are unable to stay in the area. Rather than improving the city for all, gentrification only benefits the wealthiest.

In conclusion, gentrification predominantly has a negative impact on cities. It forces long-term residents from their homes, results in areas losing their individual character, and only provides real benefits for those with the most money. The government needs to find a way to ensure that redevelopment of the city can have a positive effect for everyone.

C Find the phrases the writer used to introduce the counter argument and rebuttal in the example essay. Use the information in the box to help you.

Using counter-arguments and rebuttals

In order to strengthen your argument in a persuasive essay, you can anticipate the points that could be used to support the opposite side of the argument (the counter-arguments) and respond with your answer to those arguments (a rebuttal). The rebuttal must respond directly to the counter argument.

Introduce a counter argument with phrases like:

- *Opponents/Supporters of .... claim/argue/believe that ...*
- *Some studies have shown that ...*
- *There is an argument that ...*

Introduce a rebuttal with phrases like:

- *However, this is only partially true.*
- *Studies have shown this is not true.*
- *Nevertheless, ...*

WRITING

A PREPARE Work in pairs. Look at the essay prompt and brainstorm reasons to support each side.

> Which is better: living in the city or living in the country?

Reasons why living in the city is better	Reasons why living in the country is better

B PLAN Decide on your best points from Exercise A and make a plan of your essay.

C WRITE Write a persuasive essay to answer the essay prompt. Use a counter-argument and rebuttal in the third body paragraph. Use the example essay to help you.

D REVIEW Exchange your essay with a partner. How could your partner's essay be improved? How effective are their counter-arguments and rebuttals?

E EDIT Read your partner's comments. Rewrite any parts of your essay you think can be improved.

Audio scripts

1 TRENDS

Lesson 1.1, Listening, Exercise B

1.1 **C = Carly D = Dan**

C: So? How did the job interview go, Dan?

D: It was a breeze! I got the job. But the thing is, I start in two weeks and I don't have anything to wear. The job involves meeting important clients. But they won't take me seriously in my scruffy jeans and hoodie!

C: Sounds like you need some new clothes.

D: I know. But I'm on a tight budget until I receive my first few months' salary.

C: Well, it's easy to look good without spending a fortune. Do you have a suit?

D: No, but I saw a suit yesterday for 40% off in a sale, so I'll save almost $100 if I buy that.

C: Well, you're only saving money if you buy something you really need. If you're just buying it because it's cheap, you're throwing money down the drain. It's much better in the long run to invest in timeless classics. For example, instead of buying a cheap off-the-rack suit that you'll need to replace in a few months, save up for a tailor-made suit that will make you look great for many years.

D: OK, I admit that suit was a little cheap-looking. But it was the only one in my size. They had some nice suits in the sale, but they were all too tight or too loose for me.

C: Well, you can always buy oversized clothes – as long as they're good quality, and then take them in.

D: What do you mean, take them in?

C: It's when you unpick the seams, move the pieces of fabric closer together, and sew them back together. In fact, more generally, I'd say the best way to look good without spending a lot of money is to learn to sew. But hang on a second. Didn't you have to wear a suit for the job interview?

D: Well, it was an online interview, so I just wore a jacket from an old suit and a nice shirt and tie to create a good impression. They had no idea I was wearing baggy sweatpants under my desk!

C: Haha, no, you're kidding me! It's usually a good idea to mix and match parts of different outfits, which can save you a lot of money, but I'd say mixing a suit with a sweatsuit is taking things a little far! Do you still have the pants to go with that jacket?

D: Yeah, I actually have two old suits with perfectly good jackets but pants that I can't wear! One pair is coming apart at the seams. The other is completely worn out at the knee.

C: Hmm, it sounds like you can start your sewing lessons on those pants! Then you'll have two suits in your closet for peanuts! That's actually a good example of how to go shopping in your closet.

D: Sorry. Where?

C: In your closet. Most people have a lot of clothes that they never wear. The trick is to sort them into four categories: love, mend, sell and trash.

D: Go on.

C: 'Love' is for the clothes that make you look and feel great. 'Mend' is for the clothes that you need to adjust or repair. 'Sell' is for the clothes that you can auction online. And then 'trash' is for everything else. Basically you need to get rid of them!

D: OK, I have a lot of clothes that I could sell, but I've never used an auction website before. Do you think anyone will buy my old clothes?

C: You'd be surprised. I mean, most customers on those sites stick to the professional sellers with beautiful tailor-made sales pages created by web designers. But I actually buy most of my clothes from ugly sales pages, created by inexperienced sellers.

D: What? Are you saying I should create an ugly sales page for my second-hand clothes?

C: No, not at all. The more professional your sales page, the more you can charge for your clothes. And it needs to be a seamless process for your customers from beginning to end. So as a general rule, when you're selling clothes, it's well worth taking the time to make your sales page look good. For example, you can just use one of the off-the-rack templates from the auction site. Choose a template that catches your eye – it's much better than creating your own site from scratch.

D: OK, sounds like good advice. And when I'm buying clothes online, to replace the ones I'm selling?

C: Then you should look out for newbie sellers with bad photos – they're usually good for picking up a bargain.

D: Ah, yes, that makes sense. So are auction sites the best place to pick up cheap second-hand clothes?

C: Sometimes, but the best place to buy them is usually thrift stores, even though they're pretty exhausting! You need to know where to go if you want to avoid wearing yourself out for nothing! For instance, the best thrift stores are in expensive, exclusive neighborhoods. You'd be amazed what you can pick up there. The trick is to avoid stores in a trendy area or one with a lot of students – all the best stuff will be snapped up immediately.

D: OK, good. What about regular stores?

C: They're fine as long as you're not too choosy – the big-name stores are usually no better than others, but they charge a lot more for the same stuff! But wherever you go, don't forget to haggle to get the price down.

D: What do you mean?

C: Ask the sales clerks for a discount. I always ask, 'Is this the best you can do?' Many sales clerks are authorized to offer discounts, so it's always worth haggling. You have nothing to lose but your pride!

D: OK. I'll give it a try. Thanks.

Lesson 1.2, Listening, Exercise B

1.3 **D = Dora A = Adam**

A: Hello and welcome to the latest 'Website design podcast'. Today, I've invited Dora Cho to talk about becoming a trendsetter. As I'm sure you know, Dora's video channel is the most hyper-influential source of advice on lifestyle trends on the web. Dora, are you there?

A: Sorry. I forgot to unmute Dora's microphone. Dora?

D: Hello? Can you hear me now?

A: Yes. Sorry, Dora. Should we restart?

D: You know what? Keep going. One of the most common mistakes that new vloggers and podcasters make is to expect everything to be perfect. So they edit and re-edit everything again and again. But when things go wrong, we hear the real, authentic 'you', and that's what makes your podcast engaging. You actually need to unlearn all those rules about perfection!

A: OK. But your videos are always amazing. You seem so self-confident and relaxed. How do you do that?

D: It all comes down to experience. My first videos were pretty cheesy and amateurish. I used to be fairly disaster-prone with technology: everything that could go wrong did go wrong. But after a while, it got a lot easier! I learned everything by taking risks and making mistakes. It was frustrating at the time but you need to go through that experience. I'm a lot more tech-savvy now, but I'm still learning.

A: Great. So how did you start your vlog?

D: First of all, I set myself a target of one video every week for a year. I figured that if nobody cared after a year, I'd give up. And it did take a while to get noticed, which was frustrating. But after several months, I started to see fairly big audience numbers. By the end of the year I had 7,000 subscribers.

A: Wow! And now?

D: Six million.

A: Amazing! So what am I doing wrong with my podcasts?

D: Well, there's no need to be negative. The most important thing is that you've found your niche and you've created some excellent content.

A: Really? Oh, thank you.

D: Yeah, it's true. But if you want to move to the next level, you need to be really systematic. I mean, when do your podcasts come out?

A: It depends. Whenever I have a somewhat good idea for a podcast, then I try to make it within a few days.

D: OK, but you can't expect your listeners to check your website every day on the off-chance that you've released another episode – that's not user-friendly at all. But my followers can be absolutely sure that every Wednesday at ten o'clock, there will be a new video on my channel.

A: OK. But what if you run out of ideas?

D: I won't. I plan everything at least six months in advance, and I set alerts on my phone to tell me what to do and when. I've tried to make my system idiot-proof so that I can't mess up!

A: OK …

D: You also need to be far more social media-savvy: once you've released each episode, tell the world about it. And don't just post a link – you need to engage with your audience, too, by replying to the comments on your site. People love to feel listened to.

A: Every single comment?

D: Well, there are plenty of people who post offensive or spammy comments. The trick is to ignore them and focus on the people who want to join your community. You can also ask them what they'd like you to talk about in future podcasts. Once you have an active community behind you, you'll never run out of ideas.

A: Right. OK, so I'll do all that. But it sounds like hard work!

D: It is hard work! Not long ago, a journalist mentioned my blog in an article about overnight successes. I suppose in many people's eyes, I am an overnight success. They probably think I'm super-lucky to have hit the big time. But they don't see the years of hard work behind that success.

A: Right. So I just need to keep working hard on my podcasts, right?

D: Well, your podcasts are great, as I say, but actually I think your content would work much better as smartphone-friendly videos. I mean, you talk about website design, so we really need to be able to see what you're talking about.

A: Maybe, but I'm not as charismatic as you. I hate being in front of the camera.

D: Well, I felt awkward at first, too, but you do get used to it. I really think you should rethink and become a vlogger instead.

A: OK. I'll give it a try. Dora Cho, thanks so much for joining me today. You've given me a long list of jobs to do! I feel super-exhausted just thinking about it.

2 CREATIVITY

Lesson 2.1, Listening, Exercise C

.1 **P = Presenter C = Caroline**

P: This week's guest on *More than meets the eye* is art historian Caroline Bishop. Caroline, thanks for joining us.

C: It's my pleasure. Thank you for having me.

P: So the painting you've picked also happens to be one of the great masterpieces. Could you start by telling us its name and a little about the painter?

C: Sure. It's a painting by Velázquez, called *Las Meninas*. Velázquez is one of Spain's most important artists. He painted in a Baroque style, which means his paintings are very ornate, detailed and realistic. He mainly painted historical scenes and portraits. He painted *Las Meninas* after he'd been given a prominent position in the royal court.

P: And can you describe the painting to us?

C: Well, it depicts a scene in the artist's studio. In the center foreground we have the young Infanta Margaret Theresa, the daughter of the King and Queen – the word *Infanta* is similar in meaning to princess. The Infanta is framed on either side by her two ladies-in-waiting. Then to the right we have two other women from the royal court and a dog. Behind them are the Infanta's attendants – a chaperone and bodyguard – and further in the background, there's a royal official in a doorway.

P: OK. So, we are probably looking at the Infanta's entourage?

C: Hmm … yes we can see her entourage on the right, but to the left, we can see the artist himself, standing next to a gigantic canvas. The inclusion of the artist in the painting is one of the things that makes this such an interesting piece. It seems more like a snapshot, taken behind the scenes of the royal court, rather than the typical posed portraits of the time. It was a very original composition – groundbreaking at the time.

P: So, do you know why he chose such an unconventional composition?

C: Actually, there are several theories about this – which is one of the things I like best about the painting. There's been a lot of debate about who the subject of the painting really is. On first inspection, it seems that the Infanta is the subject – after all she's in the center of the painting. But then, if you look in the background, there appears to be a mirror that shows the King and Queen. This suggests that the artist is actually painting *their* portrait. So we, the viewer, are actually seeing the world through the eyes of the King and Queen. The Infanta and her companions are merely watching.

P: So, it's a portrait of the King and Queen, not the Infanta. Is that right?

C: Well … some people think so, yes. Even though the image of them is really small.

P: That's a very imaginative idea – and really unusual for a royal portrait I'm guessing.

C: Yes, absolutely. However … there's one other interpretation that I like. Some people believe that the scene we see is actually just the reflection in a large mirror. What we're seeing is the artist at work in his studio.

P: So this may even be a self-portrait?

C: Exactly. The point of the picture may be to show us the artist's life – this is his studio, this is what it was like when he was painting a portrait. It's actually a very complex composition. It's like a puzzle for the viewer to decide what is really happening.

P: It's fascinating – and I'm not sure which interpretation I like best. Anyway, why did you choose it as your favorite painting? Do you have a personal connection to the work?

C: Well, I first saw this painting in the Prado Gallery in Madrid over 20 years ago when I was a student. And the first time I saw it, I was astounded. It's sensational. I'd never seen anything like it. In fact, I switched to art history a couple of months later.

P: So this painting helped you to choose your career?

C: Yes, yes it did.

Lesson 2.2, Listening, Exercise A

2.5 **M = Mark L = Lauren**

L: Hi Mark, how's the dissertation going?

M: Terrible, Lauren. I'm stuck. I have no ideas today. Zero.

L: Oh, no. How awful! But did you see that article Simon shared about how people find inspiration? It's really interesting.

M: Yeah? He's always sharing self-help stuff, but…

L: No, but this one's different. It's real artists, writers, directors, musicians and dancers talking about how they come up with their ideas.

M: Hmm … So, what did they say then?

L: Oh … let me find it. Here we go. OK. This person's a fashion designer and he says, 'Inspiration can strike at any time. I sometimes get ideas when I'm out shopping or walking in the park. I always carry a pen and paper with me, so I can sketch it or write it down. Sometimes the smallest thing can trigger an idea. A flower, a smile, a color.'

M: OK. Isn't that somewhat pretentious? Can't he just use his phone to write notes? And anyway a blank notebook is still a blank notebook.

L: OK, here's an artist – he says the best time for him to get ideas is very early in the morning – when you're not exactly awake and not exactly asleep. He often sets his alarm for 4 am, so he can get into the right state of mind to have ideas.

M: What! Is he crazy? He must never get enough sleep.

L: Yeah, but come on, I know what he means. A few times, I've had a good idea just before waking up – usually when I have a problem that I'm trying to solve.

M: Well, I don't think it's going to work for my dissertation.

L: OK. But here's an actual writer. Apparently, she thinks you have to be really disciplined and get into a regular routine. You just sit down and write, because if you wait for ideas to come, you'll never do anything. She says choose a time and stick to it – even if you don't feel like it or even if your writing is terrible, you just need to shut the door, remove all distractions and write.

M: Why does she keep writing if it's terrible? I don't want my dissertation to be terrible!

L: How about this then? You should immerse yourself in other things. Do something completely different – like watch a movie. Then when you get back to your desk, you'll be refreshed and ready to be creative again.

M: That's the first thing that I agree with! I need to take a break. I think I need a change of scenery … right now.

L: Yeah, it doesn't hurt, does it? I also think it helps to talk to people – you know, bounce ideas around with someone and see if they can improve your idea. It can really help to get a fresh perspective on something.

M: Isn't that a little … scary? I don't think I want to share this dissertation until it's finished.

L: Well, it has to be someone you trust. Celia and I usually read each other's work, so we're used to helping each other. She also thinks that if you're working from a completely blank canvas, the possibilities can seem limitless, so she likes to impose some restrictions – such as using a particular genre or restricting herself to a particular format. I think she likes to set herself a challenge. That's pretty fun, don't you think?

M: OK, it's very interesting – and I guess it makes sense. It must be easier to decide what to do if you have fewer choices.

L: Yeah, and I really like the idea of giving yourself a challenge like that. There's one other thing you could do. An artist here says it's important to take risks. You might not fully understand what you're doing, but you just have to trust your instincts and run with it.

M: Is she serious? How can you make something when you don't know what you're doing?

L: Haven't you ever started doodling a picture without knowing what it was going to be?

M: Hmm … I guess so …

L: Well, I think that's what she means. So … anyway, good luck with the dissertation, Mark.

M: Thanks, Lauren!

3 PROGRESS

Lesson 3.1, Listening, Exercise B

3.1 **S = Saleswoman M = Man W = Woman**

S: Excuse me, sir. Do you ride a bike, by any chance?

M: Well, I have a bike yes. Why do you ask?

S: You just look like a very healthy and athletic person.

M: Really? Thank you. Well, I haven't ridden my bike for months. It's too wet right now.

S: Yeah, tell me about it! I bet you can't wait for the weather to warm up so you can get out on your bike, can you?

M: Uh, no. I guess not. It's not much fun biking in the rain!

S: Hmm, I know exactly what you mean. It sounds like you need some smart biking clothes.

M: Uh, sorry? I don't …

S: Smart biking clothes are made from smart materials, which change their form depending on their environment. Let me show you an example. This biking hat is made from an advanced material that responds to your body temperature. It's somewhat complicated technology, but I'll try to simplify it for you. Just imagine you're out on your bike early one morning. When you leave home, the fibers in your hat respond to the cold temperature by tightening up. That ensures there's no heat loss from your head and keeps you nice and warm. But as you warm up, the gaps between the fibers in your hat automatically enlarge to allow air to flow freely around your head, to cool you down. But then let's imagine it starts to rain. As the hat gets wet, the water strengthens the fibers and the gaps close to keep your head dry. Amazing, isn't it?

M: Yes. It sounds very inventive.

S: It is inventive! This technology is straight out of the laboratory. You won't find these in any stores for years!

M: Really?

S: No. We're still at the testing stage. Hey, would you be willing to test it for us? We'd absolutely love to hear how you do with it. It would be incredibly useful for us.

M: Uh, possibly. What would it involve?

S: You wear your hat for a few weeks while you're riding your bike, and then you fill in a five-minute questionnaire about your experiences. And of course you get to keep your hat at the end! Would that be OK?

M: Really? Yeah, why not?

S: Great! Thanks. Here's your hat. Congratulations! I just need you to sign this form to formalize our agreement.

M: OK, no problem.

S: Thanks. We're planning to sell the hats for $50 in the future, so I think you got yourself an excellent deal there, sir. I can see you're a very smart negotiator!

M: Am I? Yes, I suppose so. Thanks a lot.

S: No problem. Actually, maybe there is a problem. Did you say you never go biking in the rain?

M: Yes. Why?

S: Ah … well we really need people to describe their experiences of wearing the hat in different weather conditions over the next couple of weeks, including rain. I'm so sorry – this is really embarrassing. Should I take the hat back?

M: Uh, no. I don't mind biking in the rain once or twice. I'll just have to get a little wet, I suppose!

S: Really? Oh that would be amazing if you could. And you know what? Maybe I can help you out there. You see, we also have some smart biking jackets. They're made of tiny fibers that flatten when they're wet, making the coat completely waterproof, and they open up again when dry, enabling your skin to breathe. Again, they're not available for sale for a while, but maybe I can make an exception for you. Do you mind waiting a second while I call my boss?

M: No, not at all. Go ahead.

S: Great! Oh hi, Debbie. Listen, I have a gentleman here who's interested in buying the biking coat. I know we're not allowed to sell them yet, but … No way, huh? Are you sure? He's going to help us test our hat. Really? Oh, that's great. Thanks, Debbie! I owe you one. Good news! She says she's willing to make an exception, just for you.

M: Oh, great. Thanks. Uh, how much is it?

S: Well, we're planning to sell them for $500. But … hmm … maybe … I can offer you … a special price … to thank you for your help. I'll give you 10% off … would that be better?

M: Yes, I guess so.

S: Excellent. So that's $450, please. Will you be paying by cash or credit card?

M: Uh, credit card, I suppose.

S: Yes. Of course. Just put in your PIN here.

S: OK, perfect. Thanks. And here's your coat. Thanks so much for helping us out with the testing. I really appreciate it.

M: You're welcome. And thank you. You've been very nice. Goodbye.

S: Goodbye.

Lesson 3.2, Listening, Exercise B

.3 **P = Presenter B = Bob M = Mary J = James C = Callum S = Sonia**

P: Hello, and welcome to *The Progress Show*. According to a recent survey, despite amazing progress in technology and sharp increases in living standards, many of us believe our quality of life has actually decreased! So this week, I interviewed some people on the street about their lives. I asked them, would you say the world is generally getting better or worse? Let's hear a few extracts from those interviews.

So Bob, would you say the world is getting better or worse?

B: Worse, definitely. When I was a teenager, we always showed respect for older people. For example, no sooner had an older person gotten on the bus than we all stood up to offer the person a seat. I was on a bus the other day, and it was full of teenagers, but not one person offered me a seat. Only after they'd all gotten off the bus could I finally sit down.

P: So Mary, what's your view?

M: I'd say it's getting worse for people of my age. People of my parents' age had it much easier. There was plenty of work for everybody, and apartments and houses were much cheaper. But everyone of my age seems to be struggling for money. No way could I ever afford an apartment. It's not fair!

P: James, what do you think?

J: I feel like I'm going backwards sometimes. I mean, when I was younger, life was simple. None of our neighbors had much money, and neither did we. But we didn't need much, so we were content just to get on with life. But these days, if you don't post endless selfies of your perfect lifestyle on social media, you feel like a reject from society. It's very frustrating and stressful.

P: Callum, what's your take on this?

C: On balance, it's probably getting worse. You see such terrible things on TV all the time – crime, wars, diseases! I don't remember anything like that from my childhood. Mind you, I didn't watch much TV when I was a kid and I certainly didn't read any newspapers.

P: Sonia, how about you?

S: Worse, much worse. I remember when I was in my early twenties, life was wonderful. Not only did I have great friends, but we also did cool things all the time … and the sun always seemed to be shining. Nowadays, life's just work work work … and the weather's always terrible too!

Lesson 3.2, Listening, Exercise D

.4 **Pre = Presenter Pro = Professor**

Pre: Let's turn now to my guest, Professor Nila Martinelli, an expert in psychology. Professor, is the world really getting worse?

Pro: No, not at all. However you choose to measure people's well-being, life for the average person is getting better. But the key word there is 'average'. By no means am I suggesting that life is wonderful for everyone everywhere. But the vast majority of the world's population really is better off, year after year.

Pre: OK, so why do so many people say the opposite?

Pro: Well, it's all due to a psychological process called declinism, which is a feeling that things are declining, or getting worse. Declinism has a number of separate causes, including something called the inequality paradox. Let me give you an example. Say you live in a community where everybody has terrible healthcare and education, and so on, but overall people just accept that life is hard. But now imagine that 20% of the people suddenly become a lot better off, with comfortable lifestyles and so on. Those 20% push the average up, so according to statistics, the population seems better off. But in fact the remaining 80% feel much worse than before, because they're now aware of what they're missing.

Pre: Ah. That makes sense.

Pro: Another reason is the so-called reminiscence bump. Scientists have conducted plenty of research on this subject which shows that we build up our strongest memories in our late teens and early twenties. Our memories of early adulthood stay with us for ever. This is why so many people are nostalgic for that time in their life.

Pre: Oh … so it's almost as if we rewrite the events in our memories in order to perfect the picture of our younger days!

Pro: Exactly! One of my favorite phenomena is something I call the them-and-us delusion. If you were a well-behaved child, you're likely to remember that most other kids of your age were similarly well-behaved. But that's probably because you didn't notice their bad behavior at the time. Or you've simply erased their negative attributes and bad conduct from your memory. But when you look at a group of people from the outside, what do you notice most? The noisiest, worst-behaved ones. That explains why so many people think that kids today are worse than their own generations.

Pre: Yeah, I suppose you're right. I don't remember much about my childhood!

Pro: No – and that's normal. Children simply fail to notice things that are obvious to adults. When I was a child, never in a million years did it occur to me that my parents were worried about money or job insecurity or whatever. But that doesn't mean they never talked about those things. This is something that we might call the invisible struggle phenomenon: we don't see the problems that other people face, so we think we're the only ones with such problems. We tend to attribute other people's success to luck and we overlook all the problems they've struggled with. And of course that's a major source of inter-generational conflict: young adults always suspect that earlier generations had it much easier!

Pre: Ah. I see what you mean.

Pro: There's one last aspect of declinism, and it's called the window-on-the-world effect. It arises when people become aware of the terrible things that happen around the world. Centuries ago, people were blissfully unaware of wars and diseases in distant countries. But nowadays, we see such things on a daily basis on the news, on social media and so on. So it's not that terrible events are necessarily becoming more frequent, but rather that we're aware of those events. And for me, the fact that more and more people care about global tragedies makes it more likely that we'll do something about them. And that's my main reason for optimism that the world really is getting better, and will continue to do so.

Pre: Hmm … Professor Nila Martinelli, thanks very much for joining us.

4 INTELLIGENCE

Lesson 4.1, Listening, Exercise B

4.1 **H = Host Dr = Dr. Carter A = Amanda**

H: On this week's episode of *Ask an Expert*, we're talking about boosting your brain power. These days many products claim to make you smarter. But is it really possible? To answer the question, I'm joined today by two experts: Dr. Ramona Carter, a leading neuroscientist, and Amanda Saraha, a life coach and the author of *How to be smarter*. Thank you for joining me.

A: Thanks, John.

Dr: Thank you, John.

H: So first up, Amanda, the big question. Can people really make themselves smarter?

A: The short answer is yes, John. But the first step may actually be believing it's possible. Researchers have shown that when a group of students are told it's possible to become more intelligent, they can retain more of what they learn.

H: Dr. Carter, do you agree? Can we make ourselves brighter? One way that's very popular is brain training games.

Dr: I have to admit, I love them. But I'm skeptical about whether they have any long-term effects. The problem is that the effects are probably not transferable. So for example, if you do a lot of Sudoku, the math puzzle where you write the numbers in boxes, it's most likely that you will just become better at playing that game.

A team from Cambridge actually tried to shed some light on the impact of brain-training games. They had thousands of participants, so this was a big study doing brain training activities for at least 10 minutes a day, three times a week for six weeks. They tested them before and after. And the results showed no improvements in their test scores. In other words, their study showed that brain training didn't actually work.

A: Actually, if you don't mind me saying, that was just one study. Another study looked at older people playing a game that involved multi-tasking – they had to drive a car and look out for specific symbols as they drove. In this study, the participants showed that not only did they get better at the game, but that they also improved their attention and working memory.

Dr: Yes, you're right. But it's worth noting that this study specifically involved a video game rather than a typical brain-training game. Playing video games may affect our cognitive abilities according to research. But these kinds of games may prove to be more beneficial than dedicated brain-training games.

H: So overall, the findings about playing games are a little inconclusive right now. So, what else can we do to boost our brain power?

A: There are actually a lot of things you can do. For example, have you ever wondered why so many high achievers boast about starting the day with a workout? I strongly believe that the exercise they are doing makes them smarter and more competitive.

Dr: Well … I'd be cautious about making a direct link between high achievement and exercise, but there is a pretty clear consensus that exercise is good for the brain. Some scientists believe that exercise can help to promote the growth and formation of neurons in the hippocampus – so, as I mentioned before, if we retain the new cells that our body produces, it could affect our ability to think and remember.

H: Hmm … Is food another factor? Recently, we've seen a lot of media stories about super foods, food that you should eat to boost your brain power – fatty fish, blueberries, even chocolate. Is this true, Dr. Carter?

Dr: Um, the research is actually fairly inconclusive. Some studies have shown that eating a healthy diet has an impact on thinking ability, but claims that particular foods can impact your intelligence are mostly exaggerated or misleading.

H: Do you agree, Amanda?

A: As Dr. Carter says, we may still be in the dark about the science behind it, but I personally believe that the food we eat has a huge effect on every aspect of our lives. I know a lot of people who strongly believe that changing their diet has made them smarter.

H: OK. So maybe I do need to rethink my lunch choices. And is there anything else we can do to boost our intelligence. Amanda?

A: Well, we haven't talked about this yet, but it's actually really important to take some time out and unplug for a while. You need to disconnect from your phone and your computer and let your mind wander.

Dr: I completely agree with this. Getting enough sleep, taking some time to rest, sitting quietly or meditating has a big impact on reducing stress and anxiety, and it also helps you think. There are studies that back this up – they have shown that students who daydream do better on standardized tests than those who remain completely focused on a task.

H: So, resting can boost your brain power? That's good to know!

Lesson 4.2, Listening, Exercise B

4.4 **C = Chair E = Ella**

C: So the motion is: 'Intelligence gives people the greatest advantage in life.' Now I look to Ella to open the case against the motion.

E: Thank you very much. It's an honor to speak against the motion tonight. Right, it's easy to see why so many people believe being intelligent makes your life better. After all, we see intelligent people thriving at school. We see them getting into the college courses they want. We see them graduating with good academic certifications. And on top of that, we see the importance the world gives to certifications.

So, it may seem strange for me to stand here and argue that intelligent people aren't necessarily at an advantage in life. However, that is exactly what I'll do. In fact, there are several clear disadvantages in having a superior intellect.

Let's start with a lack of common sense. And let's talk about a chess champion. Not just any chess champion, but a chess champion that was also a child chess prodigy. She must be smart, right? Well, talk to her mother. According to her, she frequently locks her car keys inside her car. The 'nutty professor' – smart but absent-minded and eccentric – is a common stereotype of highly intelligent people. Some scientists believe that geniuses' brains are wired differently. While highly intelligent people are curious about complex puzzles and are able to troubleshoot, they can't deal with more mundane tasks. So Ms. Chess Champion could beat 15 chess players in a row … but she can't drive herself home.

Another problem faced by intelligent people is an inability to socialize. We've all known that friend at school or college. They're ready to answer in the physics class, they ask the lecturer countless questions and their voice drowns out everybody else's in the seminar. Then you take them to a party. Suddenly it seems like wishful thinking that anyone will talk to them again. Ever. Probably because they're still talking about physics. There are a few reasons why highly intelligent people are thought of as socially awkward. First, they find small talk tedious. You find them correcting other people's mistakes or trying to engage in a passionate debate at a casual social event. Second, they are incredibly self-conscious. This means they tend to overthink things and appear awkward.

And finally, there's the burden of expectation. You have a reputation to protect. If everyone thinks you're a genius, they expect you to be successful and make an impact in the world. Sometimes the pressure is just too much. Highly intelligent people can end up dropping out of education altogether and trying to hide their intellect to fit in. Or they're afraid to look stupid. So they avoid asking questions when they need to, or they try to skip the basics when they learn something new, which, of course, only creates problems down the line.

In summary, if you think that being smart means lounging in a bath tub waiting for a eureka moment, then think again. There are a lot of downsides to intelligence. Geniuses can lack common sense, find it difficult to socialize, and feel pressure to live up to expectations. I've always said myself that intelligence and happiness don't necessarily go together. This is no surprise to people who lock their keys in their car, don't have any friends to drive them and are too scared to ask. In fact, being highly intelligent makes life more not less difficult.

5 GAMES

Lesson 5.1, Listening, Exercise B

5.1 **J = Joe O = Olga L = Lin**

Part 1

J: OK, so we've been locked in. So where's the key?

L: Found it! It's at the bottom of this measuring cylinder.

J: Really?! That was easy!

L: Yeah, but there's a metal bar across the top with a combination lock attached to it. No way will we get that big key through this narrow gap.

O: So we need to figure out the combination to remove the bar, right?

L: Exactly. But even if we could do that, my arm's nowhere near long enough to reach the key at the bottom.

O: Can you tip it upside down?

L: Nah, it's attached to the wall. It can't be moved.

J: Try pulling it really hard.

O: Seriously?! That's cheating! Anyway, we'll get thrown out if anything gets broken! According to the instructions, we're not allowed to use force to move things!

J: I don't remember being given any instructions.

O: We were asked to sign a form at the front desk. Those were the instructions, Joe!

J: Ah, I wondered what that form was.

L: Didn't you read it?!

J: Uh, sorry. I just signed it.

L: Unbelievable! Anyway, there are microphones all over the place, so we're probably being listened to right now!

J: OK, so we need to get the key out of the cylinder without touching it. But that's impossible.

O: Not necessarily. Look. There's a cork attached to the key.

Part 2

O: I think the cylinder needs to be filled with water. Then the cork will float to the top, lifting the key with it.

L: Well, there's some water in this big vase, but nowhere near enough to fill that measuring cylinder.

J: What about this cooking oil? Do you think the cork will float on oil?

O: Absolutely. Bring it over here.

J: Hmm, I can't. The jug's attached to the shelf.

L: Typical! Could we use the vase to transfer the oil?

O: No. It needs to be something small enough to fit inside the jug and scoop out the oil. There must be a cup hidden somewhere. What's in that chest of drawers, Lin?

L: Let's take a look. An electric scale, a bath towel and, hmm, there's no handle on the bottom drawer. I can't open it. Any ideas?

J: Uh, maybe it'll open if we press that switch on the wall.

L: It's just a light switch, Joe! It won't … Oh amazing! You just turned all the lights off! Excellent!

J: Wait! I did it! Look up! There's a secret message on the ceiling! It must have been written in fluorescent paint – it's only visible in the dark. But it's just one word: sugar.

O: Really? There are some sugar cubes on the shelf, but how does that help us?

Part 3

L: This is ridiculous. We've been stuck in here for almost an hour. We should've been given more clues. Should we give up?

J: Give up?! No way! I told all my friends I'm great at puzzles. If we give up now, I'll be made fun of for weeks. There must be a clue somewhere – something we're missing.

O: I've figured it out! Something must have been hidden inside those sugar cubes! We need to dissolve them in water!

J: Yesss! There's some water in that vase.

O: Great! They're dissolving. And I was right. There's something there. What is it? Something metal? Aha! Two screws!

L: Screws? What are we supposed to do with them?

O: We can screw them into the holes in the drawer and use them to pull it open. Just a second.

J: You did it! You've found the cup! We're free!

L: Are you joking?! We still need to remove the metal bar from the cylinder, which means working out the combination to that lock.

J: Oh yeah, I forgot.

L: Joe! We have two minutes left! Think of something!

J: Stop yelling at me! I can't think when I'm being yelled at!

O: I suppose at least we can transfer the oil to the cylinder while we're thinking. Pass me the cup. Thanks. Ooh! There's something in the jug!

L: Yeah right! There's nothing there besides the oil. You need to get your eyes tested! Oh!

O: I was right! A glass ball. Maybe we're supposed to weigh it.

J: Great! But it's covered in oil, and so are you! Be careful not to drop it!

O: Aha, that's what the towel's for! We need to clean the oil off it first!

L: OK, but hurry up! We only have 60 seconds!

O: Calm down! OK, it weighs one kilogram 327 grams. Try that combination, Joe! One three two seven.

J: One, three, two, seven. Yes! It worked. Quick, bring the oil over! How much time do we have?

L: Forty-five seconds! Come on! Hurry up!

Lesson 5.2, Listening, Exercise C
5.4 **P = Presenter**

P: So? What did you make of puzzle A – the Take or Share game? The fairest outcome would be for both of you to choose SHARE, and to win $500 each. Sadly, it's more complicated than that. By choosing that option you're risking losing everything. It turns out that the best strategy in a one-round game is to be selfish, because you have a 50/50 chance of winning $1,000, which is better than a 50/50 chance of winning $500. The problem is, your opponent can be assumed to be having the same thoughts, so you'll both probably end up with nothing anyway!

This example comes from Game Theory, which involves using mathematical models to solve problems where your choices affect – and are affected by – other people's choices. It allows for more accurate predictions and estimates.

Coming back to puzzle A, things get really fascinating over several rounds, because now you can reward your partner's kindness, or punish his or her selfishness. For example, if you share the money in the first round, you're implying that you're willing to cooperate. It turns out that one of the best approaches over several rounds is to share in round 1 and then spend the rest of the game copying your opponent's previous move. However, it's important to acknowledge that this strategy doesn't always work.

Let's turn to puzzle B – the Talent Show Dilemma. If there's a clear favorite, you might conclude that voting for her would be a waste of your precious vote, because she's expected to win by a landslide anyway. Supposedly then the most appropriate solution is to vote for your second favorite contestant, to make the final more interesting. But if everyone follows the same strategy, no one will vote for the favorite, and she'll be eliminated! This type of thing is reported to have happened many times in real life – not just in talent shows, but also in important elections. So in such situations, I'd urge you to resist the temptation to vote tactically, and to vote for your own favorite.

What about puzzle C – the Food Truck problem? The answer seems obvious, right? You should put your truck at point B and instruct the other truck to move to point D – or vice versa. That way, you serve half the town each, and all the town's residents have one food truck fairly close. Wonderful, except that the other owner has no incentive to move her truck from point C. If you park at point B, she can simply assert that she's staying in her prime spot in the town center, and end up with three-quarters of the town's customers. The only way for you to get 50% is to park right next to her at point C! Even if a hundred new food trucks arrived, they'd each be better off by clustering together in a single point.

Finally, what about puzzle D – the road network? To reduce congestion, we need to build a new fast road between Smallton and Littlemarket, right? It's common sense, isn't it? But let's check. In the original network, there are two routes between the two big towns, so half the traffic is likely to choose each route. But in the new 'improved' network, there's now one obvious route that everyone's going to choose. So, it'll have almost twice as much traffic as either of the old routes, and the whole network will have much worse congestion than before!

6 DISCOVERIES

Lesson 6.1, Listening, Exercise B
6.1 **P = Presenter K = Kyle**

P: Today we're talking about unusual travel challenges. Forget remote beaches and idyllic islands or precarious mountain treks and volcano hiking. None of that is enough to impress anybody these days. If you really want to stand out from the crowd, you need a travel challenge. At least that's what travel journalist Kyle Chen, who's been following this trend closely, is here to tell us today. Welcome to the show, Kyle.

K: Thanks for having me, Jo.

P: So … first of all, what exactly is a travel challenge?

K: Well, basically, it's traveling with a goal or some sort of self-imposed restriction – or both in some cases.

P: OK. Can you give us some examples?

K: Sure. So you can limit yourself to a particular method of transportation, you can visit locations with a theme, or you can choose a particular route.

P: Actually, that sounds kind of fun. But why do you think these kinds of challenges are so popular all of a sudden?

K: Different reasons I guess. Well, in general, I think people want to be different. Maybe they want to have a goal to make their trip more interesting. And, I think for some of them, they want to share their adventure. Or maybe they're doing something for charity, or hoping to write a book.

P: So, can you tell us about some interesting challenges that people have done?

K: OK. Well, this was a pretty ambitious one. A guy named Adam Leyton challenged himself to visit as many countries as possible in 24 hours using public transportation.

P: Woah! I'm guessing you can't visit that many countries in 24 hours, though?

K: Well, amazingly, he visited 12.

P: Twelve countries in a day!

K: Right. It wasn't an easy 24 hours by the sound of it either. He came up against a few challenges. He had no time to sleep, on the whole, except for a couple of hours on a night train. But he had to wake up, and get off and on the train, to set foot in Czechia. He had to jog to the border with Hungary and only had 22 minutes to get from there to the Austrian border.

P: That's sounds pretty … intense. What gave him the idea to take on the challenge?

K: Supposedly, he wanted to break a record but he also wanted to raise $900 for charity.

P: Hmm … it does sounds like an incredible trip. But … the fact is, you need some spare time to plan a challenge like that. What are some other challenges you've come across?

K: Well, one of my favorite challenges is a guy named Dixe Wills. He decided he was going to visit places in Great Britain, except he was only going to visit places that started with the letter Z. And he was going to visit all of them.

P: How many places is that?

K: There are 41 apparently! He wrote a book about it called *The Z-to-Z of Great Britain*. It's a great book, actually. It's about all these obscure places you might never have heard of – small farms in the middle of nowhere, a rock on the Isles of Scilly.

P: Hmm. That sounds like an interesting read. What else have people done?

K: Well, another really quirky one is Daniel Tunnard, a British man who lives in Buenos Aires. He decided to ride all of the 140 bus lines in the city.

P: One hundred and forty bus lines? Why?

K: It's a travel challenge. It took him about six months. Remarkably, he was sometimes traveling for 14 hours at a time.

P: OK. That actually doesn't sound like much fun to me.

K: Hmm … me neither. But you have to admire his dedication. He set himself a goal and then he went through with it, taking three bus routes a day. He also blogged about his experiences – in English and Spanish – and he published a book about them. It's actually a really fascinating read.

P: Good for him. So how do these people fund their trips, on the whole?

K: Well, I think most of the examples I gave were self-funded. Mind you, traveling on the buses was actually very cheap. I think it cost about $55 altogether.

P: Right, got you.

K: However, some people ask for donations through crowdfunding sites like GoFundMe.

P: Isn't that a little … bold? Surely, you should pay for your own adventures.

K: I think it's OK. The idea is that if people enjoy reading your blog or looking at your photos, they can make a small donation. People don't have to give anything unless they want to.

P: And what would your advice be for someone thinking about trying a travel challenge?

K: OK, first it's super important to be realistic about what you can do. Think about your budget. Think about how much time you can spare. Think about what you would be comfortable doing. The most important thing is to enjoy yourself. You don't have to travel far to have an adventure.

Lesson 6.2, Listening, Exercise C

6.4 **P = Presenter**

P: Today, I'd like to talk about someone who I particularly admire. In my opinion, he's far and away one of America's greatest inventors. His innovations have fixed everyday problems but also probably saved thousands of lives. In addition, he was one of the first African-American inventors to gain public recognition for his work. His name was Garrett Morgan and he was a prolific inventor and entrepreneur who lived between 1877 and 1963. And while you may not all know his name, you're likely to have experienced his innovations.

One of Morgan's early successes was actually an accident. He was repairing a sewing machine in his store when he noticed that some oil he was using had straightened the hairs on a cloth. Realizing that he might be on to something, he decided to test the oils on something bigger. So he borrowed his neighbor's dog and used the oils to straighten its hair. It worked. So well, in fact, that his neighbor didn't recognize his own dog and tried to chase it away. Morgan bottled his new invention, labeled it 'G.A. Morgan's Hair Refiner' and he was soon selling it far and wide.

His second big success, a safety hood, turned him from an innovator into a hero. Morgan had noticed how smoke inhalation made the work of firefighters both difficult and dangerous. His solution was a hood worn over the head with two tubes that extended to the ground, where the air was breathable. He soon had an opportunity to test out his invention. An explosion in a tunnel near his home trapped 32 workers underground with smoke, dust and poisonous gases. With emergency services unable to enter the tunnel, it was truly a life-or-death situation. Morgan and his brother Frank raced to the scene and went in side-by-side, each wearing one of Morgan's safety hoods. It was a tense moment, but they soon re-emerged safe and sound with survivors. Morgan's fame began to spread slowly but surely, with his device being used by fire and police departments across the country.

Another of Morgan's life-saving inventions was an improved version of the traffic light. By and large, in the early 1920s, American roads were dangerous places. They were filled with horses, carriages and wagons – and increasingly, the newly invented automobile. On top of this, there were only two traffic signals – stop or go. Time after time there were stories of injuries and fatalities in traffic accidents. One day, Morgan and his family saw such an accident – a collision between a car and a horse-drawn carriage at a busy intersection. The driver of the car was knocked unconscious, a little girl was thrown from the carriage, and the horse had to be put down. Determined that accidents like that shouldn't happen, Morgan's innovation was to add a third light – a 'caution' light. This gave vehicles that had entered the intersection enough time to get out before the signal changed to 'go'. Morgan sold the patent to the General Electric Motor Company, which installed the new traffic lights in cities all over the country. As a result, roads became safer and many lives were saved.

So why is Morgan so widely admired? Not only did his inventions save the lives of millions, but he also put his heart and soul into the community, even running for city council. So while his life was a classic rags-to-riches story, it was also the story of a man who took a leadership role and truly cared about others.

7 EXTREMES

Lesson 7.1, Listening, Exercise B
.1 **A = Arjun C = Catina T = Tony**

T: Welcome back to *The Breakfast Show* with me, Tony Scott. Now I'd like you to meet a real-life superhero, Arjun Prasad. Good morning, Arjun. What's your story?

A: Good morning. Well, I was driving home from work about three months ago, not really paying attention to the other vehicles, when suddenly I heard a loud bang from the road behind me. I looked in my mirror and saw a car had run over a bicycle. The bicyclist was still trapped under the car, which was leaking fuel onto the road.

T: Sounds terrifying! So the car could have exploded at any second, couldn't it?

A: Exactly. So I ran over and lifted up the car while the other driver pulled the bicyclist free. As soon as she'd freed the bicyclist, I put the car down again. Then together we carried her to safety and called an ambulance. And we were just in time – the car exploded a few seconds later. A spark must have caused the fuel to catch fire.

T: My goodness! Now, you said you lifted up the car. But that's incredible. I mean, you're a big guy, aren't you? But a car!

A: Yeah. It's weird, isn't it?

T: It certainly is. This seems like a good point to introduce my second guest, Catina Ivănescu, a professor of kinesiology. Catina, how is it possible for a person to lift a car? I mean, a car weighs, what, a metric ton and a half, doesn't it?

C: Good morning. Yes, a typical family car weighs between 1,500 and 2,000 kilograms. The world record for weight-lifting is just over 500 kilograms.

T: Are you saying that Arjun lifted over three times the world record?

C: No, not at all. If he'd lifted the car above his head, that would have been a superhuman feat. But in fact Arjun just lifted part of the car a few centimeters off the ground. Three or even all four of the car's wheels were still on the ground, supporting most of the car's weight.

T: Right. So Arjun's achievement is nothing special, then?

C: Far from it! First of all, as Arjun said, it was an incredibly dangerous situation, with a high risk of an explosion at any second. So Arjun's actions were unquestionably courageous. There's no doubt that the bicyclist escaped serious injury thanks to Arjun's heroic actions. But in addition, it still takes exceptional strength to lift a car, even by a few centimeters.

T: OK. Let's conduct a little experiment now. We have here in the studio a car of the same model as the one you lifted, Arjun. Could you lift it for us now?

A: Uh, not really. I've had a bad back for several months, and the doctor advised me against doing any more heavy lifting.

T: Oh. That's a shame!

C: Why don't you lift it, Tony?

T: Me? Uh, OK. Wow! That's heavy! There's no way I could lift that!

C: Well, not here and now. But who knows? Maybe if you were in the situation Arjun found himself in, you might be able to. It's all about something called 'hysterical strength': the strength that you get in extreme situations.

T: So that's what helped Arjun, then, was it? Hysterical strength?

C: Exactly. Basically, we're all a lot stronger than we think we are. But when we push our muscles to the limit, it's really painful.

T: Yeah, I know. I was in too much pain to lift the car – it was agony!

C: But that pain is just our body's way of telling us to stop exerting ourselves before we break anything. We feel it when our muscles are operating at around 60% of their potential. But, you could, theoretically, push yourself a lot further without damaging your muscles.

T: OK. But surely it would hurt so much that you'd want to stop.

C: Exactly. But in a high-stress situation, your body is flooded with adrenaline, which blocks your body's pain sensors – but only temporarily. That's how Arjun was able to go way beyond 60% of his strength. He didn't notice the pain until the adrenaline had worn off.

A: Exactly. I literally didn't feel any pain at all until about an hour after the accident. And then every muscle in my body was in agony!

T: I'm sure. Uh, I'm just wondering, Catina. We can't harness this strength in everyday life, can we?

C: Well, world-class athletes are able to harness it to some extent. During training, they can often push themselves up to 80% of their potential. But in high-stress situations, such as when they're chasing an Olympic medal, it's often possible to go much higher. That's why so many world records are broken at such events, rather than in regular training sessions. The adrenaline blocks the pain, allowing you to go way beyond your normal limit.

T: Ah. OK, one last question, Arjun. What happened to the bicyclist?

A: She made a full recovery. When I met her last week, after a few weeks in the hospital, she said if it hadn't been for my actions, she might not be alive today. But I don't feel like a hero – I'm just a normal guy, aren't I?

T: Well, I'm not so sure about that, Arjun! Anyway, let's have a break now, shall we? We'll be back very soon.

Lesson 7.2, Listening, Exercise C
7.3 **RS = Recruitment specialist**

RS: OK, so let's look at those questions now. Interviewers often use the 'desert island' question to determine what sort of person you are. A practical survivor type might take a knife or even a satellite phone. A more creative dreamer would take something original and fun. There's no correct answer – it depends what type of employee they're looking for. Just don't pretend to be something you're not. Focus instead on the image you want to convey about yourself.

Next, the 'dinosaur' question tests your ability to avoid obvious answers. Ninety percent of people say T. Rex is the first dinosaur they think of. But unless the employer is looking to recruit cold-blooded predators, T. Rex would be pretty unsuitable as a potential employee. Almost any other answer is much better – as long as you justify it.

The 'weakness' question is an old classic. Whatever you do, don't claim to not have any weaknesses, or you'll come across as arrogant and lacking in self-awareness. A good trick is always to describe a weakness that you've overcome.

With the 'stapler' question, the key is to think beyond the obvious applications, and to explore the properties of the object in question. I wouldn't recommend saying 'a paperweight' – it's what everyone always says.

OK, so the 'pizza' question tests your ability to make estimates and work out a plan. So don't just say any old number that pops into your head. You don't need to produce an accurate answer – which would be about 150 million in this case. But of course it's better if you're in the right ballpark, which in this case would be between around 75 and 300 million.

Next, the 'not on your résumé question is a great opportunity to remind the interviewers that you're a real person, not some invented character whose life revolves around landing this particular job. It's fine to get personal, but don't forget to bring your story back to how you're suitable for the job.

Finally, for the 'worst enemy' question, it's always worth mentioning that you don't have any enemies. But resist the temptation to leave it there; talk about perceived weaknesses that are actually strengths. Demonstrate your ability to see yourself through others' eyes – a crucial skill for any employee.

Lesson 7.2, Listening, Exercise D
7.4 **I1 = Interviewer 1 O = Oscar I2 = Interviewer 2**

I1: What would you take with you to a desert island and why?

O: Uh, a notebook and a pen. I find writing poetry immensely calming, so an extended stay on a desert island, without any other people to distract me, would really get my creative juices flowing. I'd be utterly devastated if I couldn't record my ideas on paper.

I2: Thank you. If you could be any dinosaur, which dinosaur would you be?

O: Oh, a pterodactyl, a flying dinosaur, soaring high above the plains. The views would be spectacular, and the sense of freedom would be really exhilarating. But much more importantly, compared to the ground, the sky would be a relatively good place for staying out of harm's way!

I1: OK. What's your biggest weakness?

O: Hmm, well I tend to be somewhat disorganized. When I was a student, I frequently missed deadlines. But then I learned some remarkably simple techniques, and I've improved noticeably since then. For example, I make a to-do list every day, and I can't have any rewards until I've cleared my list. It takes a lot of self-discipline, but it's so satisfying to know that, at long last, there's nothing hanging over you.

I2: Thank you. Name four uses for a stapler, without the staples.

O: You could use it to pick up tissues without getting your hands dirty! You could also use it as a hammer for hitting things. I suppose you could also give it to a child as a toy – the child might have fun pressing it and listening to the noises. And I suppose you could also use it as a paperweight, to hold down papers when it's windy.

I1: Hmm. How many square meters of pizza are eaten in the US each year?

O: A standard pizza is, what, thirty centimeters across? So you could easily fit nine inside a square meter. In fact, if you cut them up, there'd be room for possibly three more in the spaces, so, twelve. That's a year's supply for me. I'm not completely sure how typical I am – I guess some people would eat that many in a single month! But if we assume I'm not radically different from the average American, then we're looking at around one square meter per person per year. The US has around 300 million people, so that's my estimate: 300 million.

I1: Not bad. What's the most interesting thing about you that we wouldn't learn from your résumé?

O: Well, I have six younger brothers and sisters, who are all really adorable. I'm the oldest, so I've spent most of my life taking care of them while my parents were working. It's been really challenging, because I never had any time to myself and it was practically impossible to study, but it's also incredibly rewarding when I see how far they've come.

I2: Great. How would your worst enemy describe you?

O: Hah! I'm not the sort of person who has outright enemies. It used to irritate me when people treated me badly, but I've learned that the best trick is to ignore them and move on! I know some people are jealous of what I've achieved and they think I'm lucky. But they haven't seen all the struggles I've been through. The people who matter know that I deserve any luck that has come my way.

I1: OK, great. Thanks. That's the end of the interview.

8 WELL-BEING

Lesson 8.1, Listening, Exercise B

8.1 **C = Cheryl J = Jake L = Luke**

L: Hey, Cheryl.

J: Hello, Cheryl. What you doing?

C: Oh, hey guys. Check out my brand new … smart watch! What do you think?

L: Cool. I've been meaning to get one of those. Is that turned on, Cheryl?

C: Um … maybe.

J: Smart watch eh? Hmm … not a hundred percent convinced about those. I mean if I want to check my email I can just look at my phone.

L: Yeah, yeah … but you can use it whenever you exercise to monitor the amount of activity you do.

J: Didn't know you were so big on fitness Cheryl.

C: Yeah, sure. I mean … I do like to stay active … and … well, OK so … You'll never guess what … I've just been commissioned to write an article about wellness technology.

L: Amazing!

J: Cool. Congratulations. But what's wellness technology?

C: Good question. So wellness technology is … technology with which we can improve our health and well-being.

J: Did you just read that somewhere?

C: Maybe. But you get the idea. There are a lot of other devices you can get to track things. Actually, you can monitor whatever you need to keep an eye on: your breathing, temperature, glucose levels in your blood, amount of sleep, pretty much everything!

J: Yeah. And it sounds a little like information overload to me.

C: Well, yes and no. Sure more information doesn't necessarily mean better health. But I've just read several news stories about people whose lives may have been saved because their smart watch alerted them to a problem. For example, on this smart watch take this handy … heart rate tracker.

L: Eighty-five beats per minute. Isn't that fairly high …

C: Not for me, Luke. No. And anyway I'm a little stressed. I'm meeting the person writing the article with me for lunch today. I'm supposed to share my ideas. But I think I'm out of new ideas!

L: Well, what about the smart swimsuit? Have you heard of that?

C: Hmm … tell me more.

L: Hang on – here it is. It's a swimsuit with a tracking tag embedded, so you can log your time and how far you swim. It will start tracking all that whenever you put the swimsuit on.

J: I don't know. What happened to just going for a swim? People are obsessively tracking everything these days. Writing down everything they eat or do. It takes over your life – when really all you need to do is get some exercise and eat healthily.

L: But I don't think wellness technology is just about fitness fads. For example, monitoring devices can help show your doctor the big picture so he or she will be more likely to pick up on any problems. And it goes beyond just tracking. Like the smart pill bottle.

C: The smart pill what? Let me write this down.

L: It's a pill bottle for medication, like the Adhere Tech bottle. It glows blue when it's time to take your medication. And … if you forget … it starts flashing red. It can also text you or email you to remind you to take medication.

J: OK, maybe that could be useful for my grandpa.

L: There are a few health devices like that now. I was also reading about this thermometer. It's basically a thermometer which a smartphone can be attached to. Here it is. It says … this device has an automated diagnosis feature whereby it checks the symptoms of the person to whom it's attached against a database. I'll send you a link to the review. And look at this – this could be a great quote for your article. 'As tech gets smarter and people get smarter about tech, this could be the decade in which we revolutionize healthcare.'

C: Yeah. Yeah. I think that would work as a tagline. Great! Thanks, guys. One last question though. Is this thing really turned on?

Lesson 8.2, Listening, Exercise B

8.3 **L = Laura B = Bill R = Rohan J = Julie**

L: Hello, everyone. This is *First Past the Post*, the sports performance podcast. My name is Laura Ford …

B: And I'm Bill Williams.

L: This week, we're talking about sports psychology. A lot of the big teams have sports psychologists these days. But what do they actually do? This week we set out to find out more.

B: First up, we spoke to Professor Rohan Kumar, a lecturer in sports psychology. Here's what we discussed …

L: So Rohan, could you explain what a sports psychologist does?

R: Certainly. Essentially, our job is to help athletes perform at the peak of their abilities. We do that by offering training and therapy. Training usually means things like encouraging positive thinking, whereas therapy could be supporting them with off-field issues – this is particularly important in the case of long-term injuries.

L: You mentioned working on positive thinking. How exactly does that work?

R: Well, athletes, even elite athletes, suffer from the same fear of failure that we all do. They have times when they doubt their abilities or get cold feet because they're anxious about competing. Our job is to help athletes cope with these feelings, so they can perform to the best of their abilities.

L: So what kind of training do you do with them?

R: Well, I said before that positive thinking is important – but that doesn't just mean encouraging people to imagine winning a game or winning a trophy. It's actually more about visualizing your performance, thinking about the individual steps that you need to take, and imagining doing each one of those steps in exactly the right way. It's all about staying calm and focused, so they can give it their best shot.

L: So you encourage them to break things down into smaller goals?

R: That's right. It helps people focus by thinking about these smaller goals rather than getting distracted by the big picture. We also work on self-talk, which means trying to get control of that little voice inside your head that says you're not good enough or that you're having a bad day. We train athletes to use positive self-talk to build self-confidence and self-belief – and if it's a team game, to talk out loud and encourage those same feelings in the rest of the team.

L: That's been really helpful. Thank you for your time, Rohan.

R: You're very welcome.

Lesson 8.2, Listening, Exercise D

.4 **B = Bill J = Julie L = Laura**

B: After Laura spoke to Professor Kumar, I spoke to Julie Matic, a sports psychologist working with a local soccer team. I should mention that Julie was speaking to me from a training session, so there's a little background noise during this interview.

B: Julie, thank you for taking the time to talk with me today.

J: No problem.

B: So, can you tell me a little about your role with the team there?

J: Well, before I started here, the team had been going through a losing streak, so one of the first things I needed to do was to help the team get over their fear of failure. I've been helping them to think about failure in a more positive way, so they don't dwell on the fact that they failed, but they try to learn from that experience, so that failure becomes a positive thing. Nobody can win every game, so it's not a disaster to lose – as long as you just think about what you can do differently next time.

B: What about working with individual players? What kinds of things do you focus on?

J: Well, the most important thing is to get to know the individuals, and encourage the coach to do the same, so that we can work out the best way to get the most out of each person. When people think about coaching, most people have a stereotypical image of a coach shouting at the players, but that's very outdated because many players won't respond positively to that kind of coaching. Different players need different approaches – some people need a lot of guidance, some need a lot of praise, others need to feel trusted and important. It's important to talk to the players – to listen to them and find the right way to work with them.

L: Apologies again for the sound quality on that interview, but she said a lot of really interesting things. I completely agree that it's important to think about the right kind of coaching to suit individual players. I need someone to nag me and tell me to up my game, but I know that's not everyone's cup of tea.

B: Yeah, actually I find that kind of coaching ends up distracting me because I get so angry with the coach. It means I don't concentrate on the game and I end up playing even worse! I prefer a more supportive approach.

L: Yeah, I can imagine that! So we also interviewed …

9 BEHAVIOR

Lesson 9.1, Vocabulary, Exercise B

.1 **M = Man W = Woman A = American**

M: I could do with some new wheels but they'd set me back at least ten grand … and I'm completely broke.

A: Hey, can you lend me ten bucks? Ah, sweet. That's awesome, dude.

W: I don't mean to gripe, but the office bash last night was a hot mess. I was so bummed!

M: This guy offered me a brand new TV for fifty bucks, so I'm like 'Sounds shady to me – it's probably hot or something.'

A: I wanted to hang out with my buddies tonight but I'm totally beat, so I guess I'll just chill out and crash instead.

W: I'm so stoked cuz I got myself a new crib. It's so cool.

Lesson 9.1, Listening, Exercise B

9.3 **L = Lisa G = Greg J = Jake H = Helen**

L: Uh, hello.

H: Hey. Come on in. I'm Helen.

J: What's up? I'm Jake.

G: Good morning. How are you doing? I'm Greg.

L: Good, thanks. I'm Lisa. Are you all here for the psychology experiment too?

G: Yeah. The organizers offered us ten bucks, so we signed up.

L: Yeah, same here.

J: I don't know what they're testing, though. Do you?

L: Something about perception skills and stuff like that. Are we supposed to wait for the experimenters?

H: Nah, there were two guys here earlier, psychology professors or whatever, and they were like 'sorry but we have to go and teach.' They left some questions in an envelope.

G: What a hot mess! Should we get going?

J: OK. Task 1: Which line is the same length as the one on the left? Easy. It's line B, isn't it?

H: Yeah, definitely B. It's obvious.

G: Yeah, it's line B. Lisa?

L: Uh, yeah. Line B.

H: Hey, those doughnuts look kind of yummy. Do you think they're for us?

L: I suppose so. Look, there's a note. It says this plate's for the 12 o'clock group and this is for the 11:30 group – that's us.

G: Cool! Mmm, yummy!

H: What's the next task? Let's see: AFC or PTU?

G: PTU, no question. What about you, Jake?

J: Definitely PTU.

H: Yeah, me too. Lisa?

L: Uh, yeah, PTU, I suppose.

J: Great. Those doughnuts were crazy yummy. Can we have some more?

L: Well, the others are supposed to be for the next group.

H: Yeah, but we could just eat them and hide the note!

J: Yeah, whatever.

G: Fine with me. Lisa?

L: Oh, go ahead then. I mean, they are yummy!

G: Cool! Well done Lisa! You passed the test!

L: What are you going on about?

H: Sorry, Lisa, but it wasn't about perception at all. It was about social pressure and conformity: how groups influence our behavior, and so on.

L: How do you know? Aren't you participants like me?

J: Nah, we're the experimenters. We were only pretending. Sorry.

L: So what do you mean, I passed the test?

G: OK, so the first part was the lines. Did you really think it was line B?

L: Not really. It seemed obvious it was line A, but then you all seemed sort of convinced it was line B. I thought my eyes were playing tricks on me in some way!

H: Yeah, that happens to more or less everyone. Sometimes it's easier to follow the crowd, in a sense, than to trust your own eyes!

L: So it was line A after all?

H: Yeah, of course it was! OK, so the second test was AFC versus PTU. Why did you go for PTU, Lisa?

L: Cuz you all chose it! I don't even know what PTU stands for. What is it?

J: PTU? Pretending to understand! Most people hate admitting they don't understand something, especially when everyone else is nodding their heads, or something like that, so you pretend. But maybe everyone else is pretending too! They're all kind of too embarrassed to admit they don't know what's going on!

L: So what's AFC?

J: Ask for clarification! Always ask, even if it makes you feel stupid!

G: Enjoy the doughnuts, Lisa?

L: Yeah, they were yummy.

G: Yummy? That's a strange word! Why do you say that?

L: Oh, you got me again! You all called them yummy, didn't you? I never say 'yummy'! Bummer!

G: Yeah, sorry. We wanted to influence your choice of words. We used a lot of slang too, and stuff like that, to get you to conform to our style of speaking.

L: Ah, yeah. I always thought 'yummy' was uncool, but when you all started using it, I thought maybe it was cool again!

H: Nah, yummy is always a lame thing to say!

J: How did you feel about eating the other group's doughnuts, Lisa?

L: Not good. But you all convinced me it was fine. It was some kind of trick again, wasn't it?

J: Yeah, sorry. That was an example of 'groupthink', where people make bad decisions as a group that they wouldn't make as individuals. That's why we agree to things we don't want to do. And it's why many business teams make such terrible decisions.

L: OK. And what was with that humming at the end?

H: Hah! That was the last task. We wanted to make you copy us. And it worked!

L: Yeah, I know. I felt kind of stupid cuz I didn't know what was going on, so I just joined in. You must think I'm some sort of sheep, copying everything you did!

G: Chill out, Lisa. Most people are just as bad as you! Anyway, a big pat on the back to you for taking part. You're the bomb! Do you want another doughnut?

Lesson 9.2, Listening, Exercise B

9.6 **P = Presenter M1 = Man 1 M2 = Man 2 W = Woman**

P: Hello and welcome to *Human Behavior*. Today we're looking at one of the most famous experiments of all time.

In the 1940s, the leading behavioral psychologist, B.F. Skinner, conducted a remarkable experiment. Some hungry pigeons were placed in a cage with a mechanism that delivered food.

The twist in this particular experiment was that the pigeons' actions had no effect whatsoever on the mechanism, which simply delivered food at regular intervals, regardless of what the pigeons did. The pigeons, of course, didn't know this, so they kept pecking and pushing and so on in a desperate attempt to make the mechanism deliver food. Inevitably, there were occasions when food appeared immediately after the pigeon had performed a particular action. That was enough to convince the pigeon that it was that action that had caused the food to be delivered, so the pigeon kept repeating it again and again. And of course, every time the mechanism delivered another serving of food, the pigeon became more and more convinced that it could influence the mechanism with its actions.

According to Skinner's report, the pigeons swung and moved around a lot, making it look like a kind of bizarre pigeon dance. Surely humans wouldn't believe such actions could influence something beyond our control … or would we?

In fact, when the experiment was repeated on humans, who received points instead of food, the results were almost identical. By the end of one experiment, the participants were convinced that they'd gotten a point for a particular combination of shrugging, fidgeting and rocking back and forth. What never seemed to occur to them was that the points were simply awarded after completely random lengths of time. If they'd just sat there and waited, they'd still have won the points just the same, without making themselves look ridiculous in the process. But of course, it wouldn't have been so entertaining to watch.

Does anything like this happen in real life? Let's hear from a few people we interviewed on the street this morning to find out.

M1: I'm a big soccer fan. I try to watch all my team's games on TV. In fact, pretty much whenever I miss a game, my team loses! So I make sure I'm sitting by the TV in time for each game, wearing my lucky soccer jersey and scarf, to bring my team luck! And it definitely works – well, most of the time, at least.

W: It started when I was young, and my aunt gave me a lucky hamster toy before a big test. I forgot to take it with me for my next test, which was a disaster! So ever since then, I've always used lucky toys in exams.

M2: I always buy my lottery tickets at exactly 11:41 on a Thursday morning. I know it sounds crazy, but every time I've won any money on the lottery, it's after buying my ticket at that time. Unfortunately, it doesn't always work, for some reason, but it certainly seems to improve my chances of winning.

P: I'm sure it does. Anyway, join us again next week on *Human Behavior* …

10 SOCIETY

Lesson 10.1, Listening, Exercise B

10.1 **D = Denise**

D: Walking along the streets of Beijing, you really get the sense of a city going through a rapid period of change. Huge skyscrapers dominate the skyline, while construction work continues all around. As the city evolves, its population has swelled to over 21 million, making Beijing one of the most populated cities in the world. And the more people there are, the more challenging it becomes to provide comfortable environments for people to live and work in.

Fortunately, researchers at the Well Living Lab on the northern outskirts of Beijing are conducting an extensive research project to identify ways that building design can make people healthier, happier and more productive. And if people feel better about their environment they have a higher inclination to interact positively with the people around them. Inside an unassuming office building, human guinea pigs are being carefully monitored inside a simulation of a typical office environment. I talked to environmental psychologist Wang Wei about how this kind of research can help with building design.

Lesson 10.1, Listening, Exercise C

10.2 **W = Wang D = Denise**

D: So, Wang Wei, what research is being done at the Well Living Lab here in Beijing?

W: They're looking at how small changes to the environment, such as changes to the lighting, air quality or noise levels affect people. They're observing people's emotional responses and using wearable technology to monitor people's physical reactions.

For example, recently they've been looking at what kind of light makes workers most productive. They experimented by using different kinds of light. They found that people strongly preferred daylight to electric light – and, as a matter of fact, other research has shown that people have a tendency to be less productive if their desk is more than 7.5 meters away from a window. They also found that certain kinds of blue lighting can have a positive effect on workers' moods.

D: What other things have psychologists learned about office environments?

W: Some fascinating research has focused on shapes and lines. Apparently, people feel more comfortable in places with round shapes and curved lines. On the other hand, straight lines and sharp edges have been shown to create feelings of fear. Other research has looked at colors. Red walls have been shown to be better suited for tasks that require accuracy and attention to detail – maybe because people associate the color red with danger, so they're more alert. Conversely, blue walls suit creative tasks – in fact, people trying to be creative in rooms with blue walls had twice as many ideas as those working in rooms with red walls.

D: And what have we learned about the design of the city?

W: People living in cities tend to have higher levels of stress, so unsurprisingly a lot of the research has looked at what can be done about this. One interesting study showed that people are more relaxed when they see lively and interesting store facades, whereas plain, monotonous facades make people anxious and give them the urge to hurry past. Other studies have looked at how spaces can facilitate more communication – because cities can be very isolating places. Some ideas include arranging spaces that encourage interaction between strangers, such as providing more seating in communal spaces. It sounds simple, but many places have had this kind of seating removed in recent years and people didn't realize the impact this would have.

D: If you don't believe the importance of thinking about these details, you only need to look back at the story of the Pruitt-Igoe housing complex that was built in Missouri in the US in the 1950s. When it opened, the complex was lauded as magnificent architectural design. Yet, when people actually began to live there, several problems with how people interacted in the space became evident – for example, the wide spaces between the different apartment buildings in the complex meant people in different buildings had little chance to interact. This meant there was no sense of shared community between residents of different buildings, and as a result, the complex quickly became a hostile and unpleasant place to live in. The project's failings were a reminder for architects to think not just about the look of buildings, but also about how people would interact within the spaces they create.

Today, various studies, like the ones being carried out in Beijing, are looking at how places make people feel and act. This research is vital for creating the buildings of the future. With so many people living close together, the environment should encourage positive feelings.

Lesson 10.2, Listening, Exercise B

0.4 **R = Robin J = Joanna Mr. E = Mr. Evans**

J: A few weeks to go and then we're done with college for good. Can't believe it.

R: Me neither. The end of an era. So … you going to work at your dad's company then?

J: Hmm … hope not. Not if I can help it, anyway. But yeah … may need to. Any idea what you're going to do?

R: Well, funny you should ask that. I've just been trying to look over my résumé and looking for some interesting stuff to apply to. The thing is I really want to do something to help people. But I haven't seen too much of that sort of thing.

J: Really? Oh OK, thought you were going to apply for something in business though, like one of those management trainee programs.

R: I don't know. I don't think all that is really for me. I'd like to make some kind of a difference in the world. You know my cousin works for a charity, right?

J: Oh yeah?

R: Yeah, a clean water organization. Anyway, we've been talking a lot recently about all the stuff she's doing and it kind of made me want do something similar too.

J: Oh, OK got you. But you wouldn't earn that much working for a charity. At least not at first. Any other ideas?

R: Well, yeah I thought about politics too.

J: Hmm. Don't know. I mean all they seem to do is argue with each other. Just don't know how much of a change you'll be making.

R: OK … and there's also social work. You know, looking out for children, vulnerable people …

J: Hmm OK…

R: I take it you're not convinced then?

J: I just think that looks like a tough job, coping with a lot of difficult situations. I couldn't do it myself personally. I was thinking … what about teaching? You'd be a great teacher. You could train to be a teacher or just volunteer in your spare time.

R: Yeah … I guess.

J: Hey, there's Mr. Evans. Isn't he the new career advisor? Why don't you talk to him?

R: Good idea. Hang on a sec … Excuse me, Mr. Evans. Would you have a minute to talk?

Mr. E: Oh hello Robin. Sure. How can I help?

R: I was wondering if you could offer me some advice. I've just been considering what to do after graduation.

Mr. E: OK. So what are you interested in doing?

R: Well I think … first and foremost I want to do a job which involves helping people, you know, that are less fortunate than myself. So I was interested in applying for a position with a charity.

Mr. E: Ah. OK. So my first question then would be: what kind of charity do you have in mind?

R: So, ideally one that campaigns for clean water … or maybe disease prevention.

Mr. E: So second question: what do you see yourself doing for them?

R: Well … I'd like to be assisting with policy making, I guess.

Mr. E: OK let me just stop you there. Of course that is one area of charity work. But it's highly competitive. And you don't have experience or a specialist certification. You're more likely to be involved in fundraising, persuading people to donate money, at least initially. And even then, it would definitely strengthen your application if you can show some commitment to their particular work.

R: Like volunteering maybe. I was thinking about some kind of volunteer work.

Mr. E: You should definitely do it.

R: Great, thanks Mr. Evans. I can look into it.

Mr. E: But let me get to my final point. You should bear in mind that working for a charity isn't the only way you can help people. If you're likely to be helping the organization get money, you may actually be able to make more of a difference pursuing a career in business. Especially with your background. Then you can commit to donating a portion of your salary to your chosen charity.

R: Hmm … I hadn't thought of that before.

Mr. E: Yes, there's a very, very interesting book about a Wall Street trader, called *The Most Good You Can Do*. If you haven't read it, you should. The guy was a philosophy student, really smart in fact. Just like you he was thinking about how to make a difference. He decided that the way he could make the biggest impact was by working hard in finance and donating money to charity. He's been able to donate over $100,000 a year to his chosen charities – and as a result touched many people's lives.

R: Thank you, I'll look it up. And thanks for the advice Mr. Evans, it's much appreciated. I definitely have a lot to think about.

Mr. E: You're welcome.

J: So, come on then. What did he say?

R: Not what I expected. At all. He said it might be better to get a normal job, you know, an office job or something like that.

J: Told you so.

R: No, but then give the money to charity.

J: Oh. Great.

R: Yep, that's what he said. Apparently, there's a guy who does that and has given over a hundred grand a year away.

J: No way!

R: Yeah I know. Crazy, right?

J: Well, it's kind of good advice. The part about an office job. I'd do that. I'm just not sure about the giving away part.

Macmillan Education Limited
4 Crinan Street
London N1 9XW

Companies and representatives throughout the world

American Language Hub Level 5 Student's Book ISBN 978-0-230-49748-1
American Language Hub Level 5 Student's Book with Student's App
ISBN 978-0-230-49752-8

Written by Jeremy Day and Graham Skerritt

The authors have asserted their right to be identified as the authors of this work in accordance with the Copyright, Designs and Patents Act 1988.

The right of Kieran Donaghy to be identified as the author of the Speaking Pages in this work has been asserted by him in accordance with the Copyright, Designs and Patents Act 1988.

First published 2020

Designed by emc design ltd
Illustrated by Daniel Limón (Beehive Illustration) p50
Cover design by Restless
Cover photoghraphs by Getty Images/Luís Henrique Boucault (bg), Plainpicture/Cavan Images
Picture research by Emily Taylor

Authentic video footage supplied by BBC Studios Distribution Limited
Café Hub videos produced by Sharp Focus

Authors' acknowledgements
Jeremy Day would like to thank the team at Macmillan Education for their support.
Graham Skerritt would like to thank the students who tried out activities and gave invaluable feedback. Thank you to the Macmillan Education Editorial team for your excellent comments and suggestions. And thank you to my family for your patience and support.

The authors and publishers would like to thank the following for permission to reproduce their photographs:

Alamy/Zoltan Gabor p65, Suat Gursozlu p156(icons), Phillip Roberts pp16–17, Science History Images p69, Visions of America p14(b), David Wall p155(t), Westend61 p2(tr); **BBC Studios Distribution Limited** p34(a, b, c, d, e); p58(a, b); **Getty Images** pp2(bl), 64, 77(3), 94–95, 106(b), 10'000 Hours p112, AFP/Adem Altan p109, AFP/Ronaldo Schemidt p118(tl), Anadolu Agency p52, Andersen Ross Photography Inc p30(james), Ascent Xmedia pp74–75, Axelle/Bauer-Griffin p20(bl), Peter Barritt p13, Nathan Benn p61, Ira Block p67(tr), Bloomberg p37, Nikolay Bogdev/EyeEm p153, Claudia Burlotti p30(bob), Caiaimage/Tom Merton p45(b), Jon Cartwright pp104, 105(tr), Matteo Colombo pp82–83(background), Ian Cuming pp70–71(background), Robert Daly p32, Markus Daniel p110(bl), Nick David p18(tl), Steve Debenport p66, Lea Dettli/EyeEm p58–59, Enrique Díaz/7cero pp10–11(background), 88–89, Digital Vision p77(5), Erik Dreyer p97, Richard Drury p30(callum), Michael England p70(c), ER Productions Limited p163, FatCamera pvi, Clare Fieseler p115(bl), Filadendron p160, Flashpop p151, Freemixer p29, Goldfaery p87(tr), Grandriver p76(2), GrapeImages p5(b), Jorg Greuel p7, Paul Harris p33, Hero Images pp30(sonia), 31, 38, 91(b), 98, Hill Street Studios p18(tr), Dave Hogan p149(tr), Hoozone p88(bl), Hoxton/Martin Barraud pp114–115(background), Hoxton/Sam Edwards p44(b), Imagemore p76(1), 106–107(background), iStockphoto/Ellerslie77 pp1, 94(tr), Izusek p158, Azman Jaka p4(b), Johner Images p85, Jupiterimages p45(cl), Jason Kempin p21(cm), Daniel Knighton p20(br), Peetatham Kongkapech pp62–63, Roos Koole p4(mr), Justin Lewis p44(cr), Lilly3 p18(bl), Littleting/Pradthana Jarusriboonchai p82, Maica pp54–55, Martin-dm p9, Maskot p8, MECKY p49, Ty Milford p79(b), Laurence Monneret p43, Moodboard p105(tm), Morfous p78(bl), Jessica Nelson p149(b), Aaron Oberlander p155(br), Orchidpoet p110(tr), PeopleImages pp42(paul), 88(tr), Javier Pierini p150, Piola666 p15(c), Photo_Concepts p53, PhotoQuest p21(bm), Pixelfit p5(ml), Busakorn Pongparnit p118-119(background), Dave Porter pp34–35, Norman Posselt pp22–23(background), Franz Pritz p73, Purestock/Punchstock p90, Gavin Quirke p152, Ken Redding p77(4), RichVintage p100, Tim Robberts pp42(caroline), 56, 105(tl), Alexis Rosenfeld p161, Jenny E. Ross p67(br), Saenman photography p14(a), Elizabeth Salleebauer p154, Audrey Saracco/EyeEm p164, Anup Shah p103, Jordan Siemens pp86–87, Skynesher pp18(br), 80(b), 91(cl), SolStock pp10(t), pp117, 116(cl), Paul Souders p162, SpVVK p113, Stocktrek Images p79(tl), SuperStock p15(e), Thehague p111, Camille Tokerud p116(br), Topical Press Agency p62(tr), Adina Tovy pp46–47(background), Tuan Tran p30(mary), Universal History Archive p70(a), Vctor Vargas/EyeEm p118(tr), Vasantytf p87(cl), Westend61 pp3, 42(gianni), 51, 81, Josef P. Willems/LOOK-foto p25, Tim Zurowski p102(tr); **Hero Images** p116(bl); **iStockphoto** pp39(r), 70(b); **PhotoDisc** pp40–41(background); **Powerstock** p102(b); **Rex Features/Shutterstock**/Mikael Buck p22(tl), Hufton Crow/View p16(cm), George Frey/EPA p15(d), Neil Hall/EPA-EFE p22(tr), Solent News pp26, 27(c,b); **Shutterstock**/Domino p57(illustrations), Gorodenkoff p40(bl), Margouillat photo pp92–93; **Stockbyte** p80(stapler); **Thinkstock** pp80(pizza), 92(tr)

Commissioned photographs in the Café Hubs by Sharp Focus pp11, 23, 35, 47, 59, 71, 83, 95, 107, 119

The author and publishers are grateful for permission to reprint the following copyright material: Graph from 'Vinyl LP Sales and Market Share' by British Phonographic Industry, 2017. © BPI (British Recorded Music Industry) Limited 2019. All rights reserved. Reprinted with permission of British Phonographic Industry, p6; Extract from 'Tim Smit: how we made the Eden Project' by Anna Tims. Originally published in The Guardian, 29 September 2014. © 2019 Guardian News & Media Limited or its affiliated companies. All rights reserved. Reprinted with permission of Guardian News & Media Limited, p16; Extract from 'Life In An Underwater Skyscraper' by Rex Features. © Rex Features Ltd. 2018. Reprinted with permission of Rex Features Ltd. UK, p27; Extract from 'Architect Unveils Plans For Spectacular Eco-Friendly Resort' by Rex Features. © Rex Features Ltd. 2018. Reprinted with permission of Rex Features Ltd. UK, p27; Extract from 'The 'Lily Pad City' - 03 Jul 2008' by Rex Features. © Rex Features Ltd. 2018. Reprinted with permission of Rex Features Ltd. UK, p27; Extract from 'From Forest Bathing to 'Halotherapy': 5 Ridiculous Wellness Trends' by Loulla-Mae Eleftherious-Smith. Originally published in The Independent, 7 October 2016. © Independent Digital News and Media Limited 2019. Reprinted with permission of Independent Digital News and Media Limited, p92; Extract from 'Political activism is as strong as ever, but now it's digital – and passionate' by Ethan Zuckerman. Originally published in The Guardian, 15 October 2013. © 2019 Guardian News & Media Limited or its affiliated companies. All rights reserved. Reprinted with permission of Guardian News & Media Limited, p120

Printed and bound in Brazil

2024

27